POLITICS ON THE
SOUTHWESTERN FRONTIER
Arkansas Territory 1819-1936

POLITICS ON THE SOUTHWESTERN FRONTIER:

Arkansas Territory, 1819-1836

by Lonnie J. White

1964

MEMPHIS, TENN.

MEMPHIS STATE UNIVERSITY PRESS

To NANCY

Preface

THIS STUDY IS AN ATTEMPT to present a detailed account of the formative period of Arkansas politics. Arkansas Territory, on the raw frontier of the early Southwest, was frequently the scene of political quarrelling, name calling, fights, and duels. During the territorial era factions developed, young politicians matured, a powerful family combination arose, and sectionalism began to divide the Territory. In consequence of the progress made in the territorial period, Arkansas was in 1836 able to change from territoriality to statehood with only minor adjustment.

The reader will find the main source for this volume to have been the Little Rock *Arkansas Gazette.* Without this newspaper, which covers the entire territorial period, a full study of early Arkansas politics would have been virtually impossible. Other fruitful sources deserving mention are the Little Rock *Arkansas Advocate,* the Arkansas *Territorial Papers,* and the printed debates in the United States Congress. Various other materials supplement these principal sources.

I am indebted to a number of people for assistance in the preparation of the manuscript. To Dr. Walter L. Brown, specialist in Arkansas history at the University of Arkansas, I owe thanks for advice and suggestion of sources. Dr. John L. Ferguson, Executive Secretary of the Arkansas History Commission, and Mrs. Margaret Smith Ross of the Little Rock *Arkansas Gazette* also gave counsel and helped in locating materials. Several persons on the library staff of the University of Texas and the manuscript staffs of the Tennessee State Library, the Joint University Libraries in Nashville, Tennessee, the Southern Historical Collection of the University of North Carolina, Duke University, the Alderman Library of the University of Virginia, and the Library of Congress assisted in my quest for materials. I am, above all, indebted to Dr. Barnes F. Lathrop, Professor of History at the University of Texas, for reading the manuscript. His suggestion of sources, his sound discerning criticisms, and his help in matters of style and organization have contributed immeasurably to the content and presentation. And finally, I am obligated to Nancy Evans White, my wife, who helped wherever possible.

LONNIE J. WHITE

Memphis, Tennessee
September 16, 1963

Contents

Preface vii

CHAPTER   PAGE

ONE   *Creating Arkansas Territory* 3

TWO   *Organizing the Territorial Government* . . 18

THREE   *The Second and Third Elections* 33

FOUR   *Politics in Flux, 1824–1827* 48

FIVE   *The Election of 1827 and the Conway-Crittenden Duel* 66

SIX   *Public Affairs, 1828–1829* 88

SEVEN   *The Controversy of 1830* 99

EIGHT   *The Election of 1831* 115

NINE   *The Legislature of 1831* 126

TEN   *The Election of 1833* 141

ELEVEN   *The Statehood Movement* 164

TWELVE   *The Territory Becomes a State* 183

THIRTEEN   *Conclusion* 201

Bibliography 206

Index 213

Illustrations

HENRY W. CONWAY   *following page*   118

ROBERT CRITTENDEN

AMBROSE H. SEVIER

JAMES MILLER

CHESTER ASHLEY

BENJAMIN JOHNSON

WILLIAM CUMMINS

ABSALOM FOWLER

WILLIAM E. WOODRUFF

CHARLES P. BERTRAND

ANDREW SCOTT

JOHN POPE

GEORGE IZARD

WILLIAM S. FULTON

THE OLD STATE HOUSE

POLITICS ON THE
SOUTHWESTERN FRONTIER
Arkansas Territory 1819–1936

CHAPTER ONE

Creating Arkansas Territory

HERNANDO DE SOTO'S SPANISH EXPEDITION crossed Arkansas in 1541 but his exploration led to no settlement. Robert Cavelier de la Salle was therefore able in 1682 to claim for France possession of the whole watershed of the Mississippi; this vast country he named Louisiana. Four years later Henri de Tonti established Arkansas Post near the mouth of the Arkansas River. Presently a governor was appointed and colonists and Negro slaves were brought into the province. French colonizing activities ended, however, in 1763 with the cession of Louisiana to Spain. Under Spanish rule the province was broken up into subdivisions in charge of military commandants; one of these was the District of Arkansas. A census taken in 1798–1799 showed a population of 368 for that district. In 1800 Spain secretly retroceded the Louisiana province to France, and three years later France sold it to the United States.[1]

Congress in 1804 divided the Louisiana Purchase into two parts—the Territory of Orleans with boundaries extending from the Gulf of Mexico northward to the thirty-third parallel, and the District of Louisiana embracing the remainder of the purchase.[2] The district, which included the area that was to become Arkansas Territory, was administered by the governor of Indiana Territory until the formation of Louisiana Territory in 1805.[3] The Arkansas country

---

[1] Fay Hempstead, *Historical Review of Arkansas* (3 vols., Chicago, 1911), I, 1–44. For a more detailed account of Spanish and French administration of Louisiana, see Louis Houck, *A History of Missouri* (3 vols., Chicago, 1908), I–II.

[2] 2 *U.S. Stat. at L.* (1845), 283–289; Clarence E. Carter, ed., *Territorial Papers of the United States,* Vol. IX, *Orleans Territory, 1803–1812* (Washington, 1940), 202–213.

[3] 2 *U.S. Stat. at L.* (1845), 331–332; *Terr. Papers,* Vol. XIII, *Louisiana-Missouri Territory, 1803–1806* (Washington, 1948), 92–95.

comprised part of Louisiana Territory until Orleans Territory was admitted into the Union as the state of Louisiana. To avoid confusion of names Louisiana Territory was in 1812 abolished and Missouri Territory created in its stead.[4]

The District of Louisiana was in 1804 divided into five smaller districts, one of them being the District of New Madrid. Two years later the legislature of Louisiana Territory created the District of Arkansas from the southern part of the District of New Madrid. Governor Meriwether Lewis made in 1808 the first appointment of district officials.[5] In 1812, when Missouri Territory was created, Governor Benjamin Howard issued a proclamation dividing it into five counties and placing the old District of Arkansas within the limits of New Madrid County.[6] A year later the Missouri territorial legislature created Arkansas County from the southern part of New Madrid County and designated Arkansas Post as county seat. Then in 1815 what is now the upper part of Arkansas was carved out of New Madrid County and set up as Lawrence County with Davidson-ville as county seat. In 1817 Davidsonville beat out Arkansas Post by a few days to become the site of the first post office established in Arkansas. The last territorial legislature in December, 1818, created from part of Arkansas County three new counties called Pulaski, Clark, and Hempstead.[7]

The first representative of Arkansas County in the territorial house was Henry Cassidy.[8] Edmund Hogan represented the county at the two subsequent legislatures. When the legislative council became elective in 1816, Arkansas County sent John Cummins; he was succeeded in the last legislature by Cassidy. Richard Murphy represented Lawrence County in the council in 1816 and Alexander S. Walker in the house; in 1818 the house members from the county were Perry G. Magness, Joseph Hardin, and John Davidson.[9]

Agitation for admission into the Union as a state began in Missouri Territory in the latter part of 1817. During the first three months of

---

[4] 2 *U.S. Stat. at L.* (1845), 743–747; *Terr. Papers, Vol. XIV, Louisiana-Missouri Territory, 1806–1814* (Washington, 1949), 552–559; Hempstead, *Historical Review of Arkansas,* I, 53.

[5] Dallas T. Herndon, *Annals of Arkansas, 1947* (Little Rock, n.d.), 67.

[6] "A Proclamation," October 1, 1812, St. Louis *Missouri Gazette*, October 3, 1812.

[7] Hempstead, *Historical Review of Arkansas,* I, 74, 76–77.

[8] Houck, *History of Missouri*, III, 6, indicates that Cassidy did not take his seat until a second session in January, 1815, but the house journal, printed in St. Louis *Missouri Gazette & Illinois Advertiser,* January 14, 1815, shows that Cassidy presented himself during the first session on December 16, 1814.

[9] Houck, *History of Missouri*, III, 2, 5–8. The councilman from Lawrence County in 1818 has not been determined.

1818 several petitions for statehood were presented in Congress.[10] One signed largely by citizens of Washington County, and presented in January, called for the erection of a state north of the parallel of 36° 30'.[11] On March 16, 1818, Delegate John Scott of Missouri Territory presented the first petition by inhabitants of southern Missouri asking for division of the Territory and establishment of their portion as a separate territory.[12]

Representative George Robertson of Kentucky offered a resolution on December 16, 1818, that a committee be appointed to consider the expediency of forming a separate territorial government for that part of Missouri Territory lying south of 36° 30'. Robertson said in a speech supporting his resolution that Missouri Territory would probably be authorized during the session in progress to form a constitution

with certain limited boundaries, the whole Territory being too extensive to be included within one State; that part of the Territory not included within the limits of the State would of course have occasion for a separate Territorial government, which, as in the case of the admission of Mississippi into the Union, had been done in regard to the Territory of Alabama. But if his expectation was disappointed, and an act should not pass at the present session to authorize the people of Missouri to form a State government, it was yet necessary thot [*sic*] a separate Territorial government should be established. This Territory, which was likely to become in time one of the most populous Territories in the Union, was, from its remoteness from the present seat of Government, almost without either law or government.[13]

Delegate Scott seconded Robertson's motion. He said that he himself had intended introducing a similar resolution when he received a memorial from the territorial legislature asking for the erection of a state in the northern section of the Territory. Scott believed "the situation" of the people in the southern portion of Missouri Territory

called loudly for the interposition of the General Government. They were not unfrequently without a competency of civil and military officers to administer justice, or keep order in the country; and although he [Scott] was not in possession of the census of the Territory, or any petition from the people of that part of it, yet he was convinced that the quantity of the population, and its respectability, justified the request; and believing . . . that it was the wish of the people, and knowing it was their interest, he hoped the

[10] Floyd Calvin Shoemaker, *Missouri's Struggle for Statehood, 1804–1821* (Jefferson City, 1916), 37–38.

[11] Houck, *History of Missouri*, III, 243–245.

[12] *Annals of Congress*, 15 Cong., 1 sess., II (March 16, 1818), 1391–1392, 1672; *House Journal*, 15 Cong., 1 sess., 345. See also *Terr. Papers*, Vol. XIX, *Arkansas Territory, 1819–1825* (Washington, 1953), 44, note 85.

[13] *Annals of Congress*, 15 Cong., 2 sess., III (December 16, 1818), 413.

House would not consider the resolution premature, but that it would be adopted.[14]

Robertson's motion passed and a committee of three with Robertson as chairman was appointed to consider separate territoriality.

Robertson's and Scott's assertions relative to the state of affairs in lower Missouri are substantiated by a statement of the editor of the *Missouri Gazette and Public Advertiser* in November, 1818, that Arkansas County had been in a "state of anarchy for months, having no sheriff in commission nor judge in attendance—and although they have a population of near 10,000 souls, they remain without weight in our councils, having only *one* member" in each branch of the legislature.[15] (Floyd C. Shoemaker believes that Arkansas and Lawrence Counties together should have had in the house "at least seven or eight representatives" instead of four.)[16]

A memorial of the Missouri territorial legislature asking that the Territory be permitted to form a state constitution was presented in the national House of Representatives on December 18, 1818.[17] It stated that the Territory possessed a population "little short of one hundred thousand souls" and boundaries that were "too extensive to admit of a convenient, proper, and equal administration of Government." Consequently, "the present interest and accommodation, as well as the future growth and prosperity" of Missouri Territory would be "greatly promoted" by its division. The line dividing the Territory should begin in the Mississippi River at the thirty-sixth parallel and run directly westward to the mouth of Big Black River, thence up White River to its intersection with the parallel of 36° 30', and thence west with that parallel to "a due north line" that would cross the Missouri River at the mouth of Wolf River.[18]

On December 21 Robertson introduced a bill for the creation of a separate territorial government for the southern portion of Missouri.[19]

[14] *Ibid.*, 414.

[15] St. Louis *Missouri Gazette and Public Advertiser,* November 13, 1818.

[16] Shoemaker, *Missouri's Struggle for Statehood,* 53, note 34.

[17] *Annals of Congress,* 15 Cong., 2 sess., III (December 18, 1818), 418.

[18] *American State Papers, Miscellaneous,* Vol. II (Washington, 1834), 557–558.

[19] *Annals of Congress,* 15 Cong., 2 sess., III (December 21, 1818), 422. Why Robertson instead of Scott should have pressed for the establishment of Arkansas Territory is not manifest, but the fact that he was later an active candidate for the territorial governorship suggests that he may have been motivated by a desire for the office. See *Terr. Papers,* XIX, 43, note 83. Shoemaker conjectures that the people in southern Missouri Territory had Robertson act for them because they "probably doubted" if Scott "would urge thirty-six degrees and thirty minutes as the dividing line, knowing already that the Missouri Territorial Legislature was asking or had asked for, territory below that parallel for the future State of Missouri." *Missouri's Struggle for Statehood,* 54, note 35.

Petitions to the same effect continued to come in. In January, 1819, four such petitions plus one asking that Arkansas Post be designated the seat of government were presented.[20]

The signers of one of the four January petitions[21] complained (1) that Arkansas County had been without a sheriff and coroner for over a year, (2) that it was inadequately represented in the territorial legislature, (3) that its citizens were over-taxed in proportion to the number of representatives they were permitted, (4) that although it paid part of the expense of two circuit courts, it did not enjoy benefit of courts, (5) that the judge required by law to reside in Arkansas County had lived elsewhere "nearly half the time since his first appointment,"[22] and (6) that the governor had in 1815–1816 mistreated settlers living south of the Arkansas River by ordering them to remove forthwith from lands belonging to Indians.[23]

The boundary indicated by these petitioners differed from that requested by the Missouri territorial legislature. Both the memorial and the petition would, however, include in Arkansas Territory not only the entire county of Arkansas but also a considerable part of Lawrence and a small portion of New Madrid. Shoemaker, who has considered the subject of Missouri's southern boundary at some length, believes that the people and representatives of Arkansas County and that part of Lawrence County up to the parallel of 36° 30' perhaps even 37° wished to be included in Arkansas Territory but that the people residing in New Madrid County below 36° 30' sincerely desired "to be attached" to Missouri. He considers also that influential landowners and politicians of southeastern Missouri desired to keep the area in both counties south of the 36° 30'. In the measure actually adopted only that part of New Madrid County below 36° 30' and north of 36° remained in Missouri.[24]

---

[20] *House Journal,* 15 Cong., 2 sess., 149, 191, 193, 202, 220. One of the four petitions requesting separate territoriality also asked that the seat of government be located at the mouth of the Cadron on the Arkansas; another asked that it be located at Arkansas Post.

[21] See *Terr. Papers,* XIX, 28, note 34. The other three petitions have not been located.

[22] The petitioners presumably referred to Judge George Bullitt, appointed in 1814. *Terr. Papers,* XIV, 741.

[23] *Ibid.,* XIX, 25–27.

[24] Shoemaker, *Missouri's Struggle for Statehood,* 48, note 28, 52–53, notes 32 and 34, 55, note 36; Houck, *History of Missouri,* I, 6–8. Houck believes that J. Hardeman Walker, an influential plantation owner near Caruthersville, was largely responsible for the inclusion in Missouri of that area south of the 36° 30'. See also Hempstead, *Historical Review of Arkansas,* I, 83.

On February 13, 1819, the House took up in Committee of the Whole an enabling bill for Missouri, whereupon James Tallmadge, Jr., of New York moved an amendment to prohibit further introduction of slavery into Missouri and to emancipate at age twenty-five all slave children born in the state. Tallmadge's motion produced "pretty wide debate" between the representatives of the free and the slave states.[25] On February 16 the House voted separately on the two clauses of the proposed amendment; both clauses passed, but the vote in each case was close, the Southerners being "almost unanimously on the negative side."[26]

On February 17, the day that the Missouri bill went to the Senate, the House in Committee of the Whole considered the bill to establish Arkansas Territory. John W. Taylor of New York forthwith moved an amendment to prohibit further introduction of slaves into Arkansas Territory and for emancipation at age twenty-five of children born of slaves in the Territory.[27] A similar motion by Representative Abner Laycock of Pennsylvania to prohibit admission of slaves into the Territory of Missouri had in 1812 failed and Northern congressmen had in 1798 sought unsuccessfully to abolish slavery in Mississippi Territory.[28]

Taylor's motion provoked a widespread debate resembling that over the Tallmadge amendment, but differing in part because the Taylor amendment sought to impose a condition on a territory instead of a state and applied to a more southern territory. Glover Moore says that fundamentally,

the chief objection to Missouri's admission as a slave state was that it lay in the same latitude with Ohio, Indiana, and Illinois—in a "sphere" of the West which the North had come to regard as rightly its own. Likewise, in the opinion of the South, the southerly location of Arkansas raised insurmountable objections to the prohibition of slavery there.[29]

Speaking in support of his motion, Taylor asserted that slavery was not necessary in Arkansas, for "wheat, corn, cotton, and tobacco"

[25] *Annals of Congress,* 15 Cong., 2 sess., III (February 13, 1819), 1166, 1169–1170.
[26] Glover Moore, *The Missouri Controversy, 1819–1821* (Lexington, 1953), 35, 40–53.
[27] *Annals of Congress,* 15 Cong., 2 sess., II (February 17, 1819), 1222. Taylor had played a prominent part in the debates over the Tallmadge amendment. Glover Moore says that Tallmadge considered himself and Taylor the "parents" of that amendment. *Missouri Controversy,* 39–40. According to the Federal census of 1820, Arkansas contained 1,617 slaves. Orville W. Taylor, *Negro Slavery in Arkansas* (Durham, 1958), 25.
[28] Moore, *Missouri Controversy,* 31–32.
[29] *Ibid.,* 60.

could be "raised in abundance, by freemen." It was only reasonable that "at least one portion of our country, capable of growing these staples, should be left open to the enterprise and industry of the North and East." Noticing that Henry Clay had expressed regret at the introduction of Taylor's amendment, and asked what Southerners had done that they should be proscribed,[30] Taylor declared that the North did not wish to proscribe the South, for "we leave them in the full enjoyment of all their rights; we only forbid them to practice wrongs: we invite them to the territory in question, but we forbid their bringing into it a population which cannot but prove its misfortune and curse." An accusation by Clay that Northerners were under the influence of "negrophobia" was false. Rather, it was to exclude this phobia from Arkansas that the amendment had been introduced.[31]

Felix Walker of North Carolina spoke in opposition to the amendment. He complained that to exclude slavery from the area west of the Mississippi River would be to deprive Southerners of "any advantages arising in the Government, or from having either part or lot, or any inheritance" in that region. Walker declared that Congress did not possess power to legislate on the property of citizens and denied that humanity would be served by prohibiting slaves to cross the Mississippi, for "in the frontier country the servant feeds as his master, and is sufficiently clothed; while in the interior of the old States the means of subsistence is scanty and improvident." He argued further that Arkansas was too far south to support a laboring white population and that its land could only be cultivated by Negroes. But the greatest objection to Taylor's amendment, Walker believed, was that it took away from the people of the Territory "the natural and Constitutional right" of legislating for themselves on the matter of slavery.[32]

Louis McLane of Delaware also spoke against restriction of slavery in Arkansas Territory. He maintained that Congress did not have power to impose such restriction because the Federal Constitution, which recognized slaves as property, said that property could not be interfered with by legislation. Moreover, the United States had agreed by the treaty of cession with France in 1803 to protect inhabitants of Louisiana in their property until they could be incorporated into the Union. Taylor's amendment amounted to virtual "emancipation

[30] Clay's speech is not recorded in the *Annals*.
[31] *Annals of Congress*, 15 Cong., 2 sess., II (February 17, 1819), 1222–1225.
[32] *Ibid.*, 1226–1227.

of the present slaves and their issue." Furthermore, the United States had agreed that the inhabitants of Louisiana in forming state governments should enjoy the same rights and immunities as other states; these rights included that of accepting or rejecting slavery; and such condition as Northerners sought to impose upon Missouri and upon Arkansas Territory (which would in time become a state) therefore violated the compact with France. McLane considered compromise the only solution to the problem. Since "gentlemen on this floor from the South and the West" had avowed their willingness to "agree upon a line which shall divide the slaveholding from the non-slave-holding States," McLane suggested a "compact," binding upon all subsequent congresses, to establish a line west of the Mississippi "north of which slavery should not be tolerated."[33]

After more debate[34] the Committee of the Whole voted separately on each clause. The clause to prohibit further introduction of slaves into Arkansas Territory was defeated 80 to 68, and the other, that slave children born in the Territory after its formation should be free at age twenty-five, was rejected "without a division."[35]

When the bill to establish Arkansas Territory was considered by the House on February 18, Taylor moved an amendment identical with his first except that only children born after the admission of Arkansas as a state should be free at age twenty-five. On the first clause, to prohibit further introduction of slavery, the House voted 71 to 70 against. The tabulation below shows that the vote was largely sectional, but that the slave states would have been defeated without help from a small number of free-state congressmen.[36]

The second clause, to free slave children at age twenty-five, passed by a vote of 75 to 73.[37] A tabulation by states shows an alignment almost identical with that on the first clause. Lewis Williams of North Carolina immediately moved to reconsider the vote on the second clause. He said that he "had voted with the majority, for the purpose of obtaining for himself the privilege of moving a reconsideration." He explained that he wished "a full expression of the opinion of the House on this important question, which could not now be obtained, as many members were out of the house." But Williams's motion

---

[33] *Ibid.*, 1227–1235.

[34] The texts of the speeches made in this debate are not recorded in *ibid.*

[35] *Ibid.*, 1235. Neither *Annals* nor *House Journal* gives a breakdown of the individual voting on the first clause.

[36] *Ibid.*, 1237–1238 (February 18, 1819).

[37] *Ibid.*, 1238.

STATE	FOR	AGAINST	NOT VOTING
New Hampshire	1	1	4
Vermont	5		
Massachusetts	11	3	6
Rhode Island	2		
Connecticut	5		2
New York	17	3	7
New Jersey	4	2	
Pennsylvania	20		3
Ohio	3	2	1
Indiana	1		
Illinois		1	
Delaware	1	1	
Maryland		6	3
Virginia		18	5
North Carolina		11	2
South Carolina		4	5
Georgia		5	1
Kentucky		8	2
Tennessee		5	1
Louisiana		1	
Mississippi			1
Total	70	71	43

was, notwithstanding some assistance from Northerners, defeated 79 to 77.[38] A tabulation by states indicates an alignment nearly identical with that on the two previous questions.

The bill was then ordered engrossed for its third and final reading. Evidently hoping to avoid possible passage of the amended bill on a final vote, Burwell Basset of Virginia moved to recommit it to a select committee. In ensuing discussion about "the course now most expedient to give the bill," William Lowndes of South Carolina moved to lay it on the table. After Lowndes assured the House that he would, "to prevent its being called up, and decided by surprise," move to take it up for final decision at twelve o'clock the next day, a vote was taken and the motion carried.[39]

No sooner had the House taken up the bill on February 19 than Robertson of Kentucky moved that it be recommitted to a select committee with instructions to strike out the clause of the Taylor amendment passed the day before. The ensuing vote resulted in an 88 to 88 deadlock which was broken by the ballot of Speaker Clay in favor of the motion. The following table shows the vote by states.[40]

[38] *Ibid.*, 1238–1239.
[39] *Ibid.*, 1239.
[40] *Ibid.*, 1272–1273 (February 19, 1819).

STATE	FOR	AGAINST	NOT VOTING
New Hampshire	1	4	1
Vermont		5	
Massachusetts	4	15	1
Rhode Island		2	
Connecticut		7	
New York	3	24	
New Jersey	2	4	
Pennsylvania	1	22	
Ohio	3	3	
Indiana		1	
Illinois	1		
Delaware	1	1	
Maryland	7		2
Virginia	23		
North Carolina	13		
South Carolina	7		2
Georgia	6		
Kentucky	9		1
Tennessee	5		1
Louisiana	1		
Mississippi	1		
Total	88	88	8

The select committee appointed by the House consisted of three slave-state and two free-state men. After Robertson as chairman promptly reported the bill without the restriction, the House voted 89 to 87 to accept the action of the committee in striking out the restriction. Again the slave-state men had won.[41]

Taylor now moved to amend the bill by a provision that slaves brought into Arkansas Territory should not remain for a period longer than nine months.[42] Ezekiel Whitman of Massachusetts spoke against Taylor's motion. He did not object on constitutional grounds, for he thought that Congress could impose any condition on admission of new states and "require any stipulation" on a territory. Nor did he hold that the question of slavery in Missouri and Arkansas should be decided on the basis of hopes or fear for the future of the institution. He himself had voted against slavery in Missouri, but not from any belief that the expansion of slavery would increase its "horrors." Indeed, slaves would be better provided for in the western country than on the Atlantic seaboard, and as slavery spread and the number of free inhabitants increased, "in the same ratio you increase

[41] *Ibid.*, 1273–1274. Thomas Culbreth of Maryland, who had not voted on Robertson's motion, balloted this time with the slave states; and Zabdiel Sampson of Massachusetts, who had voted against Robertson's motion, apparently did not vote on the committee report. Otherwise the second vote was identical with the first.

[42] *Ibid.*, 1274. This motion is not reported in the *House Journal.*

the chance for emancipation, final and total." The essential question was one of fairness between the "two great sections of the Union." The United States had acquired a vast area west of the Mississippi and each section had an "equal right to its enjoyment." If slavery were restricted there, the North would be favored; if it were not restricted, the South would be favored. "We must . . . go on as we have begun; admitting some States with, and some without, any restriction." As to Arkansas Territory he favored

no restriction . . . although I was, and still am, in favor of adopting it in relation to Missouri. The settled part of Arkansas will be south of the southerly line of Kentucky. In my opinion, to do justice to our Southern brethren, they ought to have permission to carry with them their slaves, even further north. But as Missouri extends south to this line, and we could not admit slavery in any part, and not in the whole, there seemed to be no alternative but to confine the admission of slavery to the south of that line.[43]

Upon the conclusion of Whitman's speech, Taylor "modified" his amendment to state that "neither slavery nor involuntary servitude shall hereafter be introduced" into Arkansas Territory, "otherwise than for the punishment of crimes."[44] Forthwith Charles F. Mercer of Virginia offered a proviso to Taylor's "modified" amendment that nothing contained therein should divest Arkansans "of their rights of property in the slaves which they now hold, or the natural increase thereof; nor to entitle to his freedom any slave carried therein, and held there for a period not exceeding nine months." Mercer's motion was negatived "without a division."[45] Taylor's amendment was then voted on and rejected 90 to 86.[46] A tabulation by states shows a voting pattern similar with that on the previous questions.

Refusing to give up, Taylor offered a more conciliatory amendment. Because he thought it important that a line beyond which slavery should not be permitted should be designated, he would forbid introduction of slavery "into any part of the Territories of the United States, lying north of 36 degrees and 30 minutes north latitude."[47] Since Arkansas lay south of the proposed line this amendment would impose no condition on slavery in that Territory.

Arthur Livermore of New Hampshire believed Taylor's proposal had been made "in the true spirit of compromise, which ought to be met, but suggested a different line." John Rhea of Tennessee opposed

[43] *Ibid.*, 1274–1279.
[44] *Ibid.*, 1279.
[45] *Ibid.*, 1279–1280.
[46] *Ibid.*, 1280.
[47] *Ibid.*

the amendment because he believed it was unconstitutional and inconsistent with the treaty with France. Alexander Ogle of Pennsylvania objected to it because he was against "any compromise by which slavery in any of the Territories should be recognised or sanctioned by Congress." George F. Strother of Virginia wanted Taylor's "principle" brought forward in a separate bill. William Henry Harrison of Ohio, who had consistently voted with the slave states on the Arkansas bill, proposed a line running west from the mouth of the Des Moines River to the western boundary of the United States. Philip P. Barbour of Virginia believed the amendment "partial" because it would apply "a rule to one portion and a different rule to another portion of citizens having equal rights." He would "let a future Congress act on it, as should then appear expedient." Richard C. Anderson, Jr., of Kentucky declared that the amendment offered no compromise because "its friends asked everything and gave nothing —what they got now was insured to them, and what they conceded now would not be binding on a future Congress, and the same principle might be extended by hereafter inserting it in the constitution of Arkansas when it should become a State." He would not agree to a compromise line even if "fairly proposed" because establishment of such line was contrary to the treaty with France.

Hoping to "put an end at once" to the debate Thomas W. Cobb of Georgia called for a vote on the *"previous question"* (the bill to establish Arkansas Territory as originally introduced). Though the House balloted 74 to 67 against Cobb's proposal, Taylor, believing compromise impossible, withdrew his amendment[48] and the bill passed the House on February 20 without further debate.[49]

The Senate took up the bill two days later. After being twice read it was, on motion of John J. Crittenden of Kentucky, referred to a committee composed of Charles Tait of Georgia, Jeremiah Morrow of Ohio, Thomas H. Williams of Mississippi, Ninian Edwards of Illinois, and John Williams of Tennessee.[50] Tait reported the bill on February 23 without amendment.[51]

The Arkansas bill was read a third time on February 27, but no final action was taken. Instead, the Senate considered the Missouri bill, which had passed the House with the Tallmadge amendment. By a vote of 22 to 16 the clause prohibiting further introduction of

[48] *Ibid.*, 1280–1282. Neither the *Annals of Congress* nor the *House Journal* gives the details of the vote.
[49] *Ibid.*, 1283 (February 20, 1819).
[50] *Ibid.*, III (February 22, 1819), 252.
[51] *Ibid.*, 253 (February 23, 1819).

slavery was struck out, and by a vote of 31 to 7 the gradual emancipation clause was rejected.[52]

When on March 1 the Senate resumed consideration of the Arkansas bill, James Burrill, Jr., of Rhode Island moved that it be returned to committee with instructions to insert an amendment prohibiting further introduction of slavery into Arkansas Territory. Burrill's motion was rejected 19 to 14, and the bill passed.[53] Four senators from northwestern states sided with slave-state senators to give victory to the slave states. The vote by states appears on the following table:

STATE	FOR	AGAINST	NOT VOTING
New Hampshire	1		1
Vermont	1		1
Massachusetts	1		1
Rhode Island	1		1
Connecticut	2		
New York	2		
New Jersey	2		
Pennsylvania	2		
Ohio	1	1	
Indiana	1	1	
Illinois		2	
Delaware			2
Maryland		1	1
Virginia		2	
North Carolina		2	
South Carolina		1	1
Georgia		1	1
Kentucky		2	
Tennessee		2	
Louisiana		2	
Mississippi		2	
Total	14	19	9

The balloting in both houses of Congress shows that the members from slave states consistently voted as a bloc. So also did a large majority of free-state men, but a small minority supported the slave-state position. In the Senate the slave-state victory was achieved only with the aid of senators from northwestern states, where many former Southerners had settled.[54] In the House it was accomplished only with the help of congressmen from both northwestern and northeastern states.

[52] *Ibid.*, 272–273 (February 27, 1819).

[53] *Ibid.*, 274 (March 1, 1819).

[54] Moore, *Missouri Controversy,* 52–54. Moore states that Senators Jesse B. Thomas and Ninian Edwards of Illinois, who voted with the slave states, "were not only Southerners by birth, but both were slaveholders, if indentured servants be considered slaves, which they were for all intents and purposes."

The debate on the Arkansas bill foreshadowed the famous Missouri Compromise of 1820. McLane's mention of a compromise line to divide free and slave territory west of the Mississippi was the first reference to compromise recorded in the *Annals of Congress,* and the parallel of 36°30′, suggested by Taylor to be the dividing line, was later agreed upon in the Missouri Compromise.[55]

By the provisions of the organic act, approved March 2, 1819, the Arkansas territorial government was to commence operation at Arkansas Post on July 4, 1819.[56] The new Territory was to be bounded on the east by the Mississippi River, on the west by "the western territorial boundary line," on the south by the 33° parallel, and on the north by a line beginning at the 36° on the Mississippi and running thence to the St. Francis River, up that stream to the 36°30′, and thence west along that parallel to the western boundary.

The executive power was vested in a governor appointed by the President, who should hold office for three years and reside in the Territory. The governor would serve not only as commander-in-chief of the territorial militia but also as superintendent of Indian affairs. He was to appoint all territorial officials "required by law" and to grant pardons. He could "on extraordinary occasions" convene the general assembly. He was also assigned such other powers and duties "as are, by law given to, and imposed" on the governor of Missouri Territory. A secretary, appointed by the President for a four-year term, and to be resident in the Territory, would rank as the second highest executive officer and perform all duties imposed on the secretary of Missouri Territory.

The judicial power was placed in a superior court, in such inferior courts as the legislature should establish, and in justices of the peace. Three judges, appointed by the President for four-year terms, would reside in the Territory and form the superior court. The court would have jurisdiction in criminal and penal cases, exclusive cognizance in capital cases, original jurisdiction concurrently with the inferior courts, and appellate jurisdiction in civil cases where the amount in controversy was one hundred dollars or more.

The legislative power was vested in the governor and superior

---

[55] Moore, *Missouri Controversy,* 64; Taylor, *Negro Slavery in Arkansas,* 21–22.

[56] Arkansas Post, which consisted in 1819 of three stores and about twenty houses, was during the territorial period usually referred to as the Post of Arkansas, and post office records called it the village of Arkansas until December, 1831, when it was officially designated Arkansas Post. *Terr. Papers,* XIX, 155, note 57; *Arkansas Gazette* (Little Rock), April 18, 1832; Thomas Nuttall, *A Journal of Travels into the Arkansa [sic] Territory, During the Year 1819* (Philadelphia, 1821), 75.

court judges. But when the governor was "satisfied" that a majority of the freeholders desired it, that part of the Missouri organic act of 1812 pertaining to the organization of the legislature was to be in force in Arkansas Territory. Until the Territory contained five thousand free white adult males, however, the number of representatives should not exceed nine. The house would be elected by the people while a council of nine would be appointed by the President from a list of eighteen persons nominated by the house.[57] Upon entering into the second grade of territorial government the people could elect a delegate to Congress.

The Arkansas organic act provided further that all laws in force in Missouri Territory on July 4, not inconsistent with the provisions of this act, should be in force in Arkansas Territory until modified or repealed by the Arkansas legislature; and all bounty lands in the Territory granted for military service in the War of 1812 would, while held by the patentees, or their heirs, remain exempt from taxes for three years from date of patent. The line established between land districts in Lawrence and Cape Girardeau Counties was by the organic act altered to correspond with the northern boundary of Arkansas Territory.[58]

Thus Arkansas Territory was created, to begin seventeen years of territoriality. In that period the political foundations of the future state of Arkansas would be laid.

[57] See 2 *U.S. Stat. at L.* (1845), 744–745.
[58] 3 *U.S. Stat. at L.* (1846), 493–496; *Terr. Papers*, XIX, 44–50.

CHAPTER TWO

Organizing the Territorial Government

THE FIRST STEP in the organization of a territorial government was the filling of the more important offices. Of the four men known to have been put forward for the governorship, three were Kentuckians: Robert Trimble declined being considered; Representative Solomon P. Sharp appears to have been only a nominal contender; and Representative George Robertson, who had introduced the bill to establish Arkansas Territory and was seemingly most active of the aspirants, in the end declined a tender of the position.[1] The fourth name urged was that of Brigadier General James Miller of the United States Army. Four New Hampshire congressmen assured President James Monroe on March 1, 1819, that the general was competent, deserving, and needy.[2] On March 3 Monroe gave him the post.[3]

Miller was born April 25, 1776, at Peterborough, New Hampshire, and raised on a farm. Admitted to the New Hampshire bar in 1803, he practiced law in Greenfield.[4] Having entered the army as a major in 1808, he was breveted colonel in 1812 for distinguished service against the British at Brownstown, and made brigadier gen-

---

[1] *Biographical Directory of the American Congress, 1774–1927* (Washington, 1928), 1468; Clarence E. Carter, ed., *Territorial Papers of the United States,* Vol. XIX, *Arkansas Territory, 1819–1825* (Washington, 1953), 43, note 83. Why Robertson should have declined the place after having made vigorous efforts to obtain it is not manifest.

[2] *Terr. Papers,* XIX, 42–43.

[3] *Ibid.,* 50–51.

[4] Rebecca Miller to Robert W. Trimble, June 12, 1876, Robert W. Trimble Collection, Arkansas History Commission; Benson J. Lossing, *The Pictorial Field-Book of the War of 1812* (New York, 1868), 819, note 1; communication of Arkansas Farmer, November 1, 1821, *Arkansas Gazette* (Arkansas Post), November 17, 1821.

eral in 1814 for outstanding performance at Lundy's Lane.[5] His gallantry at Chippewa, Niagara, and Fort Erie won him a gold medal from Congress. He resigned from the army June 1, 1819, shortly after his appointment as governor. An "Arkansas Farmer" described him in 1821 as "a steady, substantial man."[6]

The office of territorial secretary, though much less important and remunerative than the governorship, was seemingly the more sought after, probably because a young man of comparatively little experience might hope to be appointed.[7] Eleven men are mentioned in the Arkansas *Territorial Papers* as having either applied for or been recommended to the post.[8] The successful candidate was Robert Crittenden of Kentucky, younger brother of Senator John J. Crittenden.[9] Robert's candidacy had been pressed by Representatives Richard M. Johnson and Tunstall Quarles of Kentucky.[10]

Born in Woodford County, Kentucky, on January 1, 1797, Crittenden entered the army in 1814 and was discharged a first lieutenant the next year. In 1817–1818 he served as a captain of volunteers in the Seminole War. Having studied law with his brother at Russellville, he was admitted to the bar in 1818.[11] Albert Pike characterized Crittenden as "a thoroughly well-bred Kentucky gentleman," "sagacious and well informed."[12]

The successful candidates for superior court judgeships were Andrew Scott of Missouri Territory, Charles Jouett of Michigan

[5] Francis B. Heitman, *Historical Register and Dictionary of the United States Army, from its Organization, September 29, 1789, to March 2, 1903* (2 vols., Washington, 1903), I, 710–711; Fay Hempstead, *Historical Review of Arkansas* (3 vols., Chicago, 1911), I, 85–86; Lossing, *Pictorial Field-Book of the War of 1812*, pp. 819–824; Clara B. Eno, "Territorial Governors of Arkansas," *Arkansas Historical Quarterly*, IV (Winter, 1945), 276–277.

[6] *Gazette*, November 17, 1821. For an account of Miller's Arkansas career, see Lonnie J. White, "James Miller: Arkansas' First Territorial Governor," *Arkansas Historical Quarterly*, XIX (Spring, 1960), 12–30.

[7] Besides a salary of $2,000 per year, the governor received $1,500 as Indian superintendent. The secretary's annual salary was only $1,000. It may be that aspirants to the secretaryship considered the salary excellent in proportion to the duties of the office.

[8] For the names of other candidates and where they were from, see *Terr. Papers*, XIX, 40, note 78.

[9] *Ibid.*, 51–52, note 5. One suspects, from the fact that Robert's commission was sent to John J. Crittenden at Russellville, Kentucky, that his brother may have had a hand in his appointment.

[10] *Ibid.*, 29, 40.

[11] *Gazette* (Little Rock), January 6, 1835; *Arkansas Advocate* (Little Rock), January 2, 1835; Edwin Marshall Williams, "The Conway-Crittenden Duel," *Arkansas Historical Review*, I (February, 1934), 15–16; Farrar Newberry, "Some Notes on Robert Crittenden," *Arkansas Historical Quarterly*, XVI (Autumn, 1957), 243–244.

[12] Pike, "Robert Crittenden," in John Hallum, *Biographical and Pictorial History of Arkansas* (Albany, 1887), I, 65–66. Only one volume was published.

Territory, and Robert P. Letcher of Kentucky.[13] All three appointees were native Virginians. Letcher (b. 1788), a brother-in-law of Representative George Robertson of Kentucky, had practiced law in Lancaster, Kentucky, and sat in the state legislature in 1813–1815 and 1817.[14] Scott (b. 1788), a brother of Delegate John Scott of Missouri Territory, had served for several years as clerk of the Missouri territorial house.[15] Jouett (b. 1772) had practiced law in Charlottesville, Virginia, lived on two occasions in Kentucky, and been Indian agent in Detroit and Chicago. His appointment had been urged by members of Congress from Virginia, Mississippi, and Kentucky.[16]

Though the Arkansas territorial government was scheduled to commence operation on July 4, it was not until July 28 that the superior court judges and Secretary Robert Crittenden, acting as governor, convened in legislative session at Arkansas Post.[17] Before adjourning August 3 they made appropriations for the operation of the territorial government; declared in force in Arkansas Territory all laws of a general nature then in effect in Missouri Territory and not "repugnant" to the Arkansas organic act; established the territorial offices of auditor and treasurer; and formed two judicial circuits.[18]

To fill vacancies created by the legislative acts, Crittenden in August appointed James Woodson Bates and Neil McLane to be circuit judges; William Trimble and Henry Cassidy, circuit attorneys;

---

[13] *Terr. Papers,* XIX, 52–55. For the names of other candidates and where they were from, see *ibid.,* 14–18, 19–21, 36–37, 39, 41–42, note 80.

[14] *Biographical Directory of the American Congress,* 1221; *Terr. Papers,* XIX, 54, note 13.

[15] *Terr. Papers,* XIV, *Louisiana-Missouri Territory, 1806–1814* (Washington, 1949), 693–694; *Ibid.,* XIX, 52, note 7; Louis Houck, *A History of Missouri* (3 vols., Chicago, 1908), III, 6, 8; Hallum, *History of Arkansas,* 62. Scott was living at Potosi, Missouri Territory, at the time of his appointment.

[16] Milo M. Quaife, ed., *The John Askin Papers* (2 vols., Detroit, 1931), II, 472, note 17; *Terr. Papers,* XIX, 37, note 60, 37–38, 39–40, 53–54.

[17] Josiah H. Shinn doubts that Judge Jouett was present at the meeting of the first legislature notwithstanding the fact that all the acts passed bore his signature. In support of his assertion Shinn cites a grand jury presentment in 1820 (in *Gazette,* June 24, 1820) stating that Jouett had never taken his seat on the bench. Shinn maintains that Jouett would have "had to take his seat as a member of the court" before he could serve as a legislator, and quotes a statement from the *Gazette,* November 18, 1820, that Jouett was driven from the Territory in the spring of 1819 by mosquitoes before reaching Arkansas Post. *Pioneers and Makers of Arkansas* (Little Rock, 1908), 196–197. Actually the statement in the *Gazette* refers to the spring of 1820, not the spring of 1819; and both Crittenden's report to the Secretary of State and a petition to the President by the territorial legislature in 1820 stated that all the judges had been present at the first legislature. Petition to President, February 11, 1820, *Terr. Papers,* XIX, 144–145; Crittenden to Secretary of State, July 12, 1820, *ibid.,* 204.

[18] *Arkansas Acts,* 1819, pp. 70–82; Crittenden to Secretary of State, July 12, 1820, *Terr. Papers,* XIX, 204; *Gazette Supplement,* November 20, 1919. Two of the six acts passed were minor in character.

George W. Scott, auditor; and James Scull, treasurer. The same
month Crittenden appointed sheriffs, coroners, and clerks for the five
counties.[19]

In late October, 1819, a printer named William E. Woodruff arrived in Arkansas Post. A native of New York born in 1795, Wood-
ruff had served an apprenticeship in the printing office of the *Long
Island Star,* left New York in 1817, and made his way eventually to
Tennessee. After the creation of Arkansas Territory Woodruff had
purchased a small printing press, and this he brought with him to
Arkansas Post, where he began November 20, 1819, the weekly
Arkansas Gazette.[20] Woodruff was, for over a year in 1820–1821, associated in publishing the *Gazette* with Robert Briggs.[21] John
McArthur, a former mail contractor in Missouri Territory, had intended as early as June, 1819, to set up a press at Arkansas Post, and
had received appointment to be publisher of United States laws, but
his projected enterprise never materialized.[22] When the Secretary of
State learned of McArthur's failure, he gave the appointment of publisher of the United States laws to Woodruff and Briggs.[23]

In response to petitioning by the freeholders,[24] and to obtain their
"assistance and advice" in governing the sparsely populated Territory,[25] Acting Governor Crittenden issued on October 20 a proclamation "declaring the territory in the second grade of Government, and
directing an election to be held for Delegate to Congress and members of the General Assembly."[26] It has sometimes been supposed
that Crittenden's call for the election was illegal because the Terri-

[19] *Terr. Papers,* XIX, 789, 791–795, 801.
[20] John Lewis Ferguson, "William E. Woodruff and the Territory of Arkansas,
1819–1836" (unpublished Ph.D. dissertation, Tulane University, 1960), 1–14; *Gazette
Supplement,* November 20, 1919; Hempstead, *Historical Review of Arkansas,* I, 92–93;
Ernestine Gravley, "William Edward Woodruff, Pioneer Arkansas Journalist," *Arkansas
Historical Quarterly,* XIV (Summer, 1955), 128–129; Jesse Ryon Lucke, "Correspondence Concerning the Establishment of the First Arkansas Press," *ibid.,* 161–162; Fred W.
Allsopp, *History of the Arkansas Press for a Hundred Years and More* (Little Rock,
1922), 42–48.
[21] *Gazette,* March 4, 1820, May 12, 1821.
[22] McArthur to Secretary of State, June 25, 1819, Secretary of State to McArthur,
August 5, 1819, Woodruff and Briggs to Secretary of State, November 16, 1820, *Terr.
Papers,* XIX, 80, 93–94, 228–230.
[23] Secretary of State to Delegate Bates, November 30, 1830, *ibid.,* 240.
[24] Crittenden to Secretary of State, July 12, 1820, *ibid.,* 204; Petition to Governor,
n.d., Luther C. Gulley Collection, Arkansas History Commission; "Arkansas Territory,"
St. Louis *Missouri Gazette & Public Advertiser,* November 17, 1819; Ted R. Worley,
ed., "A Letter of Governor Miller to His Wife," *Arkansas Historical Quarterly,* XIII
(Winter, 1954), 388.
[25] Crittenden estimated the population in 1819 at "not exceeding fourteen thousand."
Crittenden, "To the Freemen of Arkansas," April 6, 1833, *Gazette,* April 24, 1833.
[26] *Ibid.,* November 20, 1819; Crittenden to Secretary of State, November 28, 1819,
and July 12, 1820, *Terr. Papers,* XIX, 122, 204–205.

tory was not of the second grade.[27] Actually, although the organic
act of March 2, 1819, provided for Arkansas Territory to commence
under the first grade of government, section six of that act stipulated
that as much of the Missouri organic act of 1812 as pertained to the
organization of a general assembly in the second grade should be
operative in Arkansas Territory, "so soon as the Governor thereof
shall be satisfied that such is the desire of a majority of the freeholders."[28]

In the election held November 20 James Woodson Bates defeated
five other candidates for the delegateship. The *Gazette* reported that
Bates received 401 votes; Stephen F. Austin, 342; Alexander S.
Walker, 226; Henry Cassidy, 156; Robert F. Slaughter, 138; and
Perly Wallis, 8. According to Editor Woodruff, Austin's candidacy
had not been announced until thirteen days before the election, and
the people in Arkansas County and two townships of Lawrence
County were not aware of his running.[29] Acting Governor Crittenden's election proclamation gave the vote as Bates, 403; Austin,
266; Walker, 156; Cassidy, 152; Slaughter, 140; and Wallis, 4. The
differences from Woodruff's figures rose mainly or entirely from the
fact that Crittenden had no official returns from Clark County, where
most of the vote had been divided between Walker and Austin.[30]

Delegate Bates, a Virginian born in 1788, had attended Yale, been
graduated from Princeton, and practiced law in Virginia. In 1816 he
had moved to St. Louis, Missouri Territory, and in 1819 came to
Arkansas Territory, where Crittenden appointed him judge of the
first judicial circuit. His brother, Frederick Bates, had been secretary
successively of Michigan, Louisiana, and Missouri Territories.[31] A
later pseudonymous writer said that Bates's successful bid for the
delegateship had been backed by Secretary Crittenden,[32] with whom
he had, according to Josiah H. Shinn, formed a law partnership.[33]

---

[27] David Y. Thomas, *Arkansas and Its People: A History, 1541–1930* (4 vols.,
New York, 1930), I, 45; Marie Cash, "Arkansas in Territorial Days," *Arkansas His-
torical Quarterly,* I (September, 1942), 225–226; Newberry, "Some Notes on Robert
Crittenden," *ibid.,* XVI, 246.

[28] *Terr. Papers,* XIX, 47; 2 *U.S. Stat. at L.* (1845), 744–745.

[29] *Gazette,* December 11, 1819.

[30] "Election Proclamation," November, 1819, *ibid.,* December 25, 1819.

[31] *Biographical Directory of the American Congress,* 679; *Terr. Papers,* XIX, 118,
note 77. Another brother, Edward, subsequently became Attorney General in President
Lincoln's cabinet.

[32] A Voter of Pulaski County, "To the Voters of Arkansas. No. VI," *Gazette,*
July 17, 1827.

[33] Shinn, *Makers of Arkansas,* 59. The only evidence in the *Gazette* to support Shinn's assertion that Bates and Crittenden were law partners is a notice by Bates

Albert Pike regarded Bates as a "genius" and a "polished, keen, brilliant writer" though a poor orator.[34]

Elected to the legislative council were Sylvanus Phillips of Arkansas County, Jacob Barkman of Clark County, David Clark of Hempstead County, Edward McDonald of Lawrence County, and John McElmurry of Pulaski County. The nine victorious candidates for the house of representatives were William O. Allen and William B. R. Horner of Arkansas County, Thomas Fish of Clark County, John English and William Stevenson of Hempstead County, Joab Hardin and Joseph Hardin, Sr., of Lawrence County, and Radford Ellis and Thomas H. Tindall of Pulaski County.[35]

While these events were taking place in Arkansas, Governor Miller had left his family in New Hampshire on September 10 and proceeded to Washington, obtaining there "sundry articles" for use in promoting friendship with the Indians. At Pittsburgh the ordnance department issued him upon an order brought from Washington 400 stand of arms, 40,000 rounds of ammunition, and 50 pistols with which to supply the territorial militia.[36] Accompanied by a party of twenty persons, many of them old army friends, he left Pittsburgh on October 17, and "was cordially received, and every mark of attention paid him" at Cincinnati, Louisville, and numerous other smaller towns all along his route. Seventy days on the Ohio, Mississippi, and Arkansas rivers brought Miller and his immigrant retinue to Arkansas Post on December 26.[37]

Miller's first official act was to call for February 7, 1820, a special session of the newly elected legislature.[38] The legislators, once duly convened and organized, selected a joint committee to inform the governor of the readiness of the plenum to receive any communication he might wish to make. He replied that he doubted the legality of the election of the council, and that consequently he wished the as-

---

referring his clients to Crittenden during his absence in Washington. *Gazette,* December 18, 1819. Bates and Crittenden in 1820 became partners in a land agency. "Land Agency," *ibid.,* July 15, 1820.

[34] Pike, "James W. Bates," in Hallum, *History of Arkansas,* 85.

[35] *Gazette,* November 27, December 4, 11, 1819, February 12, October 7, 1820.

[36] Thomas L. McKenney to Miller, September 28, 1819, and Miller's Message to Assembly, February 10, 1820, *Terr. Papers,* XIX, 110–111, 139.

[37] "Arrival of the Governor," *Gazette,* January 1, 1820; "Early Times," *ibid.,* August 17, 1873; Fay Hempstead, *A Pictorial History of Arkansas* (St. Louis, 1890), 178–180; Hallum, *History of Arkansas,* 167–168; Vivian Daniel, "The Territorial Development of Arkansas, 1819–1836" (unpublished M.A. thesis, University of Texas, 1929), 18–20.

[38] Proclamation by Miller, December 29, 1819, *Terr. Papers,* XIX, 133–134.

sembly to consider the matter.[39] His solicitude was predicated on a fear that the Arkansas organic law of March 2, 1819, which for the mode of electing the general assembly referred to the Missouri organic law of June 4, 1812, did not tacitly embrace an amendatory law of April 29, 1816, providing that in the second grade of government the people should elect both the councilmen and the representatives. The law of 1812 had required the representatives to list eighteen persons from whom the President would nominate nine as councilmen. The Arkansas organic law said nothing of the law of 1816; and if the law of 1812 was still applicable, then the members of the council had been illegally elected.

After Miller's doubts had been made known to the assembly, Secretary Crittenden defended before a joint session his call for the election of both houses. A debate following Crittenden's speech terminated in a joint resolution declaring that the legislature did not doubt the legality of the election.

The next day a legislative conference considered further the legality of the election. At the meeting, Governor Miller produced the written opinions of Judge Scott of the superior court and Judge McLane of the second judicial circuit as to the "intent and meaning" of the Arkansas organic law. McLane considered that Congress had intended that the subsequent law of 1816 should apply; Scott thought otherwise. After discussing the judges' views, the conference, at Miller's suggestion, heard behind closed doors the opinion of various lawyers. The outcome was a resolution of February 10 to the effect that the assembly would continue in being and would share with the governor any censure for doing so should the Federal government find the election illegal. In the meantime, Congress was to be memorialized for a "favorable construction" of the organic law.[40]

Addressing the assembly later in the day, Miller commended "the foresight" of his predecessor, "whose arrangements have given me the aid of your joint wisdom,"[41] and explained why he himself had not been on hand when the territorial government commenced opera-

---

[39] Miller subsequently wrote his wife that he did not discover until after he had issued his proclamation that the people "had no right" to choose the council. Worley, ed., "Letter of Miller to His Wife," *Arkansas Historical Quarterly*, XIII, 388.

[40] "The General Assembly," *Gazette*, February 12, 1820.

[41] Miller's favorable notice of Crittenden here seems to contradict Newberry's assumption in "Some Notes on Robert Crittenden," *Arkansas Historical Quarterly*, XVI, 246–247, that Miller was probably offended by Crittenden's action in advancing the Territory to the second grade. Miller himself referred to Crittenden in 1831 as "my old and steady friend." Miller to William E. Woodruff, July 19, 1831, William E. Woodruff Papers, Arkansas History Commission. See also Crittenden to T. P. Eskridge, November 5, 1833, *Advocate*, November 13, 1833.

tions. He then pointed out that the legislature must provide a code of laws for the territorial government. It should also request the Federal government to consider (1) bringing the public lands into market, (2) opening roads along postal routes, (3) making propitious Indian treaties, and (4) passing a preemption law. Observing that the national government had "generally been liberal in the encouragement of young Seminaries in other Territories," Miller suggested that "the duty we owe the rising generation" required early provision for its education. Because the status of the legislative council was in doubt, Miller thought the assembly should confine its lawmaking to matters not admitting of postponement.[42]

In a reply to Miller's message, the legislature expressed "entire satisfaction" with his appointment as governor and stated that the reasons he had given for not arriving earlier convinced them that the delay arose from unavoidable circumstances and not from "neglect." They had already acted "in a great measure" on his recommendations, and would confine their further "deliberation" to indispensable measures.[43]

On February 15, 1820, the legislature memorialized Congress asking passage of an act to declare the amendatory act of 1816 applicable to the organic act for Arkansas.[44] After the adjournment on February 24, Secretary Crittenden carried the memorial to Kentucky and forwarded it thence to Washington.[45] In response to President Monroe's request for an opinion, Attorney General William Wirt held that the law of 1816 was applicable to the Arkansas organic act, but that it would "be the better course to remove the doubt by an act of Congress."[46] The matter was finally settled as the legislature desired by an act of Congress approved April 21, 1820.[47]

Other business of the February session of the legislature included appropriations for 1820–1821; a requirement that sheriffs pay over public monies to the territorial auditor; appointment of William E. Woodruff as public printer; designating of Cadron as the county seat of Pulaski County, and Arkansas Post as the permanent county seat of Arkansas County; creation of Miller and Phillips Counties;[48] and a

---

[42] Message by Miller to Assembly, February 10, 1820, *Terr. Papers*, XIX, 138–140; "Governor's Message," *Gazette*, February 19, 1820.

[43] Assembly to Miller, n.d., *Terr. Papers*, XIX, 141.

[44] *Ibid.*, 147–148.

[45] *Gazette*, May 13, 1820; "General Assembly," *ibid.*, November 13, 1833.

[46] Attorney General to President, April 6, 1820, *Terr. Papers*, XIX, 157; *Gazette*, May 13, 1820.

[47] 3 *U.S. Stat. at L.* (1846), 565; *Terr. Papers*, XIX, 148, note 46.

[48] *Arkansas Acts*, February, 1820, pp. 83–106.

petition to the President and memorials to Congress on such matters as the judiciary, Indians, roads, and boundaries.[49]

A petition from the assembly to the President, dated February 11, 1820, complained that the Territory had been without the services of Judges Jouett and Letcher since August, 1819, and asked that they be "forced to perform" their duties and to reside in the Territory.[50] The next April, thirteen territorial legislators requested that Jouett's and Letcher's posts be declared vacant and that Jason Chamberlain and Henry Cassidy of Arkansas Territory be appointed in their stead.[51] At the June term of the superior court a grand jury presentment complained that Jouett had never taken his seat on the bench and that suitors "are unable, in many important causes to come to trial, necessarily continuing suits from time to time, multiplying expense, labor and vexation, intolerable to be borne in civilized society."[52] In October the legislature complained to Congress that the courts were "virtually shut" and asked for passage of a law to coerce attendance of appointed officials.[53]

Rumors that Letcher would resign had circulated from the time of his appointment. In a letter to Senator Richard M. Johnson of Kentucky on March 29, 1820, Representative George Robertson stated that Letcher had written him the previous December that he *"wished his resignation* to take effect" on December 6. Robertson had answered that "his office was not, as he [Letcher] expected and wished, vacated, and that he Must resign, and not express a *wish* that his resignation should take effect on a certain day." Letcher had then asked Robertson to announce his resignation effective April 1. Robertson had, he said, intended to comply with Letcher's request "in convenient time." Robertson did not believe that Letcher was

responsible for the manner in which the judicial business of the Territory has been conducted. He was not an Applicant for the Office: was surprised when he heard he was appointed—: promptly determined not to accept—and would not have gone to the country, had he not believed that it was his duty to assist in the organisation of the Govt[.] as it was ascertained that the Governor would not take on himself that responsibility—and as he therefore was advised that *his aid was indispensable.* Having made great Sacrifices in going to Arkansaw, he determined to hold the office until the business of the Territory should require a full court. This he was advised to do. He thought he *had* resigned.

[49] *Terr. Papers*, XIX, 143–145, 147–149.
[50] *Gazette*, March 11, 1820; *Terr. Papers*, XIX, 144–145.
[51] *Terr. Papers*, XIX, 170–171.
[52] *Gazette*, June 24, 1820.
[53] *Ibid.*, October 14, 1820; *Terr. Papers*, XIX, 234.

Letcher would, said Robertson, no longer consider himself in office after April 1, 1820.[54]

The reports that Letcher would resign had given rise to numerous recommendations of other persons for his post.[55] To fill the vacancy created by Letcher's resignation, Monroe on May 13 appointed Joseph Selden of the United States Army to be judge.[56] Selden, born in Virginia in 1787, had served as an officer in the War of 1812, and had remained in the army after the war.[57]

In the meantime, Judge Jouett had returned temporarily to Arkansas Territory. On May 1, 1820, he wrote President Monroe that "Pecuniary embarrassments connected with a sick family" had prevented his moving to the Territory at an earlier time and that now that he had done so his wife would not "consent to remain"; consequently he wished to resign his office effective July 4.[58] Jouett's resignation was welcomed by Editor Woodruff, who commented that "almost every person in the Territory" was aware of "the flagrant manner" in which Jouett had "neglected his duty."[59]

On August 4 President Monroe appointed John Thompson of Ohio to succeed Jouett.[60] According to an extract of a letter printed in the *Gazette,* Thompson started for the Territory but turned back at Jackson, Missouri. Editor Woodruff surmised that reports of the "unhealthiness" of the country had caused him to return home and resign.[61]

In Thompson's place, Monroe appointed Benjamin Johnson of Kentucky (b. 1784), brother of Senator Richard M. Johnson and for several years a circuit judge in his native state.[62] The arrival of Johnson and Selden in the Territory in 1821 terminated the furor arising from absentee judges.

[54] Robertson to Johnson, March 29, 1820, *Terr. Papers,* XIX, 156–157. Letcher subsequently represented Kentucky in Congress and served as governor of that state from 1840–1844. From 1849–1852 he was United States minister to Mexico.

[55] See *ibid.,* 101, note 51.

[56] *Ibid.,* 182–183. Selden was recommended by Delegate Bates. *Ibid.,* 160.

[57] *Ibid.,* 182, note 33.

[58] Jouett to President, May 1, 1820, *ibid.,* 172.

[59] *Gazette,* September 23, 1820.

[60] *Terr. Papers,* XIX, 39, note 75. See also Thompson to Secretary of State, August 30, 1820, and Secretary of State to John W. Campbell, January 12, 1821, *ibid.,* 213, 256, 249, note 42. Thompson's appointment was pressed by the Ohio delegation in Congress. *Ibid.,* 36, 39.

[61] *Gazette,* November 18, 1820.

[62] *Terr. Papers,* XIX, 258–259; Hallum, *History of Arkansas,* 43, 159. Johnson's appointment was urged by many prominent Kentuckians (including his brother), and by several influential politicians from other states. *Ibid.,* 203, 207, 211, 216, 219, 241, 252. See also John Quincy Adams, *Memoirs* (edited by Charles Francis Adams, 12 vols., Philadelphia, 1874–1877), V, 212.

During the spring of 1820 President Monroe filled other territorial offices. In April he appointed Henry W. Conway of Missouri to be receiver of public monies and William D. Simms of the District of Columbia to be register of the Arkansas land district.[63] The same month he gave the receivership of the Lawrence land district to John Trimble of Kentucky and made Hartwell Boswell, also of Kentucky, register.[64] In May Monroe appointed an Arkansan, George W. Scott, to be Federal marshal of the Territory[65] and designated Samuel C. Roane, an Arkansas Post lawyer, to be United States Attorney.[66] One notices a dominance of Kentuckians and an absence of Tennesseans in appointments to territorial office, a situation thoroughly out of harmony with the relative contributions of Kentucky and Tennessee to the general population of early Arkansas. Robert B. Walz finds that 35.7 per cent of the white migrants into Arkansas, 1834–1850, were from Tennessee, and only 4.9 per cent from Kentucky.[67] Why this should be true has not been ascertained.

In March, 1820, a duel between William O. Allen[68] and Robert C. Oden left vacant not only a seat in the territorial house of representatives but also the brigadier generalship of the territorial militia. In September, 1819, Allen had been appointed to the command of the militia pending approval of the Senate,[69] and two months later had won election as representative from Arkansas County. A seemingly trivial matter subsequently resulted in Allen's challenging Oden, an attorney, to a duel. When the encounter took place near Arkansas Post on March 10, Allen fired first and although his bullet inflicted a severe wound, Oden as he fell to the ground was nevertheless able to get off a random shot which struck Allen in the head. Oden recovered but Allen died ten days later.[70]

[63] *Terr. Papers,* XIX, 158–159, 167, note 96.

[64] Meigs to Boswell, April 24, 1820, Boswell to Meigs, June 3, 1820, and Meigs to Trimble, May 22, 1820, *ibid.,* 166, note 95, 185, note 46, 188.

[65] *Ibid.,* 187. Scott was a native of Virginia and brother of Judge Andrew Scott. *Ibid.,* 350; William F. Pope, *Early Days in Arkansas* (Little Rock, 1895), 41, note. His appointment was presumably made on the recommendation of Governor Miller, Neil McLane, William O. Allen, William Trimble, and Delegate Bates. *Terr. Papers,* XIX, 142–143, 186.

[66] *Ibid.,* 187–188. Roane, a former Tennessean, was recommended by Delegate Scott of Missouri and Delegate Bates. *Ibid.,* 55, 186; Shinn, *Makers of Arkansas,* 81–82.

[67] Robert Bradshaw Walz, "Migration into Arkansas, 1834–1880" (unpublished Ph.D. dissertation, University of Texas, 1958), 115–116.

[68] Allen was a Virginian who had lived in Louisiana Territory and had, after serving as an officer in the army from 1812 to 1818, settled at Arkansas Post. Shinn, *Makers of Arkansas,* 60–61.

[69] Adjutant General to Miller, September 28, 1819, *Terr. Papers,* XIX, 110.

[70] Pope, *Early Days in Arkansas,* 34–35; Worley, ed., "Letter of Miller to His Wife," *Arkansas Historical Quarterly,* XIII, 390; *Gazette,* March 25, July 1, 1820; Shinn,

In December the brigadier generalship of the militia was given to Edmund Hogan,[71] a former member of the Georgia legislature who had moved to Missouri Territory and been twice elected to the legislature there.[72] In the special election to fill the vacancy in the territorial house occasioned by Allen's death, Richard Peeler, Joseph Stillwell, and Elijah Morton announced as candidates,[73] but Morton presently withdrew.[74] Stillwell defeated Peeler by a vote of 94 to 82.[75]

The territorial legislature reconvened on October 2, 1820. Governor Miller was ill, and Secretary Crittenden delivered his message for him. Miller pronounced the revenue laws of the Territory defective in that they permitted the issuance of scrip "for the payment of public creditors." The scrip was already below par and the amount in circulation was increasing; unless something was done, it would soon become worthless. Miller suggested either borrowing on the faith of the Territory or levying an additional tax. The administration of justice was impeded by the lack of sufficient jails throughout most of the Territory; one ought to be provided for each county. An act prohibiting traffic in horses between whites and Indians "would materially tend to the tranquillity of our settlements bordering on Indian tribes," and perhaps prevent "in a great degree, the stealing of horses by Indians, which has been so much complained of throughout the Territory." In closing Miller said that he was returning certain bills passed at the February session that he had held pending a decision on the legality of the election. He suggested they be revised, and "where they are penal, to attach higher penalties."[76] No more is heard of these bills, but the legislature acted favorably upon Miller's other recommendations.[77]

The work of the session included also an act making the principals in duels where death resulted guilty of murder, and imposing a heavy fine and disbarment from territorial offices upon anyone issuing, accepting, or delivering a challenge; every person appointed to office in the future would be required to swear that he had not violated the

Makers of Arkansas, 62–65. Oden was subsequently indicted in the superior court for accepting Allen's challenge, but was acquitted because the prosecuting attorney could not produce the notice of challenge. *Gazette,* June 24, October 28, 1820.

[71] *Terr. Papers,* XIX, 110, note 68, 276. Governor Miller and Delegate Bates recommended Hogan for the position. *Ibid.,* 205–206, 276, note 8.

[72] *Gazette,* June 4, 1828.

[73] *Ibid.,* April 15, 29, June 24, 1820.

[74] *Ibid.,* May 20, 1820.

[75] "Official Election Returns," *ibid.,* August 26, 1820.

[76] "Governor's Message," October 3, 1820, *ibid.,* October 7, 1820.

[77] *Arkansas Acts,* 1820, pp. 101–104, 106–107, 114–117, 130–137. In response to Miller's fiscal recommendation, the legislature imposed additional taxes.

act.[78] Another measure abolished the circuit court system by establishing in each county a court of common pleas to be composed of three judges, and dividing the Territory into three superior districts to be presided over by the superior court judges.[79] Other business consisted of the creation of Crawford and Independence Counties,[80] an authorization to the governor to apportion representation for the legislature of 1823,[81] and memorials to Congress about certain aspects of the land situation.[82]

Undoubtedly the most important political issue before the October legislature was the location of the territorial capital.[83] At the February session Joab Hardin, chairman of a committee on the subject, had introduced a bill to remove the seat of government to the little village of Cadron. After some discussion the bill had passed by a vote of 5 to 4, Ellis, Joab Hardin, Tindall, Stevenson, and Joseph Hardin supporting it, with Allen, English, Fish, and Horner opposed. The council changed the bill by substituting for Cadron the undeveloped site of Little Rock. When the amended bill was returned to the house, a resolution of Joab Hardin to postpone consideration until the next session was approved by a vote of 5 to 4. Allen, Ellis, Horner, Tindall, and Joab Hardin voted for postponement, English, Fish, Stevenson, and Joseph Hardin against.[84]

At the time of the February session the townsite of Little Rock was the object of rival claims. In consequence of an earthquake in the New Madrid area of Missouri Territory in 1811, Congress had passed an act permitting sufferers to locate 160 acres on any public land in the United States. Three New Madrid certificates had subsequently fallen into the hands of William O'Hara, who had, after locating claims to the site of Little Rock, assigned a part interest to James Bryan and Stephen F. Austin.[85] The land claimed by the New Madrid proprietors overlapped in part a preemption originally made in 1814 by William Lewis and claimed in 1820 by William Russell and Benjamin Murphy.[86]

During the summer and fall of 1820 the rival claimants lobbied

[78] *Ibid.*, 110–113.
[79] *Ibid.*, 118–123.
[80] *Ibid.*, 123–128.
[81] *Ibid.*, 108–109.
[82] See *Terr. Papers,* XIX, 221, 224, 232, 233.
[83] Arkansas Post was designated by the Arkansas organic act to be the seat of government until "otherwise directed" by the territorial legislature. *Terr. Papers,* XIX, 49.
[84] "General Assembly of Arkansas," *Gazette,* March 4, 11, 1820; *ibid.,* October 14, 1820. The council proceedings are not reported in the *Gazette.*
[85] Dallas T. Herndon, *Why Little Rock Was Born* (Little Rock, 1933) 36–39.
[86] *Ibid.,* 6–7, 15–20; Margaret Smith Ross, "Cadron: An Early Town That Failed," *Arkansas Historical Quarterly,* XVI (Spring, 1957), 14–15; Myra McAlmont Vaughn,

vigorously to have Little Rock selected as the capital. By October several prominent politicians, among them Robert Crittenden, Robert C. Oden, and Andrew Scott, had involved themselves financially in the preemption claim. Other influential men, including James Miller, Chester Ashley, and Nathaniel Philbrook, had bought interests in New Madrid claims.[87]

A pseudonymous writer in the *Gazette* represented Little Rock as possessing numerous advantages to recommend its selection for the capital. The location was on an elevation which gradually ascended from the Arkansas River; the excellent harbor was free from current; the river could be navigated during most of the year up to Little Rock; the place was on the road leading from Missouri to Red River; and a heavy growth of timber and a plentiful supply of spring water were available in the neighborhood.[88]

On October 11 the house voted 6 to 3 to concur in the council's amendment to remove the capital to Little Rock. Ellis, English, Fish, Joab Hardin, Stevenson, and Tindall voted in the affirmative, Horner, Stillwell, and Joseph Hardin, in the negative.[89] One notices that Ellis, Joab Hardin, Stevenson, and Tindall had since February changed from favoring Cadron to favoring Little Rock. The bill, approved by Governor Miller on October 18, designated Little Rock the temporary seat of government after June 1, 1821, until otherwise provided by law.[90]

The October legislature also accepted certain lots for use of the Territory offered by Amos Wheeler on behalf of the New Madrid proprietors of Little Rock. Wheeler's proposal to furnish accommodations for use of the Territory was also approved, the governor being requested to take security for performance of the contract.[91]

"A History of the Old State House," *Publications of the Arkansas Historical Association,* Vol. III (Fayetteville, 1911), 249–251. Russell and Murphy held separate claims to the preemption. According to Ross, Russell subsequently dropped his claim and purchased a half interest in Murphy's.

[87] Herndon, *Why Little Rock Was Born,* 21–24; Ross, "An Early Town That Failed," *Arkansas Historical Quarterly,* XVI, 15, 20. Herndon states that Miller purchased a farm at Crystal Hill during the recess and that, according to tradition, he thenceforth pressed for Crystal Hill as the seat of territorial government. But Ross, who has used the Pulaski County deed books, says that Miller purchased an interest in New Madrid claims to the site of Little Rock on March 15, 1820, and that his purchase of land at Crystal Hill was not made until March 15, 1821. Thus it seems probable that Miller favored Little Rock. See also Diana Sherwood, "When Governor Miller Bought Crystal Hill," *Pulaski County Historical Review,* I (September, 1953), 5–8.

[88] Communication of Oscar, *Gazette,* May 27, 1820. See also "Little Rock," *ibid.,* December 29, 1821.

[89] "Arkansas General Assembly," *ibid.,* October 14, 1820.

[90] *Arkansas Acts,* 1820, p. 104.

[91] "Arkansas General Assembly," *Gazette,* October 14, 21, 1820.

The dispute between the rival claimants continued after the legislature adjourned. In June, 1821, the superior court, in a suit for trespass brought by William Russell against the New Madrid proprietors, ruled in favor of the preemption claimants. When New Madrid owners expressed their dissatisfaction with the decision by blowing up buildings and moving others that they had constructed, the preemption claimants, fearing depopulation of the town and possible removal of the capital, offered to compromise their differences.[92] The offer was accepted, and in November, 1821, the rival groups exchanged part interests in their claims.[93] Presumably in connection with this compromise, a block of land for the territorial public square was donated to the Territory.[94]

With the termination of the legislative session in October, 1820, and the settlement of the problem of locating the capital, the organizational period of the territorial government may be considered to have come to an end. The territorial offices had been filled, initial problems of the new jurisdiction had been dealt with, and a second grade government had been set in operation.

[92] Herndon, *Why Little Rock Was Born,* 132–153.

[93] *Terr. Papers,* XIX, 370. See also "Little Rock," *Gazette,* December 29, 1821. The compromise was worked out by Ashley and Russell. The preemption owners at the time of the compromise were Russell, Robert Crittenden, William Trimble, Henry W. Conway, Thomas P. Eskridge, Robert C. Oden, and Joseph Hardin. The New Madrid proprietors were Ashley, James DeBaun, Nathaniel Philbrook, Elias A. Elliott, and Henry Elliott.

[94] Establishment of Little Rock, November 20, 1821, and Transfer of New Madrid Claims, November 22, 1821, *Terr. Papers,* XIX, 358, 365–370.

CHAPTER THREE

The Second and Third Elections

JAMES WOODSON BATES announced May 5, 1821, that he would be a candidate for reelection to Congress in the forthcoming August election.[1] A week later Matthew Lyon, Indian factor at Spadre Bluff, gave notice that he too would be a candidate.[2] A third aspirant, Major William Bradford of Fort Smith, announced about three weeks before the election that he would "serve, if elected,"[3] but his entry into the contest came too late for him to be a serious contender.

Though Lyon was over seventy years of age, he was nonetheless still vigorous, and he possessed an impressive political background. Born in Ireland, he had emigrated in 1765 as a redemptioner to Connecticut, moved thence to Vermont in 1774, and participated as an officer in the Revolutionary War. He later served for more than a decade in the Vermont legislature and began publishing in 1793 the *Farmer's Library*. During two terms as Republican member of Congress (1797–1801) he was imprisoned for four months and fined for violation of the Sedition Act. In 1801 Lyon moved to western Kentucky, where he was forthwith elected to the state legislature. From 1803 to 1811 he represented Kentucky in Congress.[4] Notwithstanding his residence in Kentucky, Lyon was in 1812 an unsuccessful candidate for delegate to Congress from Missouri Territory.[5]

---

[1] *Arkansas Gazette* (Arkansas Post), May 5, 1821.

[2] *Ibid.*, May 12, 1821.

[3] *Ibid.*, July 14, 1821.

[4] *Biographical Directory of the American Congress, 1774–1927* (Washington, 1928), 1248; William A. Robinson, "Matthew Lyon," in Allen Johnson and Dumas Malone, eds., *Dictionary of American Biography* (20 vols., New York, 1928–1936), XI, 532–534; "Obituary," *Gazette* (Little Rock), August 13, 1822.

[5] St. Louis *Missouri Gazette*, October 24, 31, 1812; Fay Hempstead, *A Pictorial History of Arkansas* (St. Louis, 1890), 152.

A "virtually destitute" man in 1820, he accepted appointment to be United States Indian factor in Arkansas Territory.[6]

Lyon was the only one of the congressional candidates who issued a campaign circular through the columns of the *Gazette*. He would, he said, "aid in warding off or mitigating the evils," of an unpopular Choctaw treaty made in 1820, and would work for the establishment of postal facilities and a liberal land policy. He promised to recommend Arkansans for appointment to territorial offices and keep the electorate informed on political matters. Realizing that his advanced age might be urged against him, he admitted that time had "impaired some . . . powers," but averred that he was healthy, and of sound mind.[7]

The absence of partisan controversy and editorial comment in the *Gazette* suggests that the canvass produced little excitement. That Lyon actually campaigned, however, is attested by a trader who subsequently wrote that he saw Lyon in Little Rock in 1821 "canvassing for Congress." The trader tells us that Lyon rode into the capital on a mule, "which had thrown him into a bayou, and his appearance as he came in, covered with mud from head to foot, was a subject of much laughter for his companions and the town . . ."[8]

In the balloting on August 6 Bates defeated Lyon by a vote of 1,081 to 1,020.[9] Bradford's name was omitted from the acting governor's proclamation of the outcome of the election; but the *Gazette* reported that he received no votes in Arkansas County and four in Phillips County.[10]

The successful candidates for the legislative council were Neil McLane of Arkansas County; Daniel Mooney of Phillips County; Peyton Tucker of Independence County; Robert Andrews of Hempstead County; Clayborn Wright of Miller County; Samuel C. Roane of Clark County;[11] Benjamin Murphy of Pulaski County; James Billingsley of Crawford County; and William Janes of Lawrence

---

[6] Clarence E. Carter, ed., *Territorial Papers of the United States*, Vol. XIX, *Arkansas Territory, 1819–1825* (Washington, 1953), 183. For an account of Lyon's Arkansas career, see George L. Montagno, "Matthew Lyon's Last Frontier," *Arkansas Historical Quarterly*, XVI (Spring, 1957), 46–53.

[7] Lyon, "Fellow-Citizens of Arkansas Territory," April 30, 1821, *Gazette*, May 12, 1821.

[8] Thomas James, *Three Years Among the Indians and Mexicans* (edited by Milo M. Quaife, Chicago, 1953), 109–111.

[9] Acting Governor's election proclamation, September 10, 1821, *Gazette*, September 15, 1821.

[10] *Ibid.*, August 18, 1821.

[11] Roane and Eli Langford tied in the regular election but Roane won by six votes in a special election to break the tie. *Ibid.*, October 6, 1821.

County. Elected members of the house were William Trimble, Arkansas County; William B. R. Horner, Phillips County; Robert Bean, Independence County; John Wilson, Hempstead County; Stephen R. Wilson, Miller County; Thomas Fish, Clark County; Thomas H. Tindall, Crawford and Pulaski Counties; and John Hines and Jesse James, Lawrence County.[12] Tindall's election was, however, subsequently contested successfully by Edmund Hogan.[13]

Upon learning of his defeat, Lyon wrote Bates on October 15 that he had reason to believe that Crittenden's election proclamation was "founded on incorrect Data" and that consequently he would contest the election.[14] Two days later he asked Crittenden for a copy of the "papers" on which Crittenden had based his proclamation.[15] In a subsequent address to the people Lyon declared that he had received the vote of "a decided majority of the legal voters, voting in a legal manner," and that after it had been "allowed and asserted (by those who had a right to know best about it—those most opposed to my election) that I was elected," Crittenden had issued a proclamation declaring Bates to be the winner. Crittenden had also refused him permission to examine the returns, and the legislature had declined his request that it pass a law compelling "Attendance of Witnesses" to give testimony in cases of contested congressional elections.[16] Lyon now announced his intention of bringing the matter of the election to the attention of Congress.[17]

In a petition to Congress, dated October 24, 1821, Lyon asserted that Bates had received a total of 109 illegal votes in Pulaski, Independence, Clark, and Arkansas Counties and that in nearly every county Bates's "Official & professional advocates" had persuaded legally unqualified persons to vote for him. In Crawford County, where legal machinery for holding an election had not been established, a vote of 53 to 34 in favor of Bates had been reported. Lyon stated that he could offer no proof of his assertions because the Territory had no law to compel witnesses to give testimony in such cases and he was denied access to the election returns. These "Circumstances," he declared, led him to ask that the House set aside the election, refuse Bates his seat, and order a new election to be held.[18]

[12] "The Election," *ibid.,* September 1, 1821; *ibid.,* September 8, 1821.
[13] "The General Assembly," *ibid.,* October 13, 20, 1821.
[14] Lyon to Bates, October 15, 1821, *Terr. Papers,* XIX, 377.
[15] Lyon to Crittenden, October 17, 1821, *ibid.,* 378.
[16] See Memorial to Assembly by Lyon, October 18, 1821, *ibid.,* 376–377.
[17] Lyon to citizens of Arkansas Territory, October 22, 1821, *Gazette,* October 27, 1821.
[18] *Terr. Papers,* XIX, 374–376.

Lyon's petition was presented in the House on December 10 and referred to the Committee on Elections.[19] On December 19 the committee reported that Lyon had produced "no testimony whatever" to support his allegations, and the House concurred in a resolution offered by the committee that it be discharged from further consideration of the matter and that Lyon be given leave to withdraw his petition.[20] Thus Lyon's attempt to contest the congressional election of 1821 failed. Whether his assertions regarding voting irregularities were true it is now impossible to ascertain.[21]

In October the legislature convened for the first time at Little Rock. According to one contemporary writer, the new territorial capital consisted in 1821 of two taverns, a store, "a boarding-house or two," and less than a dozen families.[22] Meetings of the legislature were held in a newly constructed two-room log cabin.[23] Before the end of the year Little Rock would also be the headquarters of the *Arkansas Gazette.*[24]

Of the several laws passed by the legislature of 1821, those pertaining to the judiciary and finances were seemingly the most important. Presumably in response to Acting Governor Crittenden's recommendation,[25] an act was adopted authorizing the governor to borrow up to $10,000 on the faith and resources of the Territory at an annual interest rate of six per cent.[26] Another measure abolished the courts of common pleas and established in their stead two circuit courts.[27] A third did away with the superior court districts by providing for three terms yearly of the superior court to be held at the territorial capital.[28] Other business consisted of appropriating money for government expenses in 1821–1822; providing that all balloting in elections should be *viva voce;* amending the tax laws; and altering county boundaries.[29] Two memorials to Congress asked that the Quapaw reservation in Arkansas be purchased and that Hempstead,

[19] *Annals of Congress,* 17 Congress, 1 sess., I (December 10, 1821), 528–529.
[20] *Ibid.,* 564 (December 19, 1821). See also *Gazette,* February 9, 1822.
[21] Lyon died at Spadre Bluff in 1822. *Gazette,* August 13, 1822.
[22] Communication of A Friend to Improvement, *ibid.,* June 11, 1822.
[23] Myra McAlmont Vaughan, "A History of the Old State House," *Publications of the Arkansas Historical Association,* Vol. III (Fayetteville, 1911), 251.
[24] The last issue of the *Gazette* published at Arkansas Post was dated November 24, 1821, and the first number printed at Little Rock was dated December 29, 1821.
[25] See communication of Arkansas Farmer, November 1, 1821, *Gazette,* November 17, 1821. The legislative journal, which undoubtedly would have contained Crittenden's message to the legislature, was not published. See *Gazette,* February 26, 1822.
[26] *Arkansas Acts,* 1821, pp. 6–8.
[27] *Ibid.,* 3–6.
[28] *Ibid.,* 11–12.
[29] *Ibid.,* 10–11, 16–18, 20–21.

Crawford, and Miller Counties each be granted preemption right to 160 acres of public land to be used for erecting a courthouse and jail.[30]

Political events seemingly lagged during 1822, but the biennial election of 1823 brought excitement and discord exceeding that of any previous campaign. By the end of January, 1823, William Trimble, Thomas P. Eskridge, Henry W. Conway, and Major William Bradford had become candidates for delegate to Congress in the forthcoming election.[31] In order that the contending political rivals and their supporters might make known their views, Editor Woodruff offered to publish all personal communications pertaining to the canvass. The *Gazette* itself would, he said, remain neutral.[32]

The campaign was barely underway when Crittenden called at Little Rock a conference attended by Conway in which Eskridge and Trimble were induced to withdraw from the race in favor of Conway.[33] The reasons for this maneuver, which undoubtedly had an important effect upon the eventual outcome of the election, are by no means clear, especially as far as Crittenden is concerned. Dallas T. Herndon and Josiah H. Shinn would have us believe that Crittenden's motive was a desire to insure the defeat of his former associate, Delegate Bates.[34] The difficulty about this view is that Bates had informed Conway in a conversation at Greenville, Missouri, about November, 1822, while Bates was en route to Washington D.C., that he did not desire reelection, and the first known statement that Bates had changed his mind was dated Washington, February, 1823, and not

[30] *Terr. Papers*, XIX, 328, 373–374.

[31] The candidacies of Trimble, Eskridge, and Conway were first announced in the *Gazette*, January 28, 1823. The announcement of Major Bradford did not appear in the *Gazette* until April 22, 1823, but he stated in a circular letter dated April 10, 1823, printed in the *Gazette*, May 6, 1823, that his candidacy had been before the people for over a year.

[32] *Gazette*, January 28, 1823.

[33] The conference presumably occurred sometime between January 28 and February 3. Had it been held prior to January 28 Eskridge and Trimble would undoubtedly not have announced their candidacies on that date. It is certain that it was not held after February 3 because Samuel C. Roane discusses the meeting in a letter of that date to Conway. *Ibid.*, February 4, 1823. The withdrawal of Eskridge's name came only a week after his entry into the race; Trimble, on the other hand, waited three months before making a public announcement. *Ibid.*, May 6, 1823.

[34] Dallas T. Herndon, *Centennial History of Arkansas* (3 vols., Little Rock, 1922), I, 164–165; Dallas T. Herndon, *Annals of Arkansas, 1947* (4 vols., Little Rock, n.d.), I, 85; Josiah H. Shinn, *Pioneers and Makers of Arkansas* (Little Rock, 1908), 180. Neither Herndon nor Shinn undertakes to explain why Crittenden should have desired to defeat Bates, though Herndon goes on to say that some of Bates's friends subsequently charged that Crittenden set out to defeat Bates "because the delegate had refused to do Crittenden's bidding in certain matters." There is no evidence in any of the public letters printed in the *Gazette* to support this statement.

printed until July;[35] it cannot have figured in the Little Rock meeting.[36] What seems more likely is that Crittenden, believing Bates not a candidate, had switched his support to Conway, and that by using his influence to obtain the withdrawal of Eskridge and Trimble he sought to assist Conway to a victory over his most formidable opponent, Major Bradford. It is quite possible, also, that Crittenden had a genuine desire to discourage the development of factionalism in territorial politics and hoped that a reduction in the number of candidates would have that effect. Such, at any rate, was the reason that Trimble gave for withdrawing his own candidacy. And there was, as will appear in the next paragraph, talk at the conference about avoidance of a schism in the future.

The conference was followed by a rumor that Conway had unconditionally pledged himself to those present not to seek a second term. In an attempt to quash this damaging story of political bargaining, Conway requested United States District Attorney Samuel C. Roane, who had been in town at the time of the consultation, to state in writing what "the general understanding [was] on the subject of the present election."[37] Roane's reply, which Conway caused to be published in the *Gazette,* was that he had not been present at the discussion but understood from Crittenden that everyone present had agreed

to support Mr. Conway for the present election; and if, at a subsequent election, the friends of Mr. Conway thought that the interest of the Territory required it, he would not be the cause of a scism [*sic*], but would step aside, and let some other person run in [*sic*] without any opposition from him.[38]

Roane emphasized that Conway had not pledged to decline reelection though he would not run if his friends did not wish him to. Roane's explanation went unchallenged in the *Gazette* and no more is heard of the matter during the campaign.

Both Conway and Bradford possessed backgrounds recommending them for the office to which they aspired. Bradford, born in Virginia in 1771, had become by 1804 the owner of a large estate in Muhlenberg County, Kentucky. He served in the Kentucky legislature in 1801, 1803, 1810, and 1811. Entering the army as a captain in

[35] Extract of a letter from Bates to Joseph Hardin, February, 1823, in Conway, "To the Citizens of the Territory of Arkansas," July 8, 1823, *Gazette,* July 8, 1823.

[36] The controversy between Bates and Conway over what had transpired between them will be considered below in greater detail.

[37] Conway to Roane, February 3, 1823, *Gazette,* February 4, 1823.

[38] Roane to Conway, February 3, 1823, *ibid.*

1812, he was promoted to major in 1814, remained in the service after the war, and on December 25, 1817, became commandant at Fort Smith.[39] He was, as noticed above, an unsuccessful candidate for delegate in the election of 1821. On February 26, 1822, he was replaced as commanding officer of Fort Smith by Colonel Matthew Arbuckle, who found the fort in "a good state for defense" which he attributed to the skill and industry of the erstwhile commander.[40] Bradford was subsequently ordered to Pensacola but decided to resign his commission rather than leave Arkansas, where he and his family had resided for six years.[41] He did not actually resign, however, until May 1, 1824, almost nine months after the election.[42]

Conway at thirty was the younger of the two men, but had, for his age, an equally impressive record. Born in Greene County, Tennessee, on March 18, 1793, he entered the army as an ensign in 1812 and rose to the rank of first lieutenant.[43] Upon leaving the army following the war he served in the Treasury Department in Washington.[44] In 1818 he migrated to Missouri, whence he was appointed in 1820 to be receiver of public monies for the Arkansas land district.[45] Eighteen months later he also received an appointment as postmaster at Little Rock.[46] Major General Edmund P. Gaines, Commander of the Western Department, described him in 1822 as "a young man of business, sound judgment, and unimpeachable character & high standing [who] has few, if any superiors in the Arkansaw Territory."[47]

Conway presented his platform in a circular letter to the citizens of the Territory dated February 10, 1823. Declaring himself a republican and a property holder in the Territory, and promising to "watch and promote your interest with the greatest care and industry," he submitted an ambitious program which dealt primarily with the all-important subjects of Indians, land, internal improvements, and boundaries. With regard to the Indian problem, Conway pledged himself to work for the extinguishment of the Choctaw and Quapaw

---

[39] Carolyn Thomas Foreman, "William Bradford," *Arkansas Historical Quarterly,* XIII (Winter, 1954), 342; *Gazette,* November 14, 1826; Francis B. Heitman, *Historical Register and Dictionary of the United States Army, from its Organization September 29, 1789 to March 2, 1903* (2 vols., Washington, 1903), I, 238.

[40] Arbuckle to Adjutant General, March 4, 1822, *Terr. Papers,* XIX, 414.

[41] Bradford, "To the Citizens of the Territory of Arkansas," April 10, 1823, *Gazette,* May 6, 1823.

[42] Heitman, *Historical Register of the United States Army,* I, 238.

[43] *Ibid.,* 323.

[44] *Biographical Directory of the American Congress,* 842.

[45] *Terr. Papers,* XIX, 158–159.

[46] *Ibid.,* 380, note 55. Crittenden was one of his sureties.

[47] Gaines to Secretary of War, June 26, 1822, *ibid.,* 445.

titles in the Territory, and for the establishment of two military posts in strategic locations for protection. As to the land situation, he promised to labor for the adjustment of titles to unconfirmed lands; the survey and sale of the marginal lands on the Mississippi River; the establishment of a surveyor general's office; and permission for the whites to settle Lovely's Purchase. In reference to internal improvements, he assured the voters that he would seek the construction of a good wagon road from Chickasaw Bluffs to Little Rock; the opening of a road from Fort Smith to the Missouri River; and Federal cooperation in removing the raft obstructing navigation on Red River. In relation to the boundary problem, Conway hoped to procure the surveying of the northern territorial boundary and a law defining a propitious western border. He promised to urge improvement of the postal service. He would also try to obtain a list of names of persons owning military bounty lands in the Territory in order that such land owners could be taxed for territorial revenue. Finally, his main object if elected would be "to promote, if possible, the general interest of the people—no *party* views, *private* projects, nor *sectional* interest, shall in any manner, influence my public conduct."[48]

Two months after Conway's pronouncement, his competitor issued a similar circular. Bradford began by referring to his military service and legislative experience. He went on to proclaim his allegiance to Jeffersonian principles and to promise that he would not be guided by local prejudices, but instead by the will of the majority of the people. His main object, he said, would be "to promote the growth and prosperity of the country."[49] Bradford's program, like his political principles, in essence closely resembled that of his adversary, though he did not call for the building of roads nor the establishment of new military posts. He promised to endeavor to get the law granting the right of preemption extended beyond the time set for laying New Madrid claims, a provision which he said would protect the small settler from speculation.

As the campaign progressed the columns of the *Gazette* were increasingly weighted with letters by pseudonymous writers on behalf of their political favorite. A letter cleverly designed to enhance Bradford's chances appeared even before the appearance of his circular letter. The correspondent, who called himself "Pike," noted that "an all important election" would soon be held and that a majority of the

[48] *Gazette*, February 11–12, 1823.
[49] Bradford, "To the Citizens of the Territory of Arkansas," April 10, 1823, *ibid.*, May 6, 1823.

soldiers in the Territory would soon become citizens; consequently, they were greatly interested in the canvass. "Pike" asserted that the constitution did not prohibit soldiers from voting; that soldiers were citizens no less than civilians were; and that they should therefore be allowed to vote.[50] By indicating that the servicemen in the Territory should receive the privilege of the ballot, "Pike" was obviously beating the political drums for Major Bradford.

"Pike's" letter evoked an immediate response from a writer signing himself "A Legal Voter." He charged that "Pike's" communication was designed to induce Arkansans to believe that the personnel of Fort Smith were entitled to the suffrage. "Pike" should remember that the Federal constitution did not give the right to vote but left the suffrage to the discretion of the legislatures of the various states and territories. In Arkansas Territory a qualified voter must be a free white male citizen of the United States at least twenty-one years of age, must have resided in the Territory one year preceding the election, and must have paid a territorial or county tax. "A Legal Voter" doubted whether soldiers could meet these requirements.[51]

Presently "Pike" published another essay reiterating his argument in favor of the right of soldiers to vote. This time, however, he made quite plain the purpose behind the propounding of his thesis.

Major Bradford was, and is, a candidate for Congress; and if the soldiers, who know and appreciate him, are suffered to vote, there will be no doubt of his election. They know that he would protect and advance the rights of the military, as well as of the Territory.[52]

The expositions of "Pike" provoked "Thaddeus" to swing into verbal action. He charged that Bradford was "Pike" and had composed the communications in his own interest. "Thaddeus" went on to allege that Bradford had, while commandant at Fort Smith, forced a blacksmith named Riley to reenlist in the army. In 1822 Riley had sued Bradford for damages. If one might believe "Thaddeus," Bradford sought to defend himself by pleading that he was not a citizen of the Territory but an army officer, and as such, not subject to trial by civil courts; and by pleading the statute of limitations. When these pleas failed, "Thaddeus" reported, Bradford denied the charges, but the jury correctly found in favor of the plaintiff, assessing damages at $1,450. Because of Bradford's impecunious financial condition,

[50] Communication of Pike, *ibid.,* February 11–12, 1823.
[51] Communication of A Legal Voter, *ibid.,* February 18, 1823.
[52] Pike, "Pike—No. II," *ibid.,* April 15, 1823.

Riley was forced to compromise for only $800.[53] "Thaddeus's" highly critical narrative of this affair was clearly intended, whatever its truth or falsity, to injure Bradford's reputation and thereby decrease his chances in the election.

In the same issue with the "Thaddeus" letter the *Gazette* printed an article signed by "Franklin," who espoused the election of Conway purportedly "without entertaining an unfriendly sentiment" towards his opponent. Referring briefly to Conway's qualifications and his acquaintance with many prominent people in Washington, "Franklin" concluded that he was the better man for the delegateship.[54]

The assault by "Thaddeus" on Bradford brought a reply from "Senex," who saw in "Thaddeus's" piece "the introduction of a custom into this Territory, which I consider, as being the forerunner of worse times, and which has a direct tendency to promote discord and dissention [*sic*]." "Senex" maintained that the communications of "Thaddeus" and "Pike" were written by the same person and cleverly devised to jeopardize Bradford's chances. He implied that a Conway supporter had deliberately created a controversy calculated to place Bradford in a bad light before the voters. Though "Senex" declared that the artful "Thaddeus" had no worse opinion of Bradford than he himself had, he nevertheless revealed himself as a Bradford man by warning "the good people of Arkansas, to take care, lest they sanction by their vote, or in any other manner, any custom which they may have cause to deprecate hereafter."[55] "Senex" evidently sought to persuade Arkansans that a vote for Conway was a ballot for factionalism in Arkansas politics, something which many people presumably hoped to avoid.

"Senex's" implausible allegation that "Pike" and "Thaddeus" were one and the same prompted a Conway backer who called himself "A Friend to Thaddeus" to publish a rebuttal in which he positively declared that *"Conway knows not Pike, or Thaddeus, or Senex; nor for that information do I suppose he would give a solitary groat."* "A Friend to Thaddeus" claimed that "Senex" had not denied a single charge made against Bradford by "Thaddeus," and asked why not.

Is it because the task is too difficult for your skill? Is this the reason you attempt to throw dust in the people's eyes, and prevent them from viewing in all its deformity Bradford's conduct to the unfortunate Riley? Is it because

[53] Thaddeus, "To Major Bradford," *ibid.*, May 13, 1823. See also Shinn, *Makers of Arkansas*, 87.
[54] Franklin, "Delegate to Congress," *Gazette*, May 13, 1823.
[55] Senex to Editor, *ibid.*, May 20, 1823.

Bradford cannot be elected unless his character is shrouded and concealed, that you wish a stop, an eternal stop put to any writings relative to the candidates' pretensions?

"A Friend to Thaddeus" further denied that a desire to forestall factionalism was his adversary's motive in desiring an end to verbal warfare; rather he believed that "Senex" feared that Bradford could not stand the test of public discussion. He went on to accuse "Pike" of being Bradford's friend "though I do not say a judicious one. And for Pike's indiscretion, you wish to palm him on Conway."[56]

Bradford was again assailed on July 1—this time by a writer who signed himself "Civis." "Civis" sought to tear down the major's program point by point. He criticized unconvincingly Bradford's military service, his legislative background, his claim to independence in politics, and almost everything in his platform; upbraided him for not resigning his military commission; and predicted that if he were defeated in the election he would remain in the army.[57]

A rumor that Conway was the author of the several communications devised to injure Bradford's political standing was quickly denied by the *Gazette,* which declared that the letters signed by "Thaddeus," "A Friend to Thaddeus," and "Civis" were written and published while Conway was out of town.[58]

Delegate Bates had in the meantime come home from Washington to learn to his surprise that he was not considered a candidate, that Conway and Bradford had been actively campaigning for several months, and that many of his former supporters were already committed to one or the other. On June 6 he issued a statement in which he declined reelection, explaining that he had no alternative since it would be absolutely futile to attempt to correct at so late a date and among such a dispersed population the report that had been generally, "if not sedulously," circulated that he was not a candidate. Without mentioning Conway's name Bates left little doubt that he considered Conway the source of his political undoing.[59]

The reader may recall that Conway and Bates had formerly been friends, and that they had, while Bates was en route to Washington about November, 1822, discussed at Greenville, Missouri, the mat-

---

[56] A Friend to Thaddeus, "To Senex," *ibid.,* June 3, 1823.
[57] Civis, "To Major Bradford," *ibid.,* July 1, 1823.
[58] *Ibid.,* July 8, 1823.
[59] Bates, "To the People of the Territory of Arkansas," June 6, 1823, *ibid.,* June 17, 1823. Fay Hempstead, *Historical Review of Arkansas* (3 vols., Chicago, 1911), I, 107, and William F. Pope, *Early Days in Arkansas* (Little Rock, 1895), 26, erroneously state that Bates ran against Conway in this election.

ter of who should be a candidate in 1823. Conway now construed Bates's announcement as a misrepresentation of what had been said on that occasion. To vindicate himself he issued a public statement containing a report of the meeting as he recalled it. According to Conway, Bates had informed him during their discussion that some of Bates's friends desired him to stand for reelection, but that he did not wish to do so. He entreated Conway to run in his stead, in which case he would decline being a candidate and tender his support to Conway. Conway replied that although he had been solicited by some of his friends to run he had not yet made up his mind but would inform Bates of his decision by spring. After leaving Bates, Conway called on those persons at Batesville who had requested Bates to run for a third term. They agreed to give their support to Conway since it was Bates's desire that he become a candidate. As a result of the decision of Bates's followers to back him, Conway decided to enter the race and wrote Bates advising him of this decision.[60]

To support his contention that Bates had entreated him to enter the race, Conway inserted in his statement an extract from a letter dated February, 1823, from Bates to Joseph Hardin of Davidsonville. The extract revealed that Bates had proffered Conway his support, but that Conway had, as he now claimed, declined to commit himself to run, saying "it would be time enough to stir the business" when Bates returned home in the spring. Bates advised Hardin that he himself now desired to serve another term as delegate. While the extract supported Conway's contention that Bates had changed his mind about running for a third term, it also showed that Bates did not consider that he and Conway had reached an understanding; rather, they had parted "leaving the subject as open as we found it, and I feel myself under no more commitment than I did previously to the conversation."

Bates answered Conway in a letter dated July 24 which was, perhaps significantly, not published by the *Gazette* until one day after the election. He asserted that the extract of his letter to Hardin published by Conway was "substantially correct, but not sufficiently full." Bates did not deny that he had urged Conway to run in his stead, but maintained that Conway

more than once disavowed any intention of becoming a candidate; and in conclusion remarked, that it would be time enough to talk over the matter on my return in the spring. Thus we parted—leaving me under the entire

[60] Conway, "To the Citizens of the Territory of Arkansas," July 8, 1823, *Gazette*, July 8, 1823.

conviction that he had not (as he said he had not) any disposition to become a candidate as delegate to congress.

Since Bates believed that they had not come to an understanding he did not consider his subsequent decision to become a candidate a breach of promise. Bates castigated Conway for circulating a report that he had positively declined to run again, and charged that Conway, in telling Arkansans that he had the promise of Bates's support should he decide to run, was giving a deliberately false account of the interview.[61]

Nearly four weeks later Conway published part of a letter from Bates to him dated March 21, 1823, which spoke of "motives" and "views" that had led to a "disposition" on Bates's part in the previous fall "to retire." But the "contemplated event that would have authorized, perhaps required such a course, has been most miserably frustrated. All this you know. I feel a disposition once more to be a candidate."

The foregoing evidence would seem to establish the following points: (1) that Bates at the Missouri meeting did indeed offer to support Conway, (2) that since Bates at that time had expected "considerations" to preclude his running, he had little reason not to leave his proposition open, (3) but that Conway offered no clear proof that Bates had in fact left it open.

Besides making public verbal assaults on his erstwhile friend, Bates proceeded, if we may believe Conway, to campaign actively for Bradford by writing private letters unfavorable to Conway's candidacy.[62] Bates's efforts probably caused many voters to give their allegiance to Bradford.

During the canvass Conway's political enemies charged that he had entered the race at the bidding of a Missouri party to represent its interest in the event of his election; that he had joined a group in the Territory to further his and their interests; and that he was a speculator in New Madrid land claims. He and his friends denied all three accusations.[63]

The outcome of the hotly contested campaign was a victory for Conway at the polls on August 4. He received 1,300 votes to 921 for

[61] Communication of Bates, July 24, 1823, *ibid.,* August 5, 1823.

[62] Conway to Editor, August 18, 1823, *ibid.,* August 19, 1823. In a short reply dated August 28 Bates termed Conway's points "too frivolous to require investigation." *Ibid.,* September 2, 1823.

[63] William Woodward, "To the Public," July 19, 1823, *ibid.,* July 22, 1823; Thomas Mathers to Editor, July 8, 1823, *ibid.,* July 8, 1823; Conway, "To the Citizens of the Territory of Arkansas," July 8, 1823, *ibid.,* July 8, 1823.

Bradford, with 3 reported as "scattering." Bradford carried only two counties of the nine in the Territory.[64]

The choice of members of the territorial legislature created no such furor as that attending the election of a delegate to Congress. The successful candidates for the legislative council were Thomas Mathers of Pulaski County; Townsend Dickinson of independence County; William Humphreys of Lawerence County; Daniel Mooney of Phillips County; Andrew Latting of Arkansas County; John Mc-Lean of Crawford County; Samuel C. Roane of Clark County; Matthew Scrobey of Hempstead County; and Elijah Carter of Miller County. Carter's election was, however, contested successfully by David Clark.[65] The victorious candidates for the house of representatives were Ambrose H. Sevier of Pulaski County; Robert Bean of Independence County; Thomas Culp of Lawrence County; B. R. Horner of Phillips County; Terence Farrelly of Arkansas County; John Nicks of Crawford County; Henry L. Biscoe of Clark County; John Wilson of Hempstead County; and Joshua Ewing of Miller County.[66] Ewing's election was contested successfully by Thomas Polk.[67]

The newly elected legislature convened and organized October 6. The following day it met in joint session to hear the address of Acting Governor Crittenden. Crittenden began by praising the judicial system established by the legislature of 1821. Though certain defects needed correction, it had, he declared, "restored confidence in our judicial tribunals, and maintained the majesty of the law inviolate." As to fiscal matters, Crittenden observed that the territorial debt had since the last session increased from $7,500 to $7,975.30. But the territorial scrip was appreciating rapidly and its redemption next year was certain, for the military bounty lands, owned largely by speculators and non-residents, would by then be subject to taxation, and revenue from them would produce a considerable surplus in the treasury. Turning to the Indian situation, Crittenden complained that large numbers of Indians east of the Mississippi had been removed to Arkansas by the Federal government and that many citizens had been driven from their homes on the Arkansas and the White Rivers to make room for them. That the government did not realize Arkansas' true worth was also manifest in its failure to extin-

[64] "Proclamation," September 12, 1823, *ibid.*, September 16, 1823.
[65] See "Arkansas General Assembly," *ibid.*, October 7, 1823.
[66] "Election Returns," *ibid.*, August 19, 1823. Bean, Mooney, and Farrelly were elected without opposition.
[67] "Arkansas General Assembly," *Gazette-Extra,* October 11, 1823.

guish the Quapaw claim and in its sanction of the odious Choctaw treaty.[68]

In accordance with Crittenden's implied recommendation, the legislature passed an act providing for assessment of taxes on military bounty lands. It also increased the number of judicial circuits in the Territory to three, provided for appointment of permanent prosecutors, and reduced the number of superior court terms to two per year. Other business included appropriations to meet government expenses for 1823, 1824, and 1825; creation of Chicot County; revision of the tax laws; appointment of commissioners to locate the county seats of Crawford and Chicot Counties; designation of Elijah Stewart's house to be the county seat of Hempstead County; dissolution of a marriage; alteration of county boundaries; authorization to the governor to apportion representation for the legislature of 1825;[69] and petitions and memorials to Congress on such matters as land, Indians, internal improvements, boundaries, and frontier defense.[70] A bill introduced by Ambrose H. Sevier, to amend the duelling act of 1820 so as to remove the penalties for issuing, accepting, or delivering a challenge and the requirement of an oath by all officeholders that they had not violated the act, was vetoed by Acting Governor Crittenden.[71]

The events of 1821 and 1823 had undoubtedly constituted a considerable step in the evolution of Arkansas politics. Of particular consequence was the campaign of 1823. It produced a break between Conway and Bates and separated Bates and Crittenden. While Bates's public letters written during the canvass give no indication that he blamed Crittenden for his political discomfiture, they would not be politically associated again for nearly a decade.[72] Conway and Crittenden drew together as political allies. The election of 1823 also brought to the highest elective office in the Territory a capable young man whose family and family connections would subsequently come to wield a dominant influence in Arkansas politics.

[68] Acting Governor's Message, October 7, 1823, *Gazette,* October 7, 1823.

[69] *Arkansas Acts,* 1823, pp. 15–16, 17–20, 21, 29–31, 33–34, 36–38, 40–41, 47–48, 50–52, 55–56.

[70] *Gazette-Extra,* October 11, 1823; *Gazette,* October 21, 1823; *Terr. Papers,* XIX, 554–559.

[71] "Arkansas General Assembly," *Gazette,* October 14, 21, 28, 1823.

[72] See Lonnie J. White, "The Arkansas Territorial Election of 1823," *Arkansas Historical Quarterly,* XVIII (Winter, 1959), 337, note 38.

CHAPTER FOUR

Politics in Flux, 1824–1827

THE MOST SPECTACULAR EVENT of Arkansas politics in 1824 was a duel between Superior Court Judges Andrew Scott and Joseph Selden.[1] According to William F. Pope, whose information came presumably from Scott's son, an altercation occurred between Scott and Selden when, during a game of cards, Selden refused a demand made by Scott that he apologize to one of the ladies present for being rude to her. Though Selden later apologized, the "intermeddling of pretended friends . . . succeeded in reviving the quarrel, which resulted [in April] in Judge Scott['s] sending Judge Selden a challenge to fight a duel."[2] The *Gazette* afterward reported that the duel was several times postponed, but that the two men remained "at variance" while sitting together on the bench. Finally, in May, 1824, they met on the east side of the Mississippi opposite Helena. At the first fire Scott shot Selden through the heart, killing him almost instantly.[3]

In reporting the outcome of the meeting, Editor Woodruff of the *Gazette* said that the duel had been "much ridiculed" in the weeks following the challenge. He went on to denounce the practice of duelling as a "flagrant violation of the laws of God and man; at variance with, and an insult to the community." This editorial

---

[1] Scott and Selden were serving second terms as judges. Clarence E. Carter, ed., *Territorial Papers of the United States,* Vol. XIX, *Arkansas Territory, 1819–1825* (Washington, 1953), 474–475, 599–600.

[2] William F. Pope, *Early Days in Arkansas* (Little Rock, 1895), 33–34, 36–37.

[3] "The Duel," *Arkansas Gazette* (Little Rock), June 1, 1824; John Hallum, *Biographical and Pictorial History of Arkansas* (Albany, 1887), I, 62. Pope says the duel took place at the mouth of White River, but it seems probable, since the *Gazette's* account of the location was not challenged, that Pope is in error. Hallum states that the duel was fought on an island in the Mississippi near Helena.

brought immediate responses from James Woodson Bates and Robert C. Oden.[4] Because Selden had been "no fit subject of ridicule," Bates believed the piece must have been the "production of some wretched paragraphist, who . . . in a desire to get into print, libels the opinions and the feelings of my fellow-citizens."[5] Oden also resented the "imputations and slurs" against Selden, and criticized Woodruff for presuming to know the feelings of the public on the matter. Oden called on Woodruff to vindicate himself by revealing the names of his informants.[6]

Replying that the editorial was his own, Woodruff refused Oden's request to name his source of information. He had not intended to convey the idea that Scott and Selden's actions made them appear ridiculous, but rather that the affair had "a very unusual and extraordinary aspect." As high judicial officers they should, instead of violating the territorial law against duelling, have been the first to discountenance its infraction.[7] Whether or not Woodruff's reply was satisfactory to Bates and Oden, no more was heard of the matter in the *Gazette.*

To fill the vacancy created by Selden's death, President Monroe appointed, presumably on the recommendation of Delegate Henry W. Conway,[8] William Trimble, formerly of Kentucky.[9] Born about 1797,[10] a brother of Receiver John Trimble of the Lawrence land district,[11] William had in 1819–1820 been attorney for the first judicial circuit;[12] in 1821 he had been a representative from Arkansas County, and speaker of the territorial house;[13] and in 1823 he had withdrawn from the race for delegate to Congress. At the time of his appointment to the superior court he was a circuit judge.[14]

Scott continued to be judge of the superior court until 1827, when his nomination for reappointment was rejected 23 to 14 by the United States Senate. The Senate's action was based upon a report of the Judiciary Committee which cited against his having fought a fatal

[4] Pope names Oden as Selden's second while Hallum says Bates acted for Selden.

[5] Bates to Editor, June 11, 1824, *Gazette,* June 15, 1824.

[6] Oden to Editor, *ibid.*

[7] "The Late Duel," *ibid.*

[8] Conway to Secretary of State, June 23, 1824, *Terr. Papers,* XIX, 679.

[9] *Ibid.,* 681, 684–685, 735; Josiah H. Shinn, *Pioneers and Makers of Arkansas* (Little Rock, 1908), 201.

[10] Hallum, *Pictorial History of Arkansas,* 121.

[11] *Terr. Papers,* XIX, 312.

[12] *Ibid.,* 789.

[13] "The General Assembly," *Gazette,* October 13, 1821.

[14] *Terr. Papers,* XIX, 580, note 98, 679.

duel with Selden in a territory where even a challenge was forbidden.[15] A pseudonymous writer in the *Gazette* considered the Senate's proceeding "an act of injustice, inflicting a wound on the reputation and standing of one of the most faithful officers that ever belonged to any government—a man who . . . has never been an hour absent from his post."[16] Meeting as private citizens, the members of the territorial legislature approved the President's nomination of Scott, whom they declared to be entitled to "the consideration of the General Government."[17]

In Scott's stead, President Adams appointed Thomas P. Eskridge, native of Virginia who had come to Arkansas in 1820 and had, since 1821, held a circuit judgeship.[18]

Another conspicuous event in 1824 was the resignation of Governor James Miller, who had been reappointed the year before.[19] In June, 1823, Miller had, for the second time during his tenure, journeyed to New Hampshire to visit his family and friends. His stay was prolonged by illness. In the fall of 1824 Miller was a successful candidate for Congress in New Hampshire, but he subsequently decided to accept appointment as collector of the port of Salem, Massachusetts. In submitting his resignation as governor, effective December 31, 1824, he gave poor health as the reason.[20]

Miller and the New Jersey delegation in Congress recommended former Cherokee Agent David Brearly, a native of New Jersey, to be Miller's successor.[21] Senator Thomas Hart Benton of Missouri urged former Governor Alexander McNair of Missouri, and John B. C. Lucas, also of Missouri, became an applicant for the posi-

---

[15] *Senate Executive Journal*, Vol. III (December 26, 1826, January 30, February 26, 1827), 552, 564–565, 572; *Terr. Papers*, XX, *Arkansas Territory, 1825–1829* (Washington, 1954), 366, note 99. An application for Scott's removal had been made to President Monroe soon after the duel, but it was not acted upon. John Quincy Adams, *Memoirs* (edited by Charles Francis Adams, 12 vols., Philadelphia, 1874–1877), VI, 473.

[16] A Friend to Justice to Editor, *Gazette*, June 19, 1827.

[17] *Ibid.*, October 30, 1827.

[18] *Terr. Papers*, XIX, 217–218, note 40, 789, 826, XX, 412; *Gazette*, March 27, 1827. Eskridge was recommended by members of Congress from Virginia and by Delegate Conway and Secretary Crittenden. *Terr. Papers*, XX, 391–392; Crittenden to Eskridge, November 5, 1833, *Arkansas Advocate* (Little Rock), November 13, 1833.

[19] Because President Monroe neglected to renominate Miller prior to the expiration of his first term, Miller served from March 3, 1822, to January 3, 1823, without a commission. His official acts during that time were subsequently confirmed by act of Congress. Lonnie J. White, "James Miller: Arkansas' First Territorial Governor," *Arkansas Historical Quarterly*, XIX (Spring, 1960), 27.

[20] *Ibid.*, 24, 26–30; Rebecca Miller to Robert W. Trimble, February 9, 1876, Robert W. Trimble Collection, Arkansas History Commission. Miller continued as collector of the port of Salem until 1849 and died in 1851.

[21] *Terr. Papers*, XIX, 503–504, note 54, 350, 732–733, 738–739.

tion.[22] Secretary Robert Crittenden's name was put forward by members of Congress from Kentucky, Tennessee, and Illinois, and by Delegate Conway.[23] According to Secretary of State John Quincy Adams, Representative Daniel P. Cook of Illinois was also a candidate, and had been promised by a partisan of Andrew Jackson that he might have "the Government of Arkansas" if he would support Jackson in the presidential election then impending in the House of Representatives.[24]

President Monroe informed Adams in January, 1825, that he meant to nominate George Izard of Pennsylvania for the governorship. Though Adams, who was a candidate to succeed Monroe, wished Monroe "to consider whether for his own sake, rather than mine, he had not better defer" Izard's and certain other nominations until after the election because they might "be suspected at least to have a bearing on that event," Monroe nonetheless sent Izard's name to the Senate, explaining to Adams that Izard "was a federalist, and he wished on his own retirement to give some token of his disposition to conciliate that class of our citizens."[25] Izard's nomination was approved by the Senate on March 3 and President Adams commissioned him the next day.[26]

Adams wrote in his diary on March 9 that Izard did not seem "satisfied" with his appointment. His attitude was that he had "neither desired nor expected" the post but would accept it "in the hope that he would be remembered hereafter for a mission abroad."[27] According to Joel R. Poinsett of South Carolina, Izard, whom Poinsett described as "proud" and "aspiring," wished to be appointed United States minister to Mexico.[28]

Born in Richmond, England, in 1776,[29] while his father, Ralph Izard of South Carolina, was temporarily residing in England, George had been brought home to the United States in 1783 and had attended school in Charleston and Philadelphia. While doing further

---

[22] *Ibid.*, 736, note 31.
[23] *Ibid.*, 736, 742.
[24] Adams, *Memoirs*, VI, 476, 495–496.
[25] *Ibid.*, 477–478, 494.
[26] *Terr. Papers*, XX, 57–59, note 3.
[27] Adams, *Memoirs*, VI, 527–528.
[28] Poinsett to Monroe, February 8, 1825, Poinsett Papers, Henry D. Gilpin Collection, Historical Society of Pennsylvania. Poinsett himself received the ministership to Mexico. Samuel Flagg Bemis, *John Quincy Adams and the Union* (New York, 1956), 59; *Terr. Papers*, XX, 6, note 14.
[29] See Langdon Cheves, "Izard of South Carolina," *South Carolina Historical and Genealogical Magazine*, II (July, 1901), 222, note 2; Shinn, *Makers of Arkansas*, 173; Fay Hempstead, *Historical Review of Arkansas* (3 vols., Chicago, 1911), I, 103.

study in military schools in Europe, he was commissioned a second lieutenant in the United States Army. He resigned during Jefferson's administration, but in 1812 accepted reappointment, and during the war rose to the rank of major general. Leaving the army after the war, he had retired to "his country seat" near Philadelphia.[30] Delegate Richard K. Call of Florida Territory considered Izard's appointment to be not only "an act of injustice" to Secretary Crittenden, who had served as governor during Miller's absences, but also to "the people of the Territory, for I feel well assured that Izard will not suit them."[31]

While Izard was still in Pennsylvania,[32] the political campaign of 1825 began in Arkansas. On April 5 Delegate Conway announced that he would be a candidate for reelection to Congress.[33] A week later James Woodson Bates proclaimed his candidacy and in a brief statement to the electorate said that, since he was known to most of the people, he did not believe it necessary to give his political principles. He had "never dealt in secrets" and considered it to be "worse than idle, to give a long catalogue of pledges."[34]

The *Gazette* carried on April 26, 1825, a circular letter by Conway to the voters listing a dozen beneficial acts passed during his tenure as delegate. Besides these, he pointed to the establishment of two military posts on the frontier, the extinguishment of the Quapaw Indian title to land in Arkansas, and the creation of a number of post offices. Many things remained, however, "to be done . . . which I will attempt to do, if re-elected."[35]

Presently a pseudonymous writer signing himself "Thrasybulus" criticized Conway's circular as arrogant in manner and inane in matter. Various acts for which Conway claimed credit were of "questionable merit," and some had "but little relation to our concerns." "Thrasybulus" noticed that Conway had not urged establishment of a surveyor general's office for Arkansas, though one was badly needed.[36]

In reply to "Thrasybulus," "A Voter" maintained that "all the

[30] David Y. Thomas, "George Izard," in Allen Johnson and Dumas Malone, eds., *Dictionary of American Biography* (20 vols., New York, 1928–1936), IX, 523–524.
[31] Call to John J. Crittenden, February 26, 1825, John J. Crittenden Papers, Library of Congress. Izard's nomination had not yet been confirmed at the time of this letter, but Call was confident that it would be.
[32] See *Terr. Papers,* XX, 60–62.
[33] "August Election—1825," *Gazette,* April 5, 1825.
[34] Bates, "To the Voters of the Territory of Arkansas," April 12, 1825, *ibid.,* April 12, 1825.
[35] Conway, "To the Voters of the Territory of Arkansas," March 4, 1825, *ibid.,* April 26, 1825.
[36] Communication of Thrasybulus, *ibid.,* May 31, 1825.

laws . . . to which the circular has reference, were brought forward by Mr. Conway, and through his exertions . . . received the legislative sanction." After making a favorable evaluation of each accomplishment given in Conway's circular and asserting that Conway had worked for a surveyor general's office for Arkansas, "A Voter" noticed that "Thrasybulus" had been "silent as to the services rendered" by Bates, perhaps because "so little was effected" during Bates's four years in Congress "that it escaped the memory of the writer." A look at Bates's record, "A Voter" declared, showed only four acts to his credit.[37]

In a second newspaper address to the people, Bates admitted that Conway had accomplished more as delegate than he himself had, but contended that a comparison of their records was unfair because they had faced dissimiliar situations. As Arkansas' first delegate Bates had trodden an "unexplored" path, and "Whatever was reluctantly yielded even to naked right, was styled a liberality and treasured up to be quoted as a concession." He promised that he would, if elected, follow the instructions of the people; his only specific pledge was to work for establishment of a surveyor general's office for Arkansas.[38]

In a communication printed June 14 "A Citizen of Pulaski County" noticed that Acting Surveyor General William Clark for Missouri, Illinois, and Arkansas Territory had recently let contracts for surveying public lands in Arkansas and the contracts had been disseminated so hastily after the surveys had been ordered by the General Land Office that Arkansans had not known about the order until the surveyors appeared in Arkansas. Conway should, the writer averred, have informed his constituents of the impending order so that Arkansans might apply for contracts. As it was only one Arkansan had received a contract; the rest had gone to citizens of Missouri and other states. Conway had kept quiet because if he had given proper notice in Arkansas his relatives in Missouri would have been prevented from participating in the contracts to the exclusion of "almost every other person." "A Citizen of Pulaski County" said further that Conway had procured for his brother James the contract to run the Choctaw boundary and that James had also received a contract to survey public lands.[39]

Jonathan L. Bean, a land surveyor presumably from Missouri, promptly denied the truth of the assertions made by "A Citizen of Pulaski County." After declaring that he was in no way connected

[37] A Voter, "Congressional Election," *ibid.,* June 14, 1825.
[38] Bates, "To the People," June 18, 1825, *ibid.,* June 21, 1825.
[39] A Citizen of Pulaski County, "To the People of Arkansas," *ibid.,* June 14, 1825.

with Conway's kin, the Rectors[40] and the Conways, Bean stated that only three contracts had gone to Conway's relatives and that Conway could have had nothing to do with procuring them because he had not known when the land commissioner would order the surveys.[41] Two of Conway's uncles from Missouri maintained that "every insinuation" in "A Citizen of Pulaski County's" publication was *"false,* if not malicious."[42]

Presently "A Citizen of Pulaski County" denied that he had made "false insinuations" against Conway. Since Acting Surveyor General Clark, who had succeeded William Rector,[43] Conway's uncle, knew nothing about surveying, he "must . . . have been governed by others," who were acquainted with the duties of his office, "in selecting surveyors to do the work in Arkansas." "A Citizen of Pulaski County" believed that Clark had been influenced in selecting surveyors by Conway's relatives. Confident that Clark would rely on his kin for advice in giving contracts, Conway had persuaded the land commissioner to have the lands recently purchased from the Indians in Arkansas surveyed and had then said nothing about what he knew until Missourians had obtained the contracts. It seemed to "A Citizen of Pulaski County" that the "emoluments" of the surveyor general's office had been in Rector's hands so long that his relatives considered it to be "their exclusive property."[44]

The attack by Bates's supporters on Conway apparently had little popular effect, for in the election held August 1 Conway defeated Bates by an overwhelming vote of 2,105 to 519. Conway carried every county in the Territory, receiving large majorities in all except Independence and Arkansas.[45]

Elected to the legislative council were James M. Kuykendahl of Lawerence County; Johoiada Jeffery of Independence County; Alexander S. Walker of Pulaski County;[46] John W. Calvert of Phillips

[40] Delegate Conway's mother was a Rector. For an account of the Rector family, see Shinn, *Makers of Arkansas,* 370–410.

[41] Bean to Editor, June 14, 1825, *Gazette,* June 21, 1825.

[42] Stephen and W. Rector to Editor, *ibid.*

[43] Clark was appointed acting surveyor general in 1824 pending the arrival in St. Louis of William McRee of Pennsylvania. See *Terr. Papers,* XIX, 708–709, note 70, 716, note 83, 722–723, note 93, 746, 782, note 98.

[44] A Citizen of Pulaski County, "To the People of the Terr. of Arkansas," *Gazette,* July 12, 1825.

[45] Governor's Election Proclamation, September 25, 1825, *ibid.,* October 4, 1825. See also *ibid.,* September 20, 1825.

[46] Walker and Edmund Hogan tied in the regular election, but in a special election held September 12 Walker defeated Hogan 183 to 171. *Ibid.,* August 23, September 6, 20, 1825.

County; Bartley Harrington of Arkansas County; Jacob Barkman of Clark County; Daniel T. Witter of Hempstead County; Josiah Hoskins of Chicot County; William Quarles of Crawford County; and William Bradford of Miller County. Bradford's election was, however, contested successfully by Clayborn Wright.[47] The victorious aspirants to the house were John Hines, Lawrence County; Robert Bean, Independence County; Ambrose H. Sevier, Pulaski County; Henry L. Biscoe, Phillips County; William Montgomery, Arkansas and Chicot Counties; John Calaway, Clark County; John Wilson, Hempstead County; Aaron Hanscome, Miller County; and John Nicks, Crawford County.[48]

Several days after the election a pseudonymous writer asserted in the *Gazette* that notwithstanding Bates's announcement as a candidate and the many handbills that had been circulated in his behalf, he did not believe Bates had actually been a candidate. He averred that Bates's name had been put forward by a "fruitful source" at Little Rock "for the purpose of malignant detraction," and that had Bates "suffered his name to go to the People," he would not have lost the election.[49] Since Bates never publicly denied that he was a candidate, the writer's assertions seem entirely false, and one wonders what object he hoped his letter would accomplish.

In the meantime, Governor Izard had arrived in Little Rock on May 31[50] to find that Secretary Crittenden had been absent in Kentucky since April 18.[51] On June 6 he wrote Secretary of War James Barbour that in Crittenden's absence he was unable to make himself "acquainted with the Details of the public Affairs in this Quarter."[52] Nearly two weeks later he complained to Barbour that Crittenden was still absent and that government checks totaling $10,500, presumably intended to be used for Indian annuities "and other Payments," were made out to Crittenden and in the hands of a gentleman Crittenden had left in charge of his papers.[53] Not until July 1 was Izard able to report that Crittenden had returned, relieving him "from some Un-

---

[47] "Arkansas General Assembly," *ibid.,* October 11, 1825.

[48] "Election Returns," *ibid.,* August 16, 23, September 20, 1825; "Arkansas General Assembly," *ibid.,* October 4, 1825.

[49] "An Enemy to Intrigue and Detraction" to Editor, *ibid.,* August 9, 1825.

[50] "Arrival of the Governor," *ibid.,* May 31, 1825.

[51] *Ibid.,* April 19, 1825. At the time of Crittenden's departure Izard was expected to arrive within a few days.

[52] Izard to Secretary of War, June 6, 1825, *Terr. Papers,* XX, 66–67; *Publications of the Arkansas Historical Association,* Vol. I (Fayetteville, 1906), 423–424.

[53] Izard to Secretary of War, June 18, 1825, *Terr. Papers,* XX, 78–80; *Publications of the Arkansas Historical Association,* I, 424–425.

easiness respecting the pecuniary Supplies required" for his Indian superintendency.[54] The enmity later evident between Crittenden and Izard may have had its origin in Izard's irritation at finding Crittenden absent from the Territory.

While waiting for Crittenden to return, Izard had commenced organizing the territorial militia. Nothing had been done on "this important Subject" prior to his administration "except [the] commissioning [of] a number of Officers."[55] On June 10 he issued a general order instructing the commanding officers of all units in Clark, Hempstead, and Miller Counties to report in person or by letter to Brigadier General William Bradford[56] at Fort Towson, and those in the remaining counties to report to the adjutant general's office at Little Rock. To assist him in organizing the militia, Izard appointed Lieutenant Colonels Henry W. Conway and Ambrose H. Sevier as aides.[57] On June 18 he wrote the Secretary of War to ask for arms and ammunition to supplement "some boxes of both deposited in a Merchant's ware-house" in Little Rock,[58] but his request was refused on the ground that he had not furnished the War Department with an "ample return of the Militia."[59]

Despite Izard's efforts, he was seemingly never able to transform the militia into an effective organization. In October, 1827, he wrote Secretary of State Henry Clay that the "scattered state of our Population here & the constant changes of Residence among the Inhabitants make it impracticable to organize the Militia in such a manner as may render their Services prompt & efficient."[60]

The territorial legislature convened and organized October 3. The next day the members met to hear the address of Governor Izard. He informed them that the recent Quapaw treaty would soon be executed and that the Choctaws would, at a time not yet known, remove from the East to their reserve west of the Territory. In anticipation of these Indian movements he had commenced organizing the militia. The

---

[54] Izard to Secretary of War, July 1, 1825, *Terr. Papers,* XX, 83–84; *Publications of the Arkansas Historical Association,* I, 426.

[55] Izard to Secretary of War, June 18, 1825, *Terr. Papers,* XX, 79; *Publications of the Arkansas Historical Association,* I, 425. See also Margaret Smith Ross, "The Territorial Militia," *Pulaski County Historical Review,* III (September, 1955), 35–39.

[56] Bradford had in 1824 succeeded Edmund Hogan as brigadier general of the militia. *Terr. Papers,* XX, 157, note 59.

[57] General Order, June 10, 1825, *Gazette,* June 14, 1825; *Terr. Papers,* XX, 68–76.

[58] Izard to Secretary of War, June 18, 1825, *Terr. Papers,* XX, 79–80; *Publications of the Arkansas Historical Association,* I, 425.

[59] Acting Secretary of War to Izard, July 26, 1825, *Terr. Papers,* XX, 96.

[60] Izard to Secretary of State, October 16, 1827, *ibid.,* 543. See also Izard to Secretary of War, January 30, 1826, *ibid.,* 193.

proposed road to run from Memphis to Little Rock had been surveyed and he was assured that the survey would soon be acted upon.[61]

The legislature enacted several seemingly important measures. One provided for the formation of slave patrols in the townships and prohibited slaves from buying or selling property without a permit designating the property to be bought or sold.[62] A law of 1823 authorizing the governor to borrow money on the faith and resources of the Territory was repealed.[63] Another act, introduced by Ambrose H. Sevier,[64] repealed not only that part of the duelling law of 1820 which disqualified from holding office any person found guilty of issuing, delivering, or accepting a challenge but also the requirement that all officeholders swear they had not violated the act.[65]

Other business consisted of creating Conway, Crittenden, and Izard Counties; fixing the permanent seats of government for Clark and Hempstead Counties; authorizing Hartwell Boswell to erect a toll bridge on Poke Bayou in Independence County; making appropriations for 1826–1827; setting the territorial land tax on all confirmed land at $1.25 per one hundred acres and the county tax at $.25; and amending the judicial laws to redistrict the three circuits.[66] Though it had been reported before the meeting of the assembly that a charter for a bank would be applied for, the matter is not recorded in the legislative journal as having been brought up.[67]

Memorials to the President and Congress dealt with internal improvements, land, and Indians. A memorial to Congress asked that the legislature be granted authority to compel superior court judges to perform circuit duties in addition to holding superior court at the capital, and to provide for the appointment of an additional superior court judge.[68]

Governor Izard was in October called on by Secretary of War Barbour to explain why he had removed David Barber as sub-agent

[61] "Arkansas General Assembly," *Gazette,* October 4, 1825. Izard's message, in his own handwriting, is also in Luther C. Gulley Collection, Arkansas History Commission.
[62] *Arkansas Acts,* 1825, pp. 15–17.
[63] *Ibid.,* 11–12.
[64] "Arkansas General Assembly," *Gazette,* October 11, 1825.
[65] *Arkansas Acts,* 1825, p. 27.
[66] *Ibid.,* 3, 6–12, 17–20, 34–44, 48–49, 79.
[67] See *Gazette,* May 3, June 21, 1825.
[68] "Memorials," *Gazette,* November 15, 1825; *Terr. Papers,* XX, 127–132, 161, 162–165. The reason given for the request concerning the judiciary was that the three circuit courts, which had been established at territorial expense, were "scarcely sufficient for the administration of justice throughout the territory, and creates [*sic*] a territorial expenditure, which the present inhabitants . . . are not well able to bear . . . ."

of Indian affairs. Izard replied that he, like his predecessor, had employed Barber as his private secretary, but had found him to be incompetent, "frequently under the Influence of Intemperance, and neglectful of the Instructions addressed to him." After he had been twice absent without leave, Izard had dismissed him; but believing it "unnecessary for the public advantage to wound the Feelings of a good-natured and inoffensive Man," Izard had given him a more lucrative office. Izard wished that the President would now appoint Bernard Smith to be sub-agent.[69]

Presently Barbour informed Izard that his action in removing Barber was approved and that Smith had been commissioned to succeed him. Barbour informed the governor, however, that "the power that appoints, alone, had the power to cancel, or remove from Office."[70]

In May, 1826, Barber asked the Secretary of War for "a true history of this transaction." Soon after Izard's arrival he had, he said, agreed to a new arrangement whereby he was to act as the governor's private secretary while continuing to draw pay as sub-agent. Subsequently Izard had dismissed him, giving economy as "the motive." Suspecting that Izard had made a statement against him to the War Department, Barber had asked to see it and had been given "an incomplete Copy." Barber denied that he was "besotted" and lacked "clerical qualifications." Though he did not seek reinstatement to his former post, he wished to have his "name and Character" restored by an investigation of the matter.[71] There is no evidence that his request was granted.

Governor Izard also clashed with Cherokee Agent Edward W. DuVal. On October 10, 1826, Izard wrote DuVal that he had received petitions from two men complaining of DuVal's conduct in refusing to pay certain claims due them from the Cherokees. Unless DuVal satisfied the claims, Izard would retain the amount due the men "from the next remittances intended for your Agency." DuVal's conduct in these and other matters, Izard planned to bring to the attention of "the proper Department" in Washington.[72]

DuVal replied that he would welcome an investigation of his conduct for it had not been "such as your petitioners and tale-bearers

[69] Izard to Secretary of War, November 30, 1825, *Terr. Papers*, XX, 156–157. See also Izard to Thomas L. McKenney, September 16, 1825, *Publications of the Arkansas Historical Association*, I, 431.

[70] Secretary of War to Izard, January 16, 1826, *Terr. Papers*, XX, 179.

[71] Barber to Secretary of War, May 19, 1826, *ibid.*, 246–252.

[72] Izard to DuVal, October 10, 1826, *ibid.*, 346–347.

have represented it."[73] In December DuVal wrote Barbour to ask, in case an investigation was made, "the right of being heard in my defence."

> If rumor, the every-day gossip, is to select and have its victims then has the Governor run his Career & fallen a sacrifice. I might say more: if the assertions of respectable men are entitled to belief, he is, from his *habits,* not only disqualified properly to discharge the duties of his Office, but degraded below the character of a Gentleman. He is openly and without reserve proclaimed to have indulged, while here, in inebriating potations to an Extent that would be disreputable to the meanest peasant in the Community.[74]

If Izard submitted the charges of misconduct against DuVal to officials in Washington, there is no evidence that an investigation was made. DuVal continued to be agent, and he and Izard remained at odds throughout the remainder of Izard's administration.[75]

In July, 1826, Robert C. Oden, an attorney of Little Rock who expected to be a candidate for Congress in 1827, wrote former Governor James Miller that Izard's administration had been a *"great Contrast"* to Miller's. Factions had arisen and Izard was "deeply tinged in the turmoils"; Miller's course as governor had been "Cited" throughout the Territory "and brought-up in Judgment against" Izard. Oden predicted that the next twelve months would "present a Scene of trouble, & confusion hitherto unknown [in Arkansas politics]— parties will be more distinct—separate, and violent."[76]

Beginning about the fall of 1826, events moved rapidly toward fulfillment of Oden's prophecy. In August Crittenden asked for a sixty-day leave in order that he might go to Washington to settle his public accounts (which presumably had been called into question) before his nomination for a third term went before the Senate during the winter.[77] In September Secretary of State Henry Clay granted his request.[78]

In the meantime Crittenden had discovered from Izard that he objected to Crittenden's leaving because he himself planned to visit Philadelphia. If Crittenden should go to Washington, "the responsi-

[73] DuVal to Izard, October 18, 1826, *ibid.,* 347–350.
[74] DuVal to Secretary of War, December 27, 1826, *ibid.,* 345–346.
[75] See Izard to Secretary of War, June 18, 1828, *ibid.,* 698–700; DuVal to McKenney, September 16, 1828, *ibid.,* 747; Izard to DuVal, July 13, 26, 1827, and to Secretary of War, September 28, 1827, *Publications of the Arkansas Historical Association,* I, 449–450, 452.
[76] Oden to Miller, July 19, 1826, Robert W. Trimble Collection, Arkansas History Commission.
[77] Crittenden to Secretary of State, August 17, September 15, 1826, *Terr. Papers,* XX, 285–286, 287–288.
[78] Secretary of State to Crittenden, September 25, 1826, *ibid.,* 290.

bility of leaving the Territory without an executive head" would be Crittenden's.[79] Reporting this conversation to Clay on September 15, Crittenden asked what he should do. He had "no reason" to believe that Izard would "promote" his affairs at Washington and though his presence would, by forwarding his accounts, probably be "obviated," his nomination might, should this "expedient" fail, be rejected.[80]

Clay replied that since Crittenden and Izard could not come to "some arrangement" whereby the "public inconvenience of your both being absent at the same time would be prevented," Crittenden should remain in Arkansas and send his accounts to Washington by messenger. This plan would not, Clay believed, affect either way the Senate's action upon Crittenden's renomination.[81]

On November 1, 1826, Governor Izard left Little Rock for Philadelphia.[82] Then Crittenden, either in spite of Clay's letter or because he did not receive it, departed for Washington on January 9, 1827.[83] Before leaving he issued a statement to the people explaining that "Circumstances of the most imperative character, over which I have had no control, have rendered it necessary that I should visit Washington, for the purpose of adjusting my accounts"; he promised "an *expeditious* return."[84] Three days after Crittenden's departure the Senate approved his nomination to a third term.[85]

In Washington Crittenden complained to Secretary of War Barbour that Governor Izard held, contrary to the organic law and to precedent, that in the governor's absence the superintendency of Indian affairs did not devolve upon the secretary, and continued, after leaving the Territory, to disburse funds of that office through his private secretary. Izard's course, Crittenden said, had caused the "reflecting part of the community" to believe that he (Crittenden) was "deemed incapable or unworthy the confidence due me from my commission and heretofore extended to me by your department."[86] Barbour re-

---

[79] Crittenden and Izard are reported to have stopped speaking to each other at about this time. James Scull to James Miller, August 18, October 28, 1827, Robert W. Trimble Collection, Arkansas History Commission. See also Crittenden to John Pope, April 21, 1832, *Advocate,* May 2, 1832.

[80] Crittenden to Secretary of State, September 15, 1826, *Terr. Papers,* XX, 287–288.

[81] Secretary of State to Crittenden, October 24, 1826, *ibid.,* 298–299.

[82] *Gazette,* November 7, 1826. Izard had evidently received his leave from the President himself. See Izard to Secretary of State, December 13, 1826, *Terr. Papers,* XX, 324.

[83] *Gazette,* January 16, 1827.

[84] Crittenden, "To the People of Arkansas Territory," *ibid.,* January 30, 1827.

[85] *Terr. Papers,* XX, 367, note 1.

[86] Crittenden to Secretary of War, February 27, 1827, *ibid.,* 406–407.

plied that the War Department could not "interfere in any of the details" which the governor considered "proper to adopt in relation to his superintendency of Indian Affairs."[87]

Perhaps more significant than the Crittenden-Izard quarrel was a newspaper controversy arising from Crittenden's absence while Izard was away. The controversy began on February 6, 1827, when "A Citizen of Independence" complained in the *Gazette* that the commission of Charles Kelly as sheriff of Independence County had expired and that, owing to Acting Governor Crittenden's "misdeed" in leaving the Territory, the office could not be filled.[88] To this complaint "A Citizen of Pulaski" answered that Crittenden had secured a sixty-day leave to attend to his accounts in Washington and that, according to territorial law, the county coroner was to act as sheriff in case the sheriff's office became vacant. It was to be regretted, "A Citizen of Pulaski" continued, that persons who had received favors —obviously he referred to "A Citizen of Independence"—should repay their obligations by attacking the people who had conferred them.[89] Next a piece by "Conservator" asserted that Crittenden had received his leave before Izard had obtained his and that the vacancy in the sheriff's office in Independence County was not the actual reason for the attack upon Crittenden by "A Citizen of Independence."[90] "Junius" believed the real motive of "A Citizen of Independence," who had attempted "to conceal himself by an assumed weakness of [writing] style," was *"revenge* for disappointed expectations."[91]

In a short statement printed February 27, "A Citizen of Independence" maintained that, because Crittenden had commissioned the present coroner of Independence County for four years when the proper term was two, the offices of both coroner and sheriff were now vacant in that county.[92]

"Tuckahoe" averred that Crittenden's defenders had, in attempting to identify "A Citizen of Independence," alluded, without actually naming him, to Judge James Woodson Bates of the second judicial circuit.[93] The question of Bates's authorship was, however, "totally immaterial"; indeed, many people would consider it Bates's official

[87] Secretary of War to Crittenden, February 28, 1827, *ibid.,* 407.
[88] A Citizen of Independence to Editor, *Gazette,* February 6, 1827.
[89] A Citizen of Pulaski to Editor, *ibid.,* February 13, 1827.
[90] Conservator to Editor, *ibid.,* February 13, 1827.
[91] Junius to Editor, *ibid.,* February 20, 1827.
[92] A Citizen of Independence, "A Card," *ibid.,* February 27, 1827.
[93] Bates had been appointed circuit judge by Governor Izard in November, 1825. *Terr. Papers,* XIX, 826.

duty to call Crittenden's misconduct to the attention of the public. Crittenden had, "Tuckahoe" went on to assert, been an "irresponsible" executive.

He came among us, a young man with a presciency [*sic*] of imagination, but without judgment, . . . defective in education and without system or method . . . Yet he had heard of some Machievelian [*sic*] School . . . and determined to adopt its principles. He has been known to declare, that the Governor of a Territory who did [not] mould it to his plastic hand was "a fool." As a practising lawyer, he has scoured the country, scattering his commissions without, perhaps, even a *penciled* memorandum to enable him to make the registry on his return home. Ever calculating that his militia officers and justices of the peace were to constitute his household troops—his body guard in case of emergency. His administration and his personal example, has retarded the population of our country . . .[94]

A week later "Junius" addressed a communication to Bates as the author of the numbers signed "A Citizen of Independence." Bates was in error in contending that coroners were restricted to two-year terms, for it had been "established by the concurrent adjudication of all our courts, that where the term for which an officer is to hold, is not limited by law, that it shall be 'during good conduct.' " "Junius" went on to castigate Bates for "a systematic disregard of the laws." In the case of *Hawthorn* vs. *Hightower* recently decided in the circuit court of Independence County, Bates had violated the law by ruling that Hightower, the defendant, had no right to be represented by counsel, and by refusing to acknowledge a bill of exceptions and to allow it to be filed. The superior court had, however, subsequently reversed Bates's ruling. To support his allegations, "Junius" inserted a copy of a bill of exceptions on file in the superior court, signed by William Quarles, Thomas Moore, and John Reed and attested to by Richard Searcy (Hightower's counsel), stating that the circuit court had deprived Hightower of the right to counsel and refused him a bill of exceptions.[95]

On March 20 Acting Governor Crittenden arrived back in Little Rock.[96] A few weeks later Editor Woodruff, with whom Crittenden was on bad terms,[97] informed his readers that he understood from a

---

[94] Tuckahoe to Editor, *Gazette,* March 6, 1827. See also *ibid.,* April 3, 1827.

[95] Junius to Bates, *ibid.,* March 13, 1827. The issue of March 13 also contained an essay by "A Citizen of Pulaski" defending Crittenden's action in leaving the Territory and attacking Bates as devoid of "political character."

[96] *Ibid.,* March 27, 1827.

[97] The exact origin of the hostility between Crittenden and Woodruff, which would in time reach astronomical proportions, cannot be determined, but it almost certainly developed during Governor Miller's administration. Woodruff later recalled that Crittenden began pursuing an illiberal course toward him in 1820. John Lewis Ferguson

highly reliable source that before Crittenden set out for Washington he had been instructed by the Secretary of State not to leave the Territory while the governor was away.[98] Woodruff's source, directly or indirectly, was probably a statement made February 21 by Delegate Conway in the House of Representatives. Prompted by complaints from his constituents about Crittenden's absence, Conway had introduced a resolution looking toward the provision of an executive in the absence of both the governor and secretary from the Territory, and his accompanying speech alluded to Clay's letter countermanding the permission earlier given Crittenden to go to Washington. (Conway suggested that Crittenden did not receive the letter.)[99]

"Tuckahoe" continued the controversy in a communication published May 1. Observing that Crittenden had not, since his return from Washington, attempted to defend his absence, "Tuckahoe" concluded that his failure to do so nullified the efforts of his friends to defend him. In the matter of *Hawthorn* vs. *Hightower*, "Tuckahoe" denied that a bill of exceptions had, as "Junius" claimed, been tendered to Judge Bates. The alleged bill published in "Junius's" communication was incorrect in details. Two of the signers had probably not read the content of the bill and the third, though a lawyer, was scarcely respected as such in Independence County.[100]

Crittenden announced in the *Gazette* on May 8 that he would answer Bates when Governor Izard returned.[101] In the same issue Thomas W. Newton, a former Kentuckian now reading law with Crittenden and living in his home,[102] published a communication to Bates as the writer calling himself "Tuckahoe." Confessing himself to be "Junius," Newton took up Bates's denial that he had refused the bill of exceptions and observed that his account of the matter ran counter to that of four highly respected men whose signatures ap-

---

conjectures that enmity may have begun either because Crittenden supported John McArthur's plans in 1819 to establish a newspaper at Arkansas Post or because Woodruff irritated Crittenden by a neutral editorial course in the *Gazette*. The first open disagreement between the two occurred in 1821 when Acting Governor Crittenden refused to allow the amount Woodruff asked for printing in pamphlet form the laws of the legislature of 1821 and an executive proclamation. John Lewis Ferguson, "William E. Woodruff and the Territory of Arkansas, 1819–1836" (unpublished Ph.D. dissertation, Tulane University, 1960), 44–45.

[98] *Gazette*, April 10, 1827.

[99] *Register of Debates in Congress*, 19 Cong., 2 sess., III (February 21, 1827), 1332–1333.

[100] Tuckahoe to Crittenden, *Gazette*, May 1, 1827.

[101] Crittenden, "To the Public," *ibid.*, May 8, 1827.

[102] Newton was postmaster at Little Rock, clerk of Pulaski County, and secretary of the legislative council. Fay Hempstead, *A Pictorial History of Arkansas* (St. Louis, 1890), 767–768; *Terr. Papers*, XIX, 793.

peared on the bill on file in the superior court. Bates had "disgraced" his office not only "by gross ignorance" but also by "a visible intoxication on the bench."[103]

William Quarles and Richard Searcy also published letters against Bates. Quarles was presumably prompted by his belief that Bates, writing under the signature of "Tuckahoe," had been referring to him as the disreputable lawyer who had signed the bill of exceptions published by "Junius." According to Quarles, two bills of exceptions had been presented to Judge Bates in the case of *Hawthorn* vs. *Hightower* and both had been refused notwithstanding the fact that they bore the signatures of honorable men. Quarles went on to defend Crittenden's action in leaving the Territory and to deny that Bates had any "right" to "judge of the necessity of his staying or going."[104]

Searcy's communication alleged that Bates had, contrary to law, tried the case of *Hawthorn* vs. *Hightower* despite his having been the original counsel for the defendant; and that he had denied Hightower the right of counsel and refused two bills of exceptions. Searcy believed that Bates would have been removed from office had Hightower brought the matter to the attention of the governor. What person could, Searcy asked, "have respect for a Court, when they see the Judge of that Court intoxicated on the bench, and rioting with the crowd in the grog-shops and court-yards?"[105]

In an address to the public, published June 5, Crittenden did not attempt to explain his absence of the previous winter, but instead denounced Bates for using it as an excuse to assail his personal character. Bates had known that he would be *"personally"* secure in assaulting Crittenden because Crittenden was, as an officeholder, required to account for his public acts when called upon to do so. Thus Bates remained "safe from my resentment: the only notice I can *ever* take of him, will be corporeal punishment for personal obtrusion."[106]

The controversy ended in October, 1827, with a communication signed by Bates himself. Bates endeavored to justify his actions in the *Hawthorn* vs. *Hightower* case and questioned Searcy's ability to "pass on legal decisions and qualifications and fitness for official station," asserting that Searcy lacked education above that "our law prescribes for articled apprentices" and was ignorant "even of the terms of the profession to which he claims to belong." In conclusion Bates

---

[103] Newton, "To James Woodson Bates, alias 'Tuckahoe,'" *Gazette,* May 8, 1827.
[104] Quarles to Bates, May 19, 1827, *ibid.,* May 29, 1827.
[105] Searcy to Editor, June 4, 1827, *ibid.,* June 12, 1827.
[106] Crittenden, "To the Public," *ibid.,* June 5, 1827.

declared that the case would never have been mentioned, "had not the heinous sin rested on my head of being the supposed author of strictures on the official misconduct of Robert Crittenden."[107] It is to be noticed that, though he did not acknowledge authorship of the "strictures," Bates also did not deny the allegations of the Crittenden men that he had in fact written the pieces signed "A Citizen of Independence" and "Tuckahoe."

The events of 1824 down to the election campaign of 1827[108] were of considerable significance in territorial politics. The Scott-Selden duel not only left Selden's place on the superior court vacant, but also caused the Senate to refuse to approve the subsequent renomination of Scott to a third term on that court. The appointment of Izard in 1825 brought to the office of governor a man, who though undoubtedly competent, soon engaged in squabbles, which contributed to the growth of factionalism. If Crittenden was the dominant political figure in early territorial politics, as the evidence would seem to indicate, then his quarrel with Izard marked the beginning of the end of his dominance. The newspaper controversy over Crittenden's absence from the Territory in 1827 widened the breach between Crittenden and Bates, and Conway's resolution in Congress, coming at the same time, apparently caused Crittenden to feel that Conway had betrayed their friendship and to support Conway's opponent in the canvass of 1827.[109] The climax of the political turmoil of 1824–1827 would come in that election.

[107] Bates to Editor, October 10, 1827, *ibid.,* October 16, 1827.

[108] Actually though much of the newspaper controversy of 1827 over Crittenden's absence from the Territory paralleled the canvass of 1827, it began before the campaign and was carried on apart from it.

[109] See Conway, "To the People of Arkansas," July 12, 1827, *Gazette,* July 17, 1827; Walter Lee Brown, "Albert Pike's First Experiences in Arkansas," *Arkansas Historical Quarterly,* X (Spring, 1951), 77–78.

CHAPTER FIVE

The Election of 1827 and the Conway-Crittenden Duel

THE TERRITORIAL ELECTION OF 1827, more acrimonious, exciting, and significant than any previous political campaign in Arkansas, began on April 10, 1827, with Henry W. Conway's announcement that he would stand for reelection as delegate to Congress.[1] One week later Robert C. Oden proclaimed his opposing candidacy.[2] The main interest of the campaign revolved around the contest between these two.

Born about 1798,[3] Oden had practiced law in Pulaski County, Missouri Territory, in 1818–1819.[4] After the creation of Arkansas Territory, he served briefly as clerk of Pulaski County,[5] and was, ac-

[1] *Arkansas Gazette* (Little Rock), April 10, 1827.

[2] *Ibid.*, April 17, 1827. Oden stated in July, 1826, that William Bradford and Richard Searcy would also be candidates. Oden to James Miller, July 19, 1826, Robert W. Trimble Collection, Arkansas History Commission. But Bradford died before the campaign began (*Gazette,* November 14, 1826) and Searcy's candidacy was never announced.

[3] William F. Pope, *Early Days in Arkansas* (Little Rock, 1895), 34, states that Oden was "about twenty-two or twenty-three" years of age in 1820. Oden himself said that he was twenty years old when he commenced his career. Oden, "To the People of Arkansas," April 19, 1827, *Gazette,* April 24, 1827.

[4] Fay Hempstead, *A Pictorial History of Arkansas* (St. Louis, 1890), 839–840. Oden was a former Kentuckian. Many Voters, "To the Citizens of Arkansas," *Gazette,* July 10, 1833; Jaw-Bone to Editor, *ibid.*, August 11, 1830; Woodruff, "To the People of Arkansas," July 20, 1827, in Edwin Marshall Williams, "The Conway-Crittenden Duel," *Arkansas Historical Review,* I (February, 1934), 20. Oden returned to Kentucky soon after the election of 1827 and died about 1833. Lafayette to John Pope, *Arkansas Advocate* (Little Rock), May 1, 1833; Crittenden to Eskridge, November 5, 1833, *ibid.,* November 13, 1833.

[5] Clarence E. Carter, ed., *Territorial Papers of the United States,* Vol. XIX, *Arkansas Territory, 1819–1825* (Washington, 1953), 793.

cording to Josiah H. Shinn, Little Rock's first lawyer.[6] In 1820 he killed William O. Allen in a duel (above, p. 28). He was commissioned lieutenant colonel of the second Arkansas militia regiment in 1823,[7] and was, for a short time in 1823–1824, attorney for the third judicial circuit.[8] A contemporary wrote in 1828 that Oden was "probably a man of better talents than anyone in the Territory."[9]

In a letter to the people of Arkansas, dated April 19, 1827, Oden disclaimed any political connections except with "the whole body of the people," and declared, in obvious criticism of Conway, that he had not been "bribed by the *gift of office* to make Arkansas my home; nor did I come, with the hope of obtaining one." He promised to make his political views known in meeting the people during the campaign.[10] To Conway he gave notice that he intended speaking on the first day of court in Clark, Hempstead, Miller, Lawrence, Independence, Izard, Conway, and Crawford Counties; and that he would, if it could be arranged, speak "in all the counties on the Mississippi."[11]

Delegate Conway arrived in Little Rock from Washington on May 16 and left almost immediately on an electioneering tour of Clark, Hempstead, and Miller Counties. Before departing he issued a circular letter to the people setting forth some of his recent accomplishments. He had, he said, obtained appropriations to complete construction of the Memphis–Little Rock road and to build a road from Fort Smith to the Louisiana line; he had secured passage of a law allowing Arkansas two townships of land for the founding of a seminary of learning; and had brought before Congress various measures which had failed through lack of time.[12]

Conway's circular took note that Oden had charged him with improper use of government funds. As Conway explained it, the

---

[6] Josiah H. Shinn, *Pioneers and Makers of Arkansas* (Little Rock, 1908), 188. See also Dallas T. Herndon, *Why Little Rock Was Born* (Little Rock, 1933), 12–13. Oden announced in the first issue of the *Gazette* that he would practice law in the territorial superior court in Clark, Hempstead, and Arkansas Counties. *Gazette,* November 20, 1819.

[7] Roster of Militia Officers, June 10, 1825, *Terr. Papers,* Vol. XX, *Arkansas Territory, 1825–1829* (Washington, 1954), 69.

[8] *Ibid.,* XIX, 827.

[9] Hiram A. Whittington to Father, December 1, 1828, in Margaret Smith Ross, ed., "Letters of Hiram Abiff Whittington, 1827–1834," *Pulaski County Historical Society Bulletin,* No. 3 (December, 1956), 11. Whittington said that Oden had, until 1828, when he came under the influence of a minister, "been one of the most haughty, proud, self conceited, good for nothing fellows I ever knew, continually in some drunken frolic, quarrelling with every person he met."

[10] Oden, "To the People of Arkansas," April 19, 1827, *Gazette,* April 24, 1827.

[11] Oden, "To Mr. Henry W. Conway," April 21, 1827, *ibid.*

[12] Conway, "To the People of Arkansas," May 18, 1827, *ibid.,* May 22, 1827.

Secretary of War had in 1824 entrusted him with $7,000 to be used by Secretary Robert Crittenden for defraying the expenses of treating with the Quapaw Indians. Conway had given $6,400 to Crittenden and retained, with Crittenden's permission, the remaining $600. A pseudonymous writer, who signed himself "A Citizen of the Territory," quickly replied that he did not believe that Conway would swear to his version of the transaction, for Crittenden had denied giving Conway leave to retain a part of the money.[13]

Writing in defense of Conway, "A Voter of Pulaski County" declared that an affidavit made by Crittenden in Hempstead County at the outset of the campaign had not denied positively that he had given Conway permission to retain the $600.[14] Crittenden replied that instead of making an affidavit he had read a statement saying that he was " 'positively certain' " that he had not given Conway permission to retain a portion of the money. He had considered Conway's inability to produce the entire amount in 1824 a matter between Conway and the government.[15] Conway maintained in a second circular to the people that Crittenden had not only consented to his retention of the $600 but had also assured him, when he offered to hand over the money prior to his return to Washington in the fall of 1824, that it was not needed. Conway observed that he and Crittenden had, at the time, been close friends "and the understanding in relation to the money was known, as I thought, and believe, only to ourselves." In 1825, when Crittenden had favored Conway's election, "this pretended defalcation" had not been mentioned.[16]

Crittenden answered this second circular of Conway by a second public letter of his own. He professed astonishment at Conway's version of the Quapaw matter. At the time that he, Crittenden, had made the statement about it in Hempstead County Conway had been "the first man" to see the statement; they had not, it was true, been in "perfect agreement," but Conway had not considered it "expedient to animadvert upon the variance" in his speeches made "the same evening." Crittenden now said that he could not have given Conway permission to retain part of the Quapaw funds because he had no "power to control one cent of the $7000 until it had been paid me." Crittenden also questioned whether Conway could, prior to his de-

[13] A Citizen of the Territory, "To the People of Arkansas.—I," ibid., June 5, 1827.
[14] A Voter of Pulaski County, "To the Voters of Arkansas. No. I," ibid., June 12, 1827.
[15] Crittenden, "To the People of Arkansas," ibid., June 19, 1827.
[16] Conway, "To the Public," June 22, 1827, ibid., June 26, 1827.

parture for Washington in 1824, have handed over the $600 re-tained by him. Actually Crittenden had loaned $620 to Conway to make the trip, and had afterwards been told by Conway that he had been obliged to use half of that to pay debts before leaving Little Rock. Conway had now "thought proper" to make their difference "on a point of fact" an important one, and in his second circular to treat Crittenden's "feelings and character" in a manner "somewhat equivocal." If Conway

means to charge me with falsehood, or deliberate misrepresentation, in re-gard to this or any other subject, I hurl the foul imputation with scorn back upon him; and more, that if such imputation was designed by him, in that explanation, that he has uttered a foul falsehood, knowingly, and for the worst of purposes.[17]

The statement which Crittenden had made in Hempstead County appeared in a circular published for Oden at Memphis.[18] "A Voter of Pulaski County" responded by insisting that what Crittenden called a statement had been a sworn affidavit; that in it Crittenden had misstated under oath the month of his meeting with Conway in 1824; and that his entire account was therefore suspect. "A Voter of Pulaski County" said further that

Mr. Crittenden possesses the art and address of holding out the right hand of friendship and good fellowship, to many, while in the other is the poisoned chalice, with which he would, if he dare, prostrate them in death. But I will admit, that, in the case of Mr. Conway, the friendship of Mr. Crittenden was real, and I do believe Mr. Crittenden so ardent in his friendship, that he will go great lengths to accommodate his friends. ["A Voter of Pulaski County" had previously stated that he doubted the "reality" of the former Conway-Crittenden friendship.] Under this view, I believe Mr. Crittenden would not, and did not, hesitate to give his assent to Mr. Conway, to retain the 600 dollars, provided Mr. Conway would pay it into the Treasury, immediately on his arrival at Washington.[19]

"A Citizen of the Territory" quickly denied that Crittenden had sworn to the statement in Oden's circular. Conway had in Hempstead County admitted his recollection of the transaction to be erroneous.

To *affect* to believe that a man of Mr. Crittenden's character for integrity and honor, *could* be guilty of [swearing falsely] . . . argues as little for the *sense*, as it does for the *heart*, of his accuser. To say that *any* man, under *any* circumstances, would *swear falsely*, is an *awful* accusation; but to say that he

---

[17] Crittenden, "To the Public," *ibid.*, July 24, 1827.
[18] No copy has been found.
[19] A Voter of Pulaski County, "To the Voters of Arkansas. No. VI," *Gazette*, July 17, 1827.

would do so, or had done so, on a question where he could not by possibility have more interest at stake, than any other individual in the community, is an *insult* to the common sense of every *honest* man, and the heighth [*sic*] of villainous absurdity.[20]

The editor of the *Gazette* subsequently explained, probably correctly, that Crittenden's statement had not been a sworn affidavit but that he had expressed his willingness to swear to what he had said.[21]

The foregoing evidence would seem to indicate either that Conway or Crittenden was lying in 1827 or that they had completely misunderstood one another in 1824. Whatever the truth, Crittenden evidently sought, by his stand, to defend his own conduct as a public official while Conway, whose misuse of public money seems obvious, apparently hoped to shift some of the blame to Crittenden, thereby placing himself in a better light before the electorate.

"A Voter of Pulaski County" charged early in the canvass that Crittenden himself had on several occasions misused public funds: he had transferred $2,750 of government money to "a gentleman of this Territory" to buy land on which Little Rock stood; he had given the $6,400 received from Conway to a Little Rock merchant to purchase goods for the Quapaws "at a *very enormous advance*"; and he had also secretly participated in a contract for supplying corn and beef to the Quapaws during their removal from the Arkansas to Red River.

"A Voter of Pulaski County" also accused Crittenden of having united with Oden to defraud Oden's creditors in "various sales and transfers" of Little Rock property. Oden had given power of attorney to a brother-in-law "to dispose of his Little Rock town lots"; had then conveyed the same lots to Crittenden "without any consideration"; and had afterward sold part of them to William E. Woodruff, instructing Crittenden to make the conveyance. Crittenden knew at the time that he actually had no title, for, as he subsequently "acknowledged," the transfer from Oden to him had been "made for no other purpose than to prevent Oden's creditors from executing the property," and was therefore "fraudulent."[22]

Crittenden responded to this attack by demanding that Editor Woodruff tell the name of "A Voter of Pulaski County." Woodruff

[20] A Citizen of the Territory, "To the People of Arkansas. No. V," *ibid.*, July 24, 1827.

[21] Woodruff, "To the People of Arkansas," July 20, 1827, in Williams, "Conway-Crittenden Duel," *Arkansas Historical Review*, I, 22.

[22] A Voter of Pulaski County, "To the Voters of Arkansas. No. I," *Gazette*, June 12, 1827.

refused, saying that although he himself was not the author he would "sustain those charges, if you think proper to require me to do so, in a legal manner."[23]

Crittenden replied in a public address that he found it indeed perplexing to be assailed thus when he was "not a candidate for office" and when "the most mad-cap friend, Mr. Conway has, does not charge me with defamation or injustice towards him"; the only possible reason for the attack was his decision to vote for Oden and "for daring to think and act for myself . . . I have been thus vilified and abused." His refutation of the charges of official misconduct Crittenden reserved for a libel suit against Woodruff. To the accusation that he had helped Oden to manipulate certain Little Rock property he made what was more a correction than a denial. In 1824 Oden had informed Crittenden that Chester Ashley, a Little Rock attorney, held a judgment against him on "an unjust debt" but had promised to withhold execution until Oden should return from a trip to Missouri. To make sure that Ashley did not force the sacrifice of Oden's property despite his promise, Oden deeded it to Crittenden. When Oden returned Crittenden "conveyed the lots to Woodruff, at Ashley's request, Oden having sold them to him."[24]

According to "A Voter of Pulaski County," his accusations against Crittenden created much excitement. He had been threatened with "Cow-hiding, dirking, ear-cropping, and shooting"; and Woodruff, after taking responsibility for the charges made, had for three days expected to be attacked in his office.[25] "A Voter of Pulaski County" claimed that Crittenden had made an unsuccessful effort to forestall legal aid to Woodruff by attempting to engage all the best legal talent available.[26]

Late in the campaign Woodruff issued a lengthy circular reviewing the difficulty between himself and Crittenden. He had refused to

[23] Woodruff to Crittenden, June 15, 1827, in Crittenden, "To the People of Arkansas," *ibid.,* June 19, 1827, and in Woodruff, "To the People of Arkansas," July 20, 1827, in Marshall, "Conway-Crittenden Duel," *Arkansas Historical Review,* I, 24–25. According to Hiram A. Whittington, who was employed in Woodruff's printing office in 1827, Crittenden not only threatened to cut Woodruff's throat for publishing the communication against his official conduct, but also "to cut off the nose of every printer in the place and pull down the printing office." Hiram A. Whittington to Granville Whittington, July 26, 1827, in Ross, ed., "Letters of Hiram Abiff Whittington," *Pulaski County Historical Society Bulletin,* No. 3, p. 3.

[24] Crittenden, "To the People of Arkansas," *Gazette,* June 19, 1827. Crittenden and Ashley were former law partners. See *ibid.,* January 9, 1827.

[25] But Woodruff himself said that he doubted Oden's forces "ever *seriously intended* to make any attack on us." *Ibid.,* June 26, 1827.

[26] A Voter of Pulaski County, "To the Voters of Arkansas. No. II," *ibid.,* June 19, 1827.

identify "A Voter of Pulaski County" because the piece Crittenden objected to had been written at his (Woodruff's) *"suggestion* and *request,* and I felt myself as much responsible for its contents, as the *author* or *writer* of it, could possibly be."[27] Crittenden had been offered access to the *Gazette* "for the purpose of disproving the charges," and told that Woodruff "was prepared to sustain" them in court. Crittenden had chosen to go to court.

Admitting that it was not "very proper" to publish evidence "which is intended to be subsequently submitted [by Crittenden] to a jury," Woodruff nonetheless printed what he said was a certificate obtained by Crittenden from Judge Sam C. Roane of the first judicial circuit "for the purpose of disproving the charge in relation to the disposition which he is alleged to have made of the public draft for $2,750." Roane certified that he, Crittenden, and others had, in December, 1824, hoped to "make a speculation" by locating a Cherokee preemption claim to the site of Little Rock. Before Roane left for Batesville to enter the preemption Crittenden had requested him to take a government check for $2,750, get it cashed at Batesville, and bring back the money. Someone had suggested using the money in purchasing the land should the preemption be rejected. While Crittenden had said that he could not lend public money, he had nevertheless told Roane that if the money were used to purchase land it must be returned when he called for it. As it turned out, the "land was held by the pre-emption right—I [Roane] failed in negotiating the Check—and handed it over to Mr. Crittenden's order." Woodruff thought Roane's certificate "quite conclusive" that "Crittenden & Co." intended speculating with government funds. (It also showed, of course, that the money had not actually been used for speculative purposes.)

Woodruff was, he said, "credibly informed" that Crittenden had admitted to "several respectable individuals" that he had furnished T. W. Johnston with funds to purchase goods subsequently sold to the Quapaws, and that Crittenden had received $900 as his "proportionate third" of the profits from the contract for furnishing provisions to the Indians during their removal.

In explaining his part in the sale of Oden's Little Rock property, Crittenden had not, according to Woodruff, "related *all* the facts."

[27] "A Voter of Pulaski County" stated several years later that Woodruff, Ashley, and Ambrose H. Sevier supplied the information contained in his communications in 1827 and that he had agreed to write essays on conditions that he should not be revealed as author and involved in a lawsuit. A Voter of Pulaski County, "To the Public," March 10, 1832, *Advocate,* March 14, 1832.

Previous to conveying the lots to Crittenden, Oden had by power of attorney authorized his brother-in-law to dispose of Oden's "interest in the town of Little Rock"; and the brother-in-law had, unknown to Woodruff, conveyed a part of the property, including the lots subsequently conveyed to Woodruff, to someone else. Woodruff's title would have been a disputed one had not Oden "neglected to record the power of attorney or the conveyance made under it."[28]

In reference to Crittenden's complaint at being brought into the contest when not a candidate, Woodruff asserted that Crittenden would not have been attacked by Conway's friends had he "in the first instance, come out decidedly in favor of Col. Oden" instead of expressing a preference for Conway "and at the very same time" secretly planning his defeat. Seeing him "playing this *double game*," Conway's friends had "determined to remove his *mask*." Woodruff declared that he could prove by a witness that Crittenden had, only six weeks before saying that he had decided three months ago to vote for Oden, "intimated" that he would vote for Conway.[29]

While Woodruff's explanation of the reason for the attack on Crittenden may be correct, the fact that he was not assailed until he was seen to be electioneering for Oden[30] strongly suggests that the Conway men were merely endeavoring to offset his influence as Oden's most prominent supporter. Thus "A Citizen of the Territory" asserted that Crittenden had been dragged into the fray by "a *combination*" in an endeavor "to take away *his* reputation, for the gratification of *personal* pique—and to prejudice the people against Col. Oden";[31] and "A Voter of Pulaski County" said that Crittenden had been attacked because he had "authorized and sanctioned the charge of defalcation against Mr. Conway."[32]

The *Gazette* had taken no stand for either candidate at the beginning of the campaign and it was not until after Editor Woodruff's brush with Crittenden that he announced that the paper, although remaining open to communications from both factions, would support Conway. The reason Woodruff gave was Oden's conduct toward him when he had recently refused to print a circular submitted by

---

[28] According to "A Voter of Pulaski County," Oden claimed that he "never knew that his brother-in-law had disposed of any part" of his Little Rock property. "To the Voters of Arkansas. No. VI," *Gazette*, July 17, 1827.
[29] Woodruff, "To the People of Arkansas," July 20, 1827, in Williams, "Conway-Crittenden Duel," *Arkansas Historical Review*, I, 18–32.
[30] See A Voter of Pulaski County, "To the Voters of Arkansas. No. I," *Gazette*, June 12, 1827.
[31] A Citizen of the Territory, "To the People of Arkansas. No. III," *ibid.*, July 3, 1827.
[32] A Voter of Pulaski County, "To the Public," *ibid.*, June 26, 1827.

Oden, a circular containing not only "abusive and scurrilous language, affecting the character of the Editor," but also exhibiting "indecorous language, interspersed with slanderous assertions, on the character and reputation" of Chester Ashley,[33] who would have held Woodruff responsible. A charge by Oden men that Conway had influenced him to refuse Oden's circular Woodruff pronounced *"a base and malicious FALSEHOOD."*[34]

The Oden circular, when published at Memphis, contained an assertion that Governor Izard had joined in a combination with Conway, Ashley, and Woodruff to oppose Oden's candidacy. This the governor denied in the *Gazette*. If he had advanced any opinion, "it was merely to say, that, supposing the qualifications of the candidates equal, I thought the experience of Mr. Conway . . . enabled him to be more useful as a Delegate than his opponent." He had never "spoken of Mr. Oden in terms of contempt or vituperation." Had Oden bothered to inquire Izard would have assured him that he had been deceived by "some base and artful individual," and thus avoided "the ridicule attendant on the puerile and paltry menace of *'crushing for ever'* one who has always repelled, with scorn and defiance, any threats with which he has been assailed."[35]

During the campaign Oden charged that Conway had "improperly" collected and retained money due from the government to twelve Arkansans "for property stolen from them by the Osage Indians." Conway acknowledged that he had received the amount of several claims, but declared that he had "notified the individuals interested . . . that the money was in my hands" and had been authorized by them in one way or another to *"keep* their money, until I should return to the Territory."[36] "A Citizen of the Territory" subsequently asked why Conway had not informed the electorate how long he had retained the money, amounting to $3,107.81, that belonged to the Osage claimants. The answer was, of course, that he had not done so because many claimants would have complained had they known he had kept their money for a year.[37]

A charge by Oden that a widow named Lydia McFarland of Conway County would never have been forced to sell her property at a

[33] Though Woodruff did not refer to Ashley by name in this editorial, he subsequently identified him in another. See *ibid.,* July 17, 1827.

[34] *Ibid.,* June 26, 1827.

[35] Izard to Bernard Smith, July 13, 1827, *ibid.,* July 17, 1827. The "base and artful individual" may have been Crittenden.

[36] Conway, "To the People of Arkansas," May 18, 1827, *ibid.,* May 22, 1827.

[37] A Citizen of the Territory, "To the People of Arkansas.—I," *ibid.,* June 5, 1827.

sheriff's sale had not Conway withheld money due her for Osage spoliation was denied by "A Voter of Pulaski County,"[38] and by the woman's son-in-law;[39] and Oden himself was reported to have subsequently retracted the charge.[40]

In connection with another Osage claim, that of William Brice, Conway was castigated by "A Citizen of the Territory" for his failure, while in Miller County during the canvass, to call on Brice and give him his money. Brice, who was sick in bed at the time, had been obliged to pursue Conway into Hempstead County, where he learned that Conway had paid Chester Ashley half the amount due as a fee for handling the claim.[41] To this criticism Conway responded by having Woodruff publish a statement by Ashley and two relevant receipts.[42] Ashley stated that in 1824 he had agreed, in the presence of John Bowman of Miller County, to handle Brice's claim for half the amount collected. In 1825 Ashley had placed the claim in Delegate Conway's hands and Conway had obtained $700 from the government. Conway had subsequently entrusted the entire amount to Ashley and upon attending circuit court in Miller County Ashley had sent word to Brice that he had his money. Brice had overtaken Ashley in Hempstead County and a settlement made.[43] The receipts showed that Conway had delivered $700 to Ashley in May, 1827, and that Brice had received that amount from Ashley the next month.[44]

A subsequent letter from Brice admitted that he had talked to Ashley about collecting the claim and acknowledged that he had receipted to Ashley for $700; but he denied that he had employed Ashley and avowed that he actually received only $350, accepting it because he had considered "a half loaf better than none."[45] Woodruff did not believe this letter "the production of the person whose signature it bears; and we even doubt whether the signature is genuine."[46] "A Citizen of the Territory," maintaining that the letter was in Brice's handwriting, contended that Conway had not received Brice's

[38] A Voter of Pulaski County, "To Col. Robert C. Oden," *ibid.*

[39] Reuben J. Blount to Editor, July 14, 1827, *ibid.*, July 17, 1827.

[40] A Voter of Pulaski County, "To the Voters of Arkansas, No. III," *ibid.*, June 26, 1827.

[41] A Citizen of the Territory, "To the People of Arkansas. No. II," *ibid.*, June 19, 1827.

[42] Conway to Woodruff, June 23, 1827, *ibid.*, June 26, 1827.

[43] Ashley to Conway, June 20, 1827, *ibid.*

[44] Receipts by Ashley to Conway, May 22, 1827, and by Brice to Ashley, June 4, 1827, *ibid.*

[45] Brice to Conway, June 24, 1827, *ibid.*, July 3, 1827.

[46] "William Brice's Claim," *ibid.*

claim from Ashley and thereby intimated that Conway had acted improperly in giving the money to Ashley.

To support his contention, "A Citizen of the Territory" published a receipt by Conway purportedly showing that Conway had received claims of Brice and two other persons from the Osage sub-agent.[47] Woodruff believed the supposed receipt was only a memorandum which had fallen into the hands of someone who had "treasured it up as a precious morceau."[48] In support of Ashley's account of the matter, Conway had printed an affidavit by Charles Moore, a "disinterested source," stating that Brice had told Moore in 1825 that he had employed Ashley to handle his Osage claim for half the amount collected.[49] Offered as additional support for Ashley's version was a letter from Miller County intimating that Brice had a shady reputation and should not be believed.[50]

Oden was accused during the contest of attempting to buy votes by distributing gew-gaws to women and children;[51] criticized for opposition to internal improvements;[52] and represented as "destitute of that moral stability which is requisite" for congressmen.[53]

Conway was reproached for sometimes failing to meet his private business obligations. This he admitted to be true, but said that he had not wilfully disappointed anyone.[54] He was also accused of having sacrificed Miller County to the Choctaw Indians by having William Ward of Mississippi appointed commissioner to negotiate a treaty in 1825. "A Voter of Pulaski County" replied that the treaty had been made at Washington by the Secretary of War himself, and Woodruff published a body of correspondence which showed that Conway had favored extinguishing the entire Choctaw claim to land in Arkansas Territory.[55] In support of Conway's candidacy, "A

[47] A Citizen of the Territory, "To the People of Arkansas. No. IV," *ibid.*, July 17, 1827; A Citizen of the Territory, "To the People of Arkansas. No. V," *ibid.*, July 24, 1827.

[48] *Ibid.*, July 17, 1827. See also A Voter of Pulaski County, "To the Voters of Arkansas. No. VII," *ibid.*, July 31, 1827.

[49] See affidavit of Moore, July 9, 1827, *ibid.*, July 17, 1827.

[50] A Citizen of Miller County to Conway, June 21, 1827, *ibid.*, July 24, 1827. Both Brice and Moore were described by Robert Crittenden in 1825 as "highly respectable." Acting Governor Crittenden to Secretary of War, February 14, 1825, *Terr. Papers*, XIX, 774.

[51] A Voter of Pulaski County, "To the Voters of Arkansas. No. III," *Gazette*, June 26, 1827; *ibid.*, July 3, 1827.

[52] A Voter of Pulaski County, "To the Voters of Arkansas. No. III," *ibid.*, June 26, 1827; A gentleman of Hempstead County to Editor, July 16, 1827, *ibid.*, July 24, 1827.

[53] A Voter, "To the Voters of Arkansas," *ibid.*, May 29, 1827.

[54] Conway, "To the People of Arkansas," May 18, 1827, *ibid.*, May 22, 1827.

[55] *Ibid.*, June 26, 1827; Conway, "To the People of Arkansas," July 12, 1827, *ibid.*, July 17, 1827; A Voter of Pulaski County, "To the Voters of Arkansas. No. VI," *ibid.*

Farmer" enumerated sixteen beneficial acts which had passed Congress during Conway's tenure as delegate.[56]

The outcome of the hotly contested canvass was a landslide victory for Conway. The balloting in the thirteen counties on August 6 gave him 2,427 votes to 856 for Oden. Oden made a strong showing only in Miller County, which he carried, and in Pulaski and Arkansas, where the vote was moderately close.[57]

The election of members of the general assembly seems to have produced no such furor as that over the election of a delegate.[58] The successful candidates for the legislative council were William Humphreys of Lawrence County; David Litchfield of Independence County; Jacob Wolf of Izard County; Edwin T. Clark of Phillips County; George C. Barfield of Crittenden County; Terence Farrelly of Arkansas County; John Weir of Chicot County; Edmund Hogan of Pulaski County; Amos Kuykendall of Conway County; John Dillard of Crawford County; Isaac Pennington of Clark County; Daniel T. Witter of Hempstead County; and John H. Fowler of Miller County. The victorious candidates for the house of representatives were George Hudspeth, Lawrence County; John Ringgold, Independence and Izard Counties; John Johnson, Phillips and Crittenden Counties; William Montgomery, Arkansas and Chicot Counties; Ambrose H. Sevier, Pulaski and Conway Counties; Mark Bean, Crawford County; Joseph Hardin, Clark County; John Wilson, Hempstead County; and James Clark, Miller County.[59]

The animosity evinced during the campaign by the opposing factions continued after the election. When it became evident that Conway had won an overwhelming victory, "A Voter of Pulaski County" made a public statement to Crittenden attributing Oden's decisive defeat "to the blighting effects of your friendship." Crittenden's support had cost Oden "*at least* 500 votes—possibly a much greater number." Those who enjoyed Crittenden's friendship lost "the confidence of the people at large; and, on the contrary, those who are under the denunciation of your wrath rise higher in the estimation of

---

[56] A Farmer to Editor, *ibid.,* June 26, 1827.

[57] "A Proclamation," September 8, 1827, *ibid.,* September 11, 1827.

[58] Hiram A. Whittington reported, however, that "opposing candidates" never met "in the street [presumably in Little Rock] without stopping to blackguard each other," and that they often engaged in fights. Hiram A. Whittington to Granville Whittington, April 21, 1827, in Ross, ed., "Letters of Hiram A. Whittington," *Pulaski County Historical Society Bulletin,* No. 3, pp. 1–2.

[59] *Gazette,* September 18, 1827. Clark and Aaron Hanscome tied in the regular election but in a special election held August 25 Clark defeated Hanscome. "Official Election Returns," *ibid.,* September 11, 1827.

their fellow-citizens." Proof of this was the rise in public esteem of Ambrose H. Sevier and a corresponding decline in the popularity of his opponent after Crittenden had "excommunicated" Sevier from his "favor" during the campaign for the territorial house.[60]

Far more consequential than "A Voter of Pulaski County's" sneers at Crittenden's standing was a letter by Conway published in the *Gazette*. Conway professed surprise at the "harsh character" of Crittenden's address of July 24, for he had not cast any "serious imputation" on Crittenden, nor had he made a *"wilful* misrepresentation" of the Quapaw transaction; rather, he had given "an accurate statement of facts." From "subsequent events" he was now convinced

that Mr. Crittenden did, *wilfully* and *intentionally,* state what he knew to be false for the purpose of injuring my election—and more, that I believe him to be so destitute of principle, that he will resort to any measure, however base and grovelling in its nature, to accomplish his object, when it cannot be otherwise secured.[61]

Crittenden's response to Conway's provocative publication was a letter giving notice that he would challenge Conway to a duel "on or before the 20th of October."[62] According to Conway, some of Crittenden's friends subsequently approached him in an attempt to arrange a settlement, but because they insisted that Conway should ask Crittenden to withdraw the challenge, negotiation ended in failure.[63]

In the meantime another challenge had come out of the campaign. According to Fay Hempstead, Ambrose H. Sevier, Conway's cousin, had expressed a wish at a barbecue to fight the pseudonymous writer of a recent piece (presumably that signed "A Citizen of the Territory") in which Conway had been criticized.[64] When Thomas W. Newton learned of Sevier's statement, he avowed himself the author

[60] A Voter of Pulaski County, "To Mr. Robert Crittenden," *ibid.,* August 14, 1827.

[61] Conway, "To the Public," August 17, 1827, *ibid.,* August 28, 1827.

[62] Crittenden to Conway, August 28, 1827, *ibid.,* November 6, 1827. John Hallum names Conway the Challenger; quotes a purported suggestion by Crittenden that the duel be postponed until Conway had discharged his " 'obligation to the people' "; and goes on to say that Conway then called Crittenden a coward and the duel ensued. John Hallum, *Biographical and Pictorial History of Arkansas* (Albany, 1887), I, 49–50. John W. Peel, who was living at Batesville in 1827, subsequently acknowledged that he was the source of Hallum's account. John W. Peel to Jesse Turner, two undated letters, Jesse Turner Papers, Duke University Library. Peel maintained the truth of his recollection of the affair, but it seems probable, from the evidence in the *Gazette,* that Peel was mistaken, though it may be that Crittenden, after issuing his challenge notice, suggested a postponement such as Peel remembered and that Conway then called him a coward.

[63] Extract of a memorandum by Conway, *Gazette,* November 13, 1827.

[64] Sevier was Oden's former law partner. See *ibid.,* February 6, 1827.

of the publication in question. The two met at Point Remove Creek above Little Rock on September 4. Newton had George W. Jones as second, Oden as friend, and Dr. William P. Reyburn as surgeon. Sevier had Wharton Rector as second and Dr. Nimrod Menefee as physician. After the combatants fired once "without effect," their friends interfered and the challenge was withdrawn.[65]

On the morning of October 29, 1827, a week after he started from Little Rock to Washington,[66] Delegate Conway met Secretary Crittenden on the east side of the Mississippi River "almost opposite" the mouth of White River. According to C. F. M. Noland, who received his information from John Ringgold, the duelists "fought with pistols [at] 18 feet." Wharton Rector was Conway's second and Benjamin Desha acted for Crittenden. Conway "fired a little before" Crittenden and "shot the upper Button hole out of his coat." Crittenden's bullet hit Conway "six or eight inches below the top of his shoulders," struck a tooth brush, and broke a rib; the ball and part of the brush then fell "downwards." Crittenden's surgeon believed the wound would be fatal, but Conway's surgeon thought it not "mortal" and predicted that he would shortly be able to resume his journey by water.[67]

Noland said further that Ashley was "supposed to have played a double game" during the controversy and that Crittenden had written him "one of the most abusive letters I ever heard of." William Montgomery and Sylvanus Phillips were "supposed to have been concerned" in Conway's decision to fight Crittenden.[68]

The *Gazette* reported on November 6 that Crittenden and Conway, fighting "at the distance of ten yards," had fired simultane-

[65] Hempstead, *Pictorial History of Arkansas,* 212–213; George W. Jones to Fay Hempstead, April 9, 1888, *Pulaski County Historical Review,* I (June, 1953), 8–9; Newton to William Noland, September 8, 1827, Berkeley-Noland Papers, Alderman Library, University of Virginia; *Gazette,* September 11, 1827; Newton to John Pope, April 10, 1832, *ibid.,* May 9, 1832; Diana Sherwood, "The Code-Duello in Arkansas," *Arkansas Historical Quarterly,* VI (Summer, 1947), 190–192.

[66] *Gazette,* October 30, 1827.

[67] According to Albert Pike, Conway was a "very good shot" while Crittenden was a quite poor one. "Albert Pike's Autobiography," *New Age Magazine,* XXXVIII (February, 1930), 103.

[68] C. F. M. Noland to William Noland, November 4, 1827, Berkeley-Noland Papers, Alderman Library, University of Virginia. According to James Scull, territorial treasurer, Thomas Crittenden of Kentucky, Robert's brother, challenged Ashley on his brother's behalf, and Oden challenged Ashley on his own part, but Ashley refused both calls on the grounds that he was a family man while his challengers were not. Writing on October 28, Scull predicted that Robert Crittenden himself would, if he survived the duel with Conway, challenge Ashley; but there is no evidence that he actually did so. Scull to James Miller, August 18, October 28, 1827, Robert W. Trimble Collection, Arkansas History Commission.

ously.[69] Crittenden's "pistol took effect in Mr. Conway's right side, between the 5th and 6th ribs." The first report had been that Conway would not long survive, but a subsequent letter from Conway's surgeon said that the wound was "severe, but not dangerous." A few days later Wharton and Elias Rector arrived in Little Rock from William Montgomery's home near the mouth of White River, where Conway had been taken, with the optimistic report that he would probably be able to continue his journey within "two or three weeks."[70] News soon came, however, that he had died on November 9.[71]

Conway had left with Woodruff two letters plus Crittenden's notice of challenge, requesting that they be published immediately after the duel "to show to the public" that the duel "was not of his seeking and that he had been forced into the course which he has pursued, by Mr. Crittenden."[72] In one of the letters William Montgomery reported to Conway a conversation with Crittenden the previous July in which Crittenden stated that he "had tried every way to get you to challenge him, and if you did not, he would challenge you."[73] In the other letter Sylvanus Phillips informed Conway of a similar conversation with Crittenden during the same month. Crittenden had also said, according to Phillips, that he had sent for two men, one of whom "was a fiery fellow . . . and if his brains should be blown out it would not be so much difference."[74] (Apparently Phillips meant to imply that Crittenden had intended to have an attempt made upon Conway's life.)

The publication of this correspondence brought from Crittenden an immediate denial that he had "long since" deliberately sought the duel. He believed that Montgomery had either "forgotten" their conversation or else misunderstood him. What he had said was that he expected a serious difficulty with Conway over his "first offensive publication," for "I considered it due myself to require Mr. Conway's

[69] That the two duelists fought ten yards apart and fired simultaneously is supported by a statement of Crittenden's second that Woodruff's facts were correct. Desha to Woodruff, *Gazette*, November 13, 1827. On the other hand Hallum, who presumably received his information from Elias N. Conway, agrees with Noland that Conway fired "an instant in advance" of Crittenden. Hallum, *History of Arkansas,* 50. See also H. H. Crittenden, compiler, *The Crittenden Memoirs* (New York, 1936), 474.

[70] *Gazette,* November 6, 1827.

[71] *Ibid.,* November 6, 13, 1827.

[72] *Ibid.,* November 6, 1827.

[73] Montgomery to Conway, August, 1827, *ibid.* For a somewhat uncomplimentary characterization of Montgomery, see G. W. Featherstonhaugh, *Excursion Through the Slave States . . .* (2 vols., London, 1844), II, 58–59.

[74] Phillips to Conway, October 20, 1827, *Gazette,* November 6, 1827.

retraction of the imputations in that publication, which I believed *he would not make.*" Phillips's letter, Crittenden asserted, did not contain "one word of truth." He had gone to Phillips County expressly to denounce Phillips, and would not have given him his confidence. Several persons, including Elias Rector, had been present during his conversation with Phillips and would, Crittenden implied, sustain his account. He regretted that Conway had not given him an opportunity to explain the letters. Two attempts to adjust the difficulty had failed, "but not through any fault of mine. I was anxious for peace. I am no adventurer for the worthless fame resulting from civil broil. I have a family, and my death would have been their ruin."[75]

The newly elected legislature had convened October 1 and organized.[76] The next day Thomas W. Newton, secretary of the council, read Governor Izard's message to a joint meeting of the two houses. The governor said that he had hoped to be able to announce that the Territory's population had reached the size required for admission as a state; but because the settlements were "so sparse and the means of access to the country so extended," census takers had been unable to determine accurately the number of inhabitants. He predicted, however, that Arkansas would become a state in 1829.

Congress had passed an act granting to the Territory two townships of land for a seminary of learning, and the governor would locate the land "without delay." Some of the land reserved by the national government for endowment of schools had been settled and improved. Rentals might be charged for the use of this land and the proceeds placed in a fund to support country schools. The law pertaining to the sale of land for non-payment of taxes should be altered by the assembly to allow owners more time to redeem land sold for taxes and to provide for the appointment of a receiver to handle redemption money.

On miscellaneous points the governor recommended securing a loan to redeem a debt of $5,054 in outstanding scrip; reported that an irregular expedition organized on the southwestern border under the

---

[75] Crittenden, "To the Public," *ibid.*, November 13, 1827. According to Woodruff, Rector disavowed Crittenden's assertion that he had been present at Crittenden's conversation with Phillips, declaring instead that he had arrived just as Crittenden concluded his "harangue." *Ibid.* In a subsequent statement Phillips maintained the correctness of the content of his letter to Conway and denied that he and Crittenden had been unfriendly at the time of their conversation. Phillips, "To the Public," June 26, 1828, *ibid.*, July 9, 1828.

[76] "The General Assembly," *ibid.*, October 2, 1827.

direction of Mexico to raid the Comanche Indians had dispersed soon after entering Texas; and assured the assembly that persons acquainted with the region were confident that a road from Memphis to Little Rock that "can be conveniently travelled during at least two thirds of the year, may be effected," though it might be found necessary to diverge from the course laid out by commissioners for the proposed road.[77]

None of Izard's recommendations was adopted by the legislature. That body did, however, change the land laws to provide that all lands previously "struck off" to the Territory, owing to a lack of bidders, might, upon payment of all taxes, charges, and interest due, be redeemed by former owners within one year from the date of the act, and that lands falling to the Territory in the future might, upon like payment, be redeemed within two years from date of ownership by the Territory. Purchasers of land sold by the Territory for non-payment of taxes were required to designate an agent living in the county where the land was located to receive redemption money.[78] Another act prohibited claimants of land who had not been in possession for seven years from bringing suit for recovery of their land against persons who had for seven years actually occupied it.[79]

The court system was revised by an act dividing the Territory into four judicial circuits and assigning the three superior court judges to the first three circuits and a fourth judge, to be appointed by the governor, to the remaining circuit.[80] In addition to circuit court duties, the superior court judges were required to hold superior court two terms annually at Little Rock. Slaves were excluded from "any execution or other process" except by circuit or superior courts.[81]

Other measures imposed a nominal fine upon persons appointed to slave patrols who did not begin performing their duty within ten days after notification of appointment; required militia battalions to muster annually and companies to assemble twice yearly; created Lovely, St. Francis, and Lafayette Counties; divided the Quapaw purchase between Arkansas and Pulaski Counties; appointed commissioners to superintend construction of a court house for Pulaski County; dissolved a marriage; amended the tax laws; appropriated

---

[77] "Governor's Message," *ibid.*

[78] *Arkansas Acts,* 1827, pp. 64–69.

[79] *Ibid.,* 69–70.

[80] *Ibid.,* 33–38. This act was in accordance with the opinion in 1826 of the Committee on Territories to whom the memorial of the legislature of 1825 concerning the judiciary had been referred. *Terr. Papers,* XX, 202–203.

[81] *Arkansas Acts,* 1827, pp. 41–43.

money for 1828–1829 and part of 1826–1827; and provided for election in Lawrence County of commissioners to select a permanent site for the seat of justice.[82]

Memorials to the President and Congress dealt with internal improvements, Indians, and land, and asked for an act of Congress to (1) provide an additional superior court judge for Arkansas, (2) make the superior court "exclusively an Appellate Court" without original jurisdiction, and (3) allow appeals to the United States Supreme Court.[83]

Governor Izard announced on November 13 that a special election would be held the next month to fill the vacancy caused by Delegate Conway's death.[84] Ambrose H. Sevier, Richard Searcy, Andrew Scott, Benjamin Desha, and Alexander S. Walker announced as candidates. Desha and Walker presently withdrew, and John Nicks, brigadier general of the militia,[85] declined the request of a meeting of citizens of Crawford and Lovely Counties that he run.[86]

Born in Greene County, Tennessee, in 1801, Sevier had migrated to Missouri in 1820 and to Little Rock the next year. He was clerk of the territorial house in 1821 and served in 1824–1825 as attorney for the third judicial circuit. Elected for three consecutive terms to the territorial house, he was in 1827 made speaker. He married in September, 1827, a daughter of Superior Court Judge Benjamin Johnson.[87]

In a circular letter to the people, Sevier modestly avowed that he had "little" to recommend him for their "confidence," but promised that he would, if elected, "exert all the talents I possess, to advance the interests of the Territory." He would press for enactment of laws embracing the requests made in recent legislative memorials and in particular for appointment of an additional superior court judge. Should he find it necessary, he would secure revision of the organic law to compel superior court judges to perform circuit duties. He would strive for a road to run from the Territory's northern boundary via Washington in Hempstead County to the Louisiana line and for acquisition of Lovely's Purchase and Choctaw lands remaining in the

[82] *Ibid.*, 5–15, 52–54, 57–60, 70–71, 73–74, 76–77.

[83] *Terr. Papers*, XX, 570–580; *Gazette*, November 6, 1827. The financial inability of the Territory to support the existing judicial system was the reason given for requesting an additional judge.

[84] Executive Proclamation, November 13, 1827, *Gazette*, November 13, 1827.

[85] *Terr. Papers*, XX, 647, note 26.

[86] *Gazette*, November 20, 27, December 24, 1827, January 1, 1828.

[87] *Biographical Directory of the American Congress, 1774–1927* (Washington, 1928), 1509; *Terr. Papers*, XIX, 827; Shinn, *Makers of Arkansas*, 204.

Territory. For better protection against the Indians, the frontier garrisons should be augmented.[88]

Searcy was a native of Tennessee, about thirty years old, who had migrated to Lawrence County, Missouri Territory, in 1817. He subsequently served as clerk of Lawrence and Independence Counties and judge of the first and second judicial circuits.[89]

Searcy issued a circular pledging himself to work for purchase of Choctaw lands in Arkansas; establishment of a permanent western boundary for the Cherokee reservation in order that Lovely's Purchase might be opened for settlement; enlargement of frontier garrisons; graduation of the price of public lands; removal of navigational obstructions in Red River; payment of territorial legislators by the national government; appointment of an additional superior court judge; and, if necessary, an act to compel superior court judges to hold circuit courts. Searcy declared that he did not belong to "any party."[90] He had, however, recently been identified with Crittenden in a controversy (above, pp. 64–65) and two pseudonymous writers asserted several years later that Searcy was in 1827 backed by Crittenden.[91]

Scott began his circular by asserting that he had been one of the "first and warmest" supporters of Conway's political career. He next called attention to the fact that he had not, during eight years as superior court judge, "been known to be absent one day from my duty when business called." Declaring himself "aloof" from "party," he promised, if elected, to labor for removal of the Indians from Arkansas; preemption rights for actual settlers to the time of the organization of the Territory; removal of obstructions in Red River; opening of roads; extension of time for liquidation of Spanish and French land claims under the congressional act of 1824 as amended in 1826; payment of members of the territorial legislature by the national government; and fulfillment of the requests in the memorials of the legislature of 1827.[92]

[88] Sevier, "To the People of Arkansas," November 20, 1827, *Gazette,* November 27, 1827.

[89] *Terr. Papers,* XIX, 789, 792, 798, 826; *Gazette,* January 9, 1833; Hallum, *History of Arkansas,* 241. Searcy died in 1832. "Obituary," *Advocate,* January 6, 1833; *Gazette,* January 9, 1833.

[90] Searcy, "To the People of Arkansas Territory," November 23, 1827, *Gazette,* November 27, 1827.

[91] Publius to Editor, *ibid.,* December 12, 1832; Jaw-Bone to Editor, *ibid.,* July 7, 1830.

[92] Scott, "To the Independent Voters of the Territory of Arkansas," November 24, 1827, *ibid.,* November 27, 1827.

Soon after the issuance of the campaign circulars, a communication signed by "A Radical" appeared in the *Gazette*. Espousing the election of Searcy, "A Radical" averred that he was the only candidate who had never participated in a duel and "was not attached to any particular set of men and measures." Possessing a "temperate, correct and moral character," Searcy had "arrived to the present public estimation, by his own exertions, integrity and acquirements . . ." The electorate must not be deceived by Sevier's "pleasant, agreeable electioneering way." No one would deny that Sevier had "a 'liquorice' use of his tongue, with a tolerable vivid imagination," but many would doubt that he was "a man of solidity of mind and understanding." Moreover, no one would contend that he was an enlightened politician. By opposing the territorial judiciary act of 1827, which had been meant to reduce expenses, Sevier had "run counter to the will" of a majority of the people.[93]

The next issue of the *Gazette* carried an unsigned essay, written in biblical style, supporting Sevier and criticizing Scott and Searcy. Though Scott had said he was not connected with faction, the people believed that he had been politically opposed to Conway. Moreover, Scott was guilty of saying in his circular that Arkansas would not become a state for eight or ten more years. Scott was not well enough known, the essayist concluded, to be a strong contender for the delegateship. As for Searcy, he too had opposed Conway, and he was the source, although not the author, of the piece signed "A Radical." "A Radical's" assertions that Sevier lacked solidity of mind and was not an enlightened politician were quite contrary to fact; actually these defects were to be found in Searcy, not in Sevier. Furthermore, Sevier's alleged " 'glib tongue and bright imagination' " were assets rather than liabilities.[94]

Under the heading "Public Sentiment" Editor Woodruff printed several letters from citizens of various parts of the Territory. A resident of Hempstead County believed that Sevier would receive more support in that county than Conway had because the people did not wish to see Conway's enemies benefited by his death. An inhabitant of Independence County claimed that northern Arkansas would back Searcy. A citizen of Villemont, who believed that Sevier would carry the counties adjoining the Mississippi, reported circulation of a rumor that before the Conway-Crittenden duel a caucus held in Little

[93] Communication of A Radical, November 26, 1827, *ibid.,* December 4, 1827.
[94] Unsigned communication, *ibid.,* December 11, 1827.

Rock had nominated Sevier to run for delegate in case Conway was killed.[95]

The outcome of the election on December 17 was a victory for Sevier, who received 939 votes to 883 for Searcy and 116 for Scott.[96] Of the sixteen counties, Sevier carried eleven, Searcy, five. Woodruff attributed the light vote to bad weather which kept many people away from the polls, and believed that a large number of voters who favored Scott voted for Searcy because they thought Scott "stood no chance of being elected."[97] Though the outcome of the regular election had suggested an overwhelming vindication of Conway by the people to the detriment of Crittenden, one wonders, in view of the close vote in this special election, whether Arkansans had not in fact been more concerned with Conway's past performance as delegate and Oden's qualifications and principles than with the charges exchanged during the campaign.

The tumultuous politics of 1827 subsequently produced another fatal encounter. Edmund Hogan and Andrew Scott, who had been competing candidates for the legislative council in the regular election, met in a Little Rock store on May 31, 1828, and, according to Editor Woodruff, fell into an argument over the "events" of the August election. Scott said that one of Hogan's assertions "could not be proved, and that any person who made it, was a LIAR!" Forthwith Hogan, who was considerably the larger man, knocked Scott to the floor. Upon arising, Scott drew a spear from his cane and plunged it four times into Hogan's body, killing him.[98] According to William F. Pope, Scott was arrested but subsequently released, "evidently" because the killing was considered to have been a case of self-defense.[99]

The *Gazette* announced in January, 1828, that Crittenden had agreed to drop his $25,000 libel suit against Woodruff[100] and that

---

[95] "Public Sentiment," *ibid.,* December 4, 1827.

[96] "A Proclamation," January 19, 1828, *ibid.,* January 23, 1828. The returns for Hempstead and Lafayette Counties, which Sevier carried, were reported together.

[97] "Election Returns," *ibid.,* December 25, 1827. Hallum conjectures that Searcy would have defeated Sevier had Sevier not received the support of James Woodson Bates. Hallum, *History of Arkansas,* 241. See also Bates to William Noland, December 25, 1827, Berkeley-Noland Papers, Alderman Library, University of Virginia.

[98] *Gazette,* June 4, 1828.

[99] Pope, *Early Days in Arkansas,* 33, 41–43. Pope, who presumably received his information from Scott's son, says the argument between Hogan and Scott had begun when Hogan charged Scott with being the source of a report that a barbecue sponsored by Sevier men during the special election had been held for "the purpose of influencing and buying votes" for Sevier. Pope's account of the affair contains various small errors.

[100] *Gazette,* July 10, 1827.

Woodruff was in return "entirely withdrawing all that is contained in 'A Voter of Pulaski county,' derogatory to Mr. Crittenden."[101] "A Voter of Pulaski County" would several years later be identified by Woodruff as Dr. Matthew Cunningham, a prominent physician of Little Rock.[102] An indictment brought against Crittenden by the United States in the territorial superior court for sending a challenge to fight a duel was quashed in October, 1828, because it did not "conclude 'against the peace and dignity' " of the United States and the challenge notice did not designate a specific date for the duel to take place.[103]

The election of 1827 was probably the most important election held in the territorial period. Though the Conway-Crittenden break may have originated earlier, the campaign brought it into the open and solidified the Conway and the Crittenden factions into two distinct political camps. The Conway faction continued after Conway's death under the capable leadership of Sevier, who would subsequently rise to a political stature greater than that of his predecessor.

[101] *Ibid.,* January 23, 1828. For further information on Crittenden and Woodruff's agreement, see *ibid.,* March 7, 1832; *Advocate,* February 29, March 14, 1832.

[102] *Gazette,* September 5, 1832; *Advocate,* March 14, 28, 1832; David Y. Thomas, *Arkansas and Its People* (4 vols., New York, 1930), II, 802.

[103] *United States v. Robert Crittenden,* in Samuel H. Hempstead, compiler, *Reports of Cases Argued and Determined in the United States Superior Court for the Territory of Arkansas, from 1820 to 1836 . . .* (Boston, 1856), 61.

CHAPTER SIX

Public Affairs, 1828–1829

GOVERNOR IZARD issued in June, 1828, a proclamation calling an election for August 4 to fill vacancies in the legislature and a special session of that body to meet October 6.[1] In the election, John Dunlap, Robert Burton, and William Hickman were chosen to occupy the council seats from which John Dillard, Daniel T. Witter, and John H. Fowler had resigned. Elected to Edmund Hogan's place in the council was Dr. John H. Cocke. Joseph Henderson won without opposition Delegate Sevier's seat in the house.[2] A subsequent election held in Lawrence County to fill a vacancy in the council caused by the death of William Humphreys resulted in a tie vote, and the legislature met before another election could be held.[3]

Governor Izard's message of October 7 informed the assembly that the special session had been called because the northwestern portion of the Territory lately ceded by the Cherokees required organization and because this new area plus a recent act of Congress relating to the territorial judiciary necessitated alterations in the existing court system.[4]

Izard expected that the legislature would immediately comply with his wishes and adjourn. When it did not do so, he sent another message, dated October 17, advising the two houses that the "only object of your being convened at this time, was, that you might act

---

[1] Proclamation, June 20, 1828, *Arkansas Gazette* (Little Rock), June 25, 1828.
[2] *Ibid.*, August 13, 20, September 2, 1828. Hickman defeated James S. Conway for his seat.
[3] *Ibid.*, October 7, 1828.
[4] "The General Assembly," *ibid.*

without delay on the two subjects submitted to you." The "unnecessary protraction" of the session caused by taking up other matters
would cost more "than can be compensated for by any saving produced" by the measures of economy passed at the 1827 session.[5]

Obviously irked by Izard's rebuke, the two houses adopted before
they adjourned on October 22 four resolutions asserting that the
governor's attempt to exercise "dictatorial power" over the legislature
was "inconsistent with the principles of Free Government"; holding
that a special session might act upon any matter "for the good government of the Territory"; regretting that it had been necessary to pro-
tract the present session; and deploring the action that had required
the spreading of "these resolutions on our Journals."[6]

The squabble with Izard did not prevent passage of the measures
for which the session had been called. The judiciary act of 1827 was
repealed, the Territory was divided into four circuits presided over
by superior court judges, and the superior court, now largely an appellate court, was required to hold two terms annually at the capital.[7]
The land acquired from the Cherokees was assigned to Izard, Independence, Conway, and Crawford Counties. Other acts abolished
Lovely County and created Washington and Sevier Counties; provided for the records of Lovely County to be transferred to Washington County; appointed commissioners to locate a permanent seat of
justice for Lawrence County; defined the boundary between Pulaski
and Conway Counties; and made appropriations for 1828.[8] Several
memorials to Congress dealt with land matters.[9]

Governor Izard, after an illness caused by the gout, died on
November 22.[10] In reporting the event to Secretary of State Clay
three days later, Acting Governor Crittenden asked appointment to
succeed Izard. In support of his request he said that he had acted as
chief executive during half his tenure as secretary and had, he believed, given satisfaction to the Federal government and the people

---

[5] "General Assembly," *ibid.,* October 21, 1828.

[6] *Ibid.,* October 28, 1828.

[7] Congress had granted the request of the territorial legislature of 1827 for an addi-
tional superior court judge and other changes in the judiciary in an act approved
April 17, 1828. 4 *U.S. Stat. at L.* (1846), 261–262. President Adams gave the new
judgeship to James Woodson Bates, who had supported Sevier in the special election.
Clarence E. Carter, ed., *Territorial Papers of the United States,* Vol. XX, *Arkansas
Territory, 1825–1829* (Washington, 1954), 683–684; Bates to William Noland,
December 25, 1827, Berkeley-Noland Papers, Alderman Library, University of Virginia.

[8] *Arkansas Acts,* 1828, pp. 8–9, 15–21, 31–39, 43–45.

[9] *Terr. Papers,* XX, 775–777; *Gazette,* November 4, 1828.

[10] "Death of Gov. Izard," *Gazette,* November 25, 1825; *Terr. Papers,* XX, 595.

of the Territory.[11] The same day Andrew Scott applied for the governorship.[12]

Delegate Sevier informed the Secretary of State on January 1, 1829, that he had received numerous letters from constituents insisting that whoever should be appointed governor come from outside the Territory. There was, Sevier observed, scarcely a qualified person in Arkansas who was not heavily involved in factional politics.

I want a man unconnected with any of our quarrels—who will be disposed to give us peace rather than war—I want neither my party to *ride* or to be ridden—as would be the case if either a partizan of mine or *Mr. Crittenden* should be elevated to that office—I don[']t disguise it—I have an unconquerable hatred for *Mr. Crittenden,* and the same aversion exists with two thirds of our citizens—He has got the credit of having caused nearly every duel that has taken place in Arkansas—His hands are stained with our lamented Conway[']s blood—I care but little who the president appoints provided he is from a slave state—is a western or southern man—

Sevier went on to recommend William Carroll, formerly governor of Tennessee, a man whom he had known "from my childhood."[13]

Editor Woodruff reported early in February a rumor that Carroll, of whom he thought well, would probably be tendered the governorship. He advised the four Crittenden "adherents" who were candidates for the post "not to make any calculations on receiving the appointment, as we conceive the contingency quite as improbable as that the Arkansas river should turn and run up stream."[14]

Despite the fact that his own term was almost at an end, President Adams undertook to fill the governorship, submitting to the Senate the name of Hutchins G. Burton, formerly governor of North Carolina. But Burton's nomination was not confirmed, presumably because the Senate wished to give the privilege of making the selection to the incoming President, Andrew Jackson, who would take

[11] Crittenden to Secretary of State, November 25, 1828, *Terr. Papers,* XX, 796. Worden Pope observed in a letter to the President in 1829 that Arkansas Territory had for the most part been "governed by Deputy." Worden Pope to President, May 31, 1829, microfilm copies of Andrew Jackson Papers, University of Texas Library.

[12] Scott to Secretary of State, November 25, 1828, *Terr. Papers,* XX, 797.

[13] Sevier to Secretary of State, January 1, 1828[9], *ibid.,* 822–824. According to a pseudonymous writer in 1831, Sevier considered "having" Chester Ashley appointed governor, but decided against it when Senator Elias K. Kane advised Sevier he had known Ashley "*too well*" when Ashley lived in Illinois. Virginius to Editor, *Arkansas Advocate* (Little Rock), May 18, 1831.

[14] *Gazette,* February 3, 1829. Woodruff did not name the candidates to whom he referred.

office in March.[15] The North Carolina delegation in Congress continued to support Burton,[16] but President Jackson promptly appointed John Pope of Kentucky.[17]

Pope was unquestionably better prepared for the post than either of
his predecessors. Born in Virginia in 1770, he had migrated with
his parents about nine years later to Kentucky, where he eventually
began the practice of law at Shelbyville. Though a former Federalist,
he was chosen a presidential elector in 1800 and voted for Thomas
Jefferson. After serving a number of years in the state legislature,
Pope was sent in 1807 to the United States Senate for a full six-year
term. Later he was appointed secretary of state in Kentucky, and
was again several times a member of the state legislature.

Pope was a brother-in-law to John Quincy Adams (they had
married sisters) and his zealous supporter until Adams in 1825
chose Pope's long time political enemy, Henry Clay, to be Secretary
of State. Pope then became a Jackson partisan and played an important part in swinging Kentucky to Jackson in the election of 1828.[18]

Pope received his appointment with some indecision. He had been
mentioned in connection with "a seat in the national Judiciary," had
wished to be United States Attorney General, and had even suggested
to Jackson that William T. Barry of Kentucky, about whom he spoke
rather condescendingly, be given the position in Arkansas.[19] Now he
understood that he himself was no better than Jackson's second
choice, the place having been first offered to another Kentuckian,
Charles A. Wickliffe. Besides, friends in Kentucky wished him to
enter Congress.[20] On April 8 he ventured to inform the acting
secretary of state he would accept the appointment,[21] but even after

[15] *Terr. Papers*, XX, 858, note 46. Sevier had written Woodruff that he believed the
Senate would not act upon a nomination by the outgoing President. *Gazette*, Febru-
ary 18, 1829. See also Sevier to Editor, December 27, 1828, *ibid.*, January 27, 1829;
James Iredell to President, March 4, 1829, *Terr. Papers*, XX, 858.

[16] *Terr. Papers*, XX, 859. Two other candidates, A. Butler and James M. Bradford
of Louisiana, also applied for the governorship.

[17] *Ibid.*, Vol. XXI, *Arkansas Territory, 1829–1836* (Washington, 1954), 3, note 3.

[18] Orval W. Baylor, *John Pope, Kentuckian: His Life and Times, 1770–1845*
(Cynthiana, Kentucky, 1943), 1–328; *Biographical Directory of the American Con-
gress, 1774–1927* (Washington, 1928), 1422; *Terr. Papers*, Vol. XIX, *Arkansas
Territory, 1819–1825* (Washington, 1953), 100–101, note 50; U. M. Rose, "John
Pope—An Unfinished Sketch," *Publications of the Arkansas Historical Association*,
IV (Conway, 1917), 290–292.

[19] See Pope to Jackson, February 19, 1829, John Spencer Bassett, ed., *Correspondence
of Andrew Jackson* (7 vols., Washington, 1926–1935), IV, 5–6, 8; microfilm copies of
Jackson Papers, University of Texas Library.

[20] Baylor, *John Pope*, 277–316, 329–332.

[21] *Terr. Papers*, XXI, 14.

setting out for Arkansas he was tempted to relinquish his commission in order to run for Congress. Fearing, however, that a congressional race would mean "a heated electioneering contest in which the Democratic vote was likely to be divided," he continued on to Arkansas, arriving in Little Rock on May 31.[22]

A few weeks after Pope's appointment, President Jackson removed Crittenden[23] from the secretaryship and commissioned in his stead William S. Fulton of Alabama.[24] Born in Maryland in 1795, Fulton had graduated from Baltimore College in 1813 and served at Fort McHenry during the War of 1812. Having moved to Tennessee, he was admitted to the bar in 1817 and the next year acted as General Andrew Jackson's "military secretary" in the Florida venture. In 1820 Fulton settled in Alabama, where he became editor of the Florence *Gazette,* a member of the state legislature in 1821, and county judge in 1822.[25] He arrived in Little Rock to assume his duties as secretary on May 21, 1829.[26]

Because Fulton's appointment was made during a recess of Congress, his commission would expire at the end of the ensuing session of the Senate. In January, 1830, Jackson nominated him for a regular term. On March 17 Senator David Barton of Missouri moved to refer the nomination to the Judiciary Committee with instructions to investigate the cause of Crittenden's removal. The motion was defeated 25 to 17. Barton then moved that the nomination be referred to Jackson with a request that he advise the Senate of the reason for Crittenden's removal. This motion met exactly the same fate as the first one, and Fulton's nomination was then confirmed by a vote of 26 to 17.[27]

Ambrose H. Sevier, William Cummins, and Richard Searcy an-

[22] Baylor, *John Pope,* 332–339. Pope told friends while en route to Arkansas in Louisville that he would "decline" the governorship if he were elected to Congress, but would not remain in Kentucky to participate in the campaign, though he would maintain his residence in Kentucky by deferring removal of his family to Arkansas. Pope to Benjamin Duncan, May 20, 1829, in Louisville *Public Advertiser,* reprinted in *Gazette,* June 17, 1829.

[23] Crittenden's removal had, according to Woodruff, been anticipated in Arkansas because Jackson "was never known to uphold one who had proved ungrateful to him." "Changes Among Indian Agents," *Gazette,* May 6, 1829.

[24] *Terr. Papers,* XXI, 13–14, 16.

[25] *Biographical Directory of the American Congress,* 994; Correspondence to Editor, December 12, 1836, *Pennsylvanian,* reprinted in *Gazette,* January 17, 1837; Dallas T. Herndon, *Centennial History of Arkansas* (3 vols., Little Rock, 1922), I, 193.

[26] *Gazette,* May 27, 1829.

[27] *Senate Executive Journal,* Vol. IV (January 5, March 17, 1830), 42, 70–71; *Terr. Papers,* XXI, 198, note 38. Sevier subsequently wrote Woodruff that Fulton's appointment was the first test of the President's power to remove from office. Sevier to Editor, March 18, 1830, *Gazette,* April 20, 1830.

nounced in March, 1829, that they would be candidates for Congress.[28] Cummins, however, subsequently withdrew,[29] leaving the contest to be waged by the two men who had been the strongest competitors in the special election of 1827. Searcy declared himself not connected with any interest save that of the people, but two later writers were probably justified in speaking of him as the candidate of the Crittenden faction.[30]

Sevier during his short tenure as delegate had undoubtedly succeeded in enhancing his chances of victory by obtaining certain highly important legislation for Arkansas. Besides the act, already noticed, giving the Territory an additional superior court judge,[31] a law approved May 24, 1828, made provision for the Federal government to compensate members of the territorial legislature.[32] A third act, approved January 21, 1829, authorized, with certain exceptions, popular election of all civil and military officers previously appointed by the governor; the exceptions were the auditor, the treasurer, and the justices of the peace all of whom were henceforth to be selected by the legislature.[33] A donation law gave 320 acres of land in Arkansas to settlers living on land no longer a part of the Territory by virtue of the Cherokee treaty of 1828.[34] According to Woodruff, Sevier's success in getting these laws enacted had "astonished every body."[35] A pseudonymous writer believed Arkansas owed more to Sevier's "untiring exertions" than to the work of any previous delegate.[36]

In a circular letter to the citizens of Arkansas Sevier claimed credit for several more measures beneficial to the Territory. The court established to adjudicate French and Spanish land claims had been extended for two more years. An appropriation of $25,000 had been voted to improve navigation of Red River. Running of the boundary between Arkansas and Louisiana had been authorized.

[28] *Gazette,* March 25, 1829.

[29] *Ibid.,* April 22, 1829.

[30] Searcy, "To the People of Arkansas Territory," April 15, 1829, *ibid.,* April 22, 1829; Publius to Editor, *ibid.,* December 12, 1832; Jaw-Bone to Editor, *ibid.,* July 7, 1830.

[31] Sevier discussed his part in getting this act passed in Sevier to gentleman of Little Rock, April 4, 1828, *ibid.,* May 21, 1828.

[32] 4 *U.S. Stat. at L.* (1846), 303.

[33] *Ibid.,* 332–333. Sevier wrote Woodruff while the franchise bill was going through Congress that it would prevent the territorial executive from using his appointive power to "build up partizans, and control public opinion." Sevier to Editor, December 23, 27, 1828, *Gazette,* January 27, 1829.

[34] 4 *U.S. Stat. at L.* (1846), 306–307, 329.

[35] "Enfranchisement of the People of Arkansas," *Gazette,* February 10, 1829.

[36] One of the People, "Ambrose Hundley Sevier," *ibid.,* March 11, 1829.

That other desirable bills had failed was not from any want of effort on his part. Because an error in the donation law was being talked about by "a few who use it as a hobby to oppose my re-election," Sevier explained in some detail that the mistake was unintentional. He had neglected to have a provision included to prohibit persons receiving donations from locating on improvements. But he had, upon discovering the "omission," succeeded in having it corrected at the next session.[37]

Searcy's circular stated that he had been induced to run again by the "flattering vote" given him in the special election of 1827 and by the "solicitations" of citizens from all parts of the Territory. He promised to work for an alteration of the western boundary of the Territory; graduation of the price of public lands; greater frontier protection; roads from Missouri to Fort Smith, from St. Louis to Red River, and from Helena to the mouth of the Cache; compensation to settlers who had been forced to remove from lands ceded to the Choctaws; and reclamation of lands bordering the Mississippi. He would endeavor "to facilitate our progress to State government, so soon as our population and resources will permit." He believed the nation's Indian policy should be changed to extend "our laws and civil jurisdiction" over the Indians.[38]

Though the campaign proved to be unusually tranquil, several newspaper exchanges did occur. David Rorer, an attorney of Pulaski County and a candidate for the territorial house, charged that Sevier, Woodruff, and Chester Ashley had, in order that they might speculate in Lovely claims, in June, 1828, conspired temporarily to withhold from the public news of the fact that location on improvements was not prohibited by the donation act of 1828. Woodruff admitted that they had agreed to keep the matter secret until it could be announced in the *Gazette,* but averred that they had done so for the purpose of preventing speculators from buying claims of settlers ignorant of the law and then locating on valuable improvements.[39]

An attempt was also made to show by one of his own letters that Searcy had been implicated in an unethical land speculation.[40] Searcy replied that the transaction in question had subsequently been can-

[37] Sevier, "To the Citizens of Arkansas," April 9, 1829, *ibid.,* April 15, 1829.

[38] Searcy, "To the People of Arkansas Territory," April 15, 1829, *ibid.,* April 22, 1829.

[39] See "Communication," *ibid.,* May 27, 1829; Rorer to Editor, June 6, 1829, *ibid.,* June 10, 1829.

[40] John Dillard to Woodruff, July 22, 1829, Searcy to Townsend Dickinson, August 21, 1828, *ibid.,* July 29, 1829.

celed and that the letter was published on the eve of the election in an attempt to create an impression among the people that he had been speculating in Lovely claims. He had, he declared, purchased only one claim.[41]

In the election on August 3 Sevier defeated Searcy by a vote of 2,064 to 1,756. The victor carried eleven of the seventeen counties in the Territory.[42] In accordance with an executive proclamation re-apportioning representation among the several counties,[43] the voters choose for the territorial house twenty-three representatives instead of the previous nine.[44]

The newly elected legislature convened and organized October 5.[45] Governor Pope had returned to Kentucky in June to bring out his family,[46] and did not arrive back in Little Rock until October 7.[47] The next day he sent by his private secretary, Dr. John T. Fulton, a brief message to the legislature pointing out that the law recently passed by Congress pertaining to election of civil and military officials be-came effective December 1, 1829, and recommending that the legisla-ture provide for the holding of elections.[48]

Pope submitted a second and much longer message on October 13.

[41] Searcy, "To the Public," July 28, 1829, *ibid.*

[42] Election Proclamation, September 15, 1829, *ibid.,* September 16, 1829.

[43] Executive Proclamation, June 2, 1829, *ibid.,* June 3, 1829. Under the organic act the electorate could choose only nine representatives prior to the time the Territory should contain 5,000 free white male adults; then the number went up to one repre-sentative for every 500 free white males. 2 *U.S. Stat. at L.* (1845), 744–745. Governor Pope reapportioned representation on the basis of a recent census.

[44] Elected to the house were George S. Hudspeth and John Rodney, Lawrence County; Mark Bean, Jesse L. Cravens, and Richard C. S. Brown, Crawford County; Caleb S. Manly and Charles McArthur, Independence County; Alexander S. Walker and Wharton Rector, Pulaski County; Robert Livingston, Izard County; John Alexander, Washington County; Thomas Mathers, Conway County; William D. Ferguson, Crit-tenden County; Wright W. Elliott, St. Francis County; Edwin T. Clark, Phillips County; William Montgomery, Arkansas County; Benjamin L. Miles, Chicot County; John Spear and Joseph Hardin, Clark County; John Wilson and Elijah King, Hempstead County; James Byrnside, Lafayette County; James Clark, Miller and Sevier Counties. The victorious candidates for the council were Coleman Stubblefield, Lawrence County; Gilbert Marshall, Crawford County; Aaron Gillett, Independence County; Charles Caldwell, Pulaski County; Jacob Wolf, Izard County; James Billingsley, Washington County; Amos Kuykendall, Conway County; George C. Barfield, Crittenden County; John Johnson, St. Francis County; Fleetwood Hanks, Phillips County; Terence Farrelly, Arkansas County; John Weir, Chicot County; Davis Fish, Clark County; George Hill, Hempstead County; Jesse Douglass, Lafayette County; Benjamin Patton, Sevier County; and George F. Lawton, Miller County. "The Next General Assembly," *Gazette,* August 26, 1829; "Official Election Returns," *ibid.,* September 23, 1829. Hanks' election was contested unsuccessfully by Sylvanus Phillips. "The General Assembly," *ibid.,* October 13, 1829.

[45] "The General Assembly," *ibid.,* October 6, 1829.

[46] *Ibid.,* July 1, 1829.

[47] *Ibid.,* October 6, 13, 1829. Pope's return was delayed by bad roads and weather.

[48] "General Assembly," *ibid.,* October 13, 1829.

After promising to do all in his power "to advance the prosperity of the Territory" and to hasten the coming of statehood, he offered a number of recommendations. The militia law required revision to make the organization of the militia more complete and "the musters less frequent and more efficient." The Secretary of War should be asked to establish a new military post in Arkansas Territory below Fort Gibson.

The opening and maintenance of roads from the Mississippi to the interior of the Territory demanded the attention of the assembly. The Memphis-Little Rock road, upon which the governor had recently travelled, could be made "a good practicable route, [passable] at all seasons of the year." Also necessary was a road from Helena to intersect the Memphis-Little Rock road, another from Little Rock to Chicot, and a third from Little Rock to the Missouri line via Batesville and Davidsonville.

Remarking the inadequacy of the privately owned building in which the assembly met, Pope suggested a request to Congress to appropriate money for a state house. Congress should also be asked to authorize long-term leases of seminary lands in order to encourage improvements and provide revenue for "the education of the rising generation of this Territory." To induce the erection at Hot Springs of buildings suitable to accommodate the sick, Pope suggested that Congress be requested either to donate the place to the Territory or to authorize the Territory to lease it. Pope thought the Federal government should give public land to actual settlers instead of requiring them to buy it.

Pope urged the legislature to investigate fiscal concerns and adopt measures to redeem the territorial scrip, then selling at about sixty cents on the dollar, and restore public credit. The revenue laws should be revised to provide for "a more equal and just rule of taxation." Non-resident landowners in particular were entitled "to some indulgence, and a more liberal and just [tax] policy."

With respect to the judiciary Pope noted that the increase in the number of counties which augmented the work of superior court judges dictated a reduction in the number of circuit court terms. Perhaps county courts should be established to look after local concerns. Certainly the statute laws should be revised and a digest prepared. Because gambling disturbed the peace of the capital and injured the reputation of the Territory, a stringent law was needed to suppress gambling equipment. Something should also be done to discourage the carrying of deadly weapons.[49]

[49] *Ibid.*

Most of Pope's recommendations seem to have been acted upon favorably. The legislature adopted measures seeking to prevent gambling and betting; establishing county courts; amending the judiciary act of 1828; dividing the militia into two brigades; scheduling elections in January, 1830, to offices made elective by the franchise law; creating Pope, Hot Spring, Union, Monroe, Jefferson, and Jackson Counties; prescribing the death penalty for the stealing of horses or Negro slaves; amending the tax laws; attaching that portion of Sevier County south of Red River to Miller County; declaring free navigation of the Little Missouri River; making free male Negroes liable to work on roads the same as whites; requiring all cotton gins to be enclosed by a fence while in operation; authorizing county judges to appoint trustees to lease school lands for periods not exceeding five years; and appropriating money for part of 1829 and for 1830–1831.[50] A bill to extend the jurisdiction of circuit courts in criminal cases was vetoed by Governor Pope, and one to call in territorial scrip and treasury warrants and discontinue paying interest on future issues of scrip was indefinitely postponed.[51]

Besides passing seventy acts, the assembly drew up twenty-four memorials to the President or the Congress dealing with such matters as land, Indians, internal improvements, and frontier defense; and one memorial to Congress asked a donation of land to pay for a state house.[52] A resolution requested Delegate Sevier to seek an act of Congress making justices of the peace elective.[53] Richard C. Byrd was chosen to be auditor, and James Scull, the incumbent, was continued as territorial treasurer.[54] The legislature adjourned on November 21 after an "unusually" protracted "and laborious session of 48 days."[55] During the session Little Rock had been orderly, and Woodruff had "seldom witnessed more harmony and good feeling in our social intercourse."[56]

One event of the session had been a public dinner in honor of Governor Pope. In the course of his speech on that occasion Pope said that he was not involved in the political divisions of the Territory and "would rather allay than foment discord." He also claimed, somewhat immodestly, that "while many other appointments of the President are condemned, all parties concur in conceding that the

[50] *Arkansas Acts,* 1829, pp. 3–25, 38–54, 60–62, 66–71, 80–83, 87–88, 91, 96–97, 102–103, 106–110, 127–133.
[51] "General Assembly," *Gazette,* November 17, 24, 1829.
[52] "Memorials," *ibid.,* November 24, 1829; *Terr. Papers,* XXI, 87–96, 99, 101.
[53] *Arkansas Acts,* 1829, pp. 136–137.
[54] *Gazette,* November 10, 1829.
[55] *Ibid.,* November 24, 1829.
[56] "The General Assembly," *ibid.,* November 10, 1829.

office of Governor of Arkansas is well filled." His position as governor he compared to that of an overseer of a plantation.[57] Pope's remarks would later be recalled by his political enemies.

In December the *Gazette* announced that Governor Pope, having departed for Kentucky to "complete the arrangement of his private affairs," would probably go to Washington before his return to Arkansas in the spring. A "large portion" of the members of the recent legislature had "strongly urged" him to do so because they believed that his experience, ability, and "high standing" would give his representations great weight and that his cooperation with Delegate Sevier "might be highly beneficial in promoting the interests of our Territory" at the next session of Congress.[58] Pope's activities in Washington would subsequently be a subject of controversy.

The two years following the turbulent election year of 1827 had been comparatively quiet ones in territorial politics. They had witnessed, however, several notable developments. Crittenden's prestige and influence had undoubtedly been lessened by his removal from office. The appointment of Pope and Fulton, both Jackson men in national politics, had brought to the executive branch of territorial government two capable politicians who would later play important roles in factional struggles. And finally, Sevier's success in securing important legislation in Congress and winning reelection to a second term had enhanced his political standing.

[57] "Dinner to Gov. Pope," October 21, 1829, *ibid.,* October 27, 1829.

[58] *Ibid.,* December 9, 1829. But Charles Caldwell, president of the legislative council, subsequently asserted that Woodruff's remarks were "erroneous so far as they relate to me, and I believe them to be so, so far as they relate to the great majority of the members of the Legislature." Caldwell to Editor, *ibid.,* March 2, 1830.

CHAPTER SEVEN

The Controversy of 1830

THE *Gazette* late in 1829 carried a prospectus announcing that Charles P. Bertrand would establish at Little Rock a weekly newspaper to be called the *Arkansas Advocate*.[1] A New Yorker born in 1808, Bertrand had nine years later been brought by his mother and stepfather to Missouri Territory and thence to Little Rock in 1820. He had subsequently worked for Woodruff on the *Gazette* and read law with Robert Crittenden; in 1836 he would marry a sister of Crittenden's wife.[2]

Soon after the appearance, on March 31, 1830, of the first issue of the *Advocate,* Editor Bertrand became involved in a quarrel with Editor Woodruff of the *Gazette.* The difficulty originated over a publication in the *Advocate* signed "Fourche." "Fourche" professed to believe that Bertrand had, in his prospectus, been inconsistent in disavowing any party connection and at the same time avowing a predilection for President Jackson. Why, "Fourche" asked, did Governor Pope and Secretary Fulton, both Jackson men, patronize the *Gazette,* which opposed Jackson.[3]

Bertrand replied that he had meant to say in his prospectus that

[1] *Arkansas Gazette* (Little Rock), November 10, 1829. The proposal to establish the *Advocate* was the second to be made since the establishment of the *Gazette.* John H. Wilkins & Company had in September, 1821, announced plans to publish a weekly newspaper at Davidsonville to be called the *Arkansas Herald,* but there is no evidence that the proposed enterprise ever materialized. *Gazette,* September 22, 1821.

[2] Margaret Smith Ross, "The Cunninghams: Little Rock's First Family," *Pulaski County Historical Review,* I (June, 1953), 11–15; Fred W. Allsopp, *History of the Arkansas Press for a Hundred Years and More* (Little Rock, 1922), 544.

[3] Fourche to Editor, *Arkansas Advocate* (Little Rock), May 19, 1830. "Fourche" was in 1833 identified as Dr. William P. Reyburn who claimed he was assisted in preparing one "Fourche" number by Crittenden. *Gazette,* June 12, 1833; *Advocate,* June 19, 1833.

the *Advocate* would be neutral only in territorial politics. He supposed that Pope had used his influence to secure the public printing for the *Gazette* because " 'Money makes the mare go,' " and that Fulton "perhaps, feels himself bound to follow in the footsteps" of the "Overseer of the Plantation."[4]

"Fourche" responded that he hoped Bertrand would not stand by and permit "a petty Territorial party" adhering to Adams to enjoy the spoils of office to the detriment of true Jackson men. It was "a political enigma" that Bertrand, "a Jackson Editor," should be "proscribed" by Pope, "a Jackson Executive," to "make room" for Woodruff, "an Adams Editor."[5]

Woodruff retorted that "certain *new-light* Jackson-men" were, in an effort to draw away a portion of the *Gazette's* patronage, attempting to create an impression among the people that he was opposed to the Jackson administration. He had, he admitted, favored Adams over Jackson in 1828, but his doubts concerning Jackson's "capacity for civil employments" had since been removed. In national politics he wished to keep the *Gazette* "strictly *neutral*" because Arkansas as a territory had no voice in national affairs.[6]

Presently the *Advocate* threatened to publish a "little book" which Bertrand said would show where "some of the *present democrats,* stood in regard to truly republican principles, a few years since, and probably" Woodruff's name "may be conspicious on its title page, and your ideas found throughout the volume."[7] Though Woodruff made no reply to this threat, Bertrand continued to taunt him on the point,[8] and subsequently seized upon a reference by Woodruff to "the scenes of 1827"[9] to announce that he intended to give in "our promised *Little Book*" a "more minute history" of "those by-gone times."[10]

Woodruff surmised that one of Bertrand's "secrets" concerned a shoot-out in Woodruff's office on January 17, 1828, when John T. Garrett had been killed[11] while attempting to assassinate Chester

[4] *Advocate,* May 19, 1830.
[5] Fourche to Editor, *ibid.,* June 2, 1830.
[6] *Gazette,* June 8, 1830.
[7] *Advocate,* June 16, 1830.
[8] *Ibid.,* June 23, 1830.
[9] See *Gazette,* July 7, 1830.
[10] "Little Billy—Again," *Advocate,* July 14, 1830.
[11] Woodruff later claimed that Garrett had accidently shot himself while Woodruff struggled with him in an attempt to prevent his killing Ashley. Dr. Matthew Cunningham, on the contrary, alleged that Woodruff himself had shot Garrett during the fray. The Voter of Pulaski County, "To Wm. E. Woodruff," *Advocate,* March 28, 1832; "To the Swearing Editor," *ibid.,* April 11, 1832; *Gazette,* April 4, 18, September 5, 1832.

Ashley.[12] It was well known in Little Rock that the attempted assassination "was *prompted* and *planned* by a *certain gentleman* [presumably Crittenden],[13] who shall be nameless." The "little book" Bertrand referred to was the forty or fifty depositions that had been taken after the shooting. If Bertrand wished him to, Woodruff would publish them; but he would not be responsible for the effect on a *"certain gentleman."*[14] One notices that although Bertrand subsequently took note of Woodruff's editorial, he did not accept Woodruff's offer to publish the material in question.[15]

The Woodruff-Bertrand quarrel took a new turn with the appearance in the *Advocate* of "Diodorus Siculus." Noticing that "Little Billy" had complained about newspaper assaults on private character, "Diodorus Siculus" charged that Woodruff had himself been guilty of them. In 1827 he had promised the people that he would sustain charges made by "A Voter of Pulaski County" against Robert Crittenden; unable to do so, he had been forced to recant.[16] A second communication from "Diodorus Siculus" maintained that Woodruff had known when he promised to sustain "A Voter of Pulaski County" that a duel between Crittenden and Conway must take place, and that he had not expected Crittenden to win. When Crittenden, who had instituted a libel suit against Woodruff, came off victorious, Woodruff had only "one forlorn hope left," and that was to compromise with Crittenden; Woodruff's mediator was Chester Ashley who arranged for Woodruff to publicly retract "A Voter of Pulaski County's" charges in return for Crittenden's promise to withdraw his libel suit. Woodruff's inability to sustain the charges was proof that Woodruff was a *" 'slanderer* and *defamer.' "*[17]

Woodruff did not respond to "Diodorus Siculus" but instead noticed a statement by Bertrand that he would surrender a correspond-

---

[12] Neither Garrett's nor Ashley's name was actually mentioned in Woodruff's editorial, but they were undoubtedly the persons meant. See The Voter of Pulaski County, "To Wm. E. Woodruff," *Advocate,* March 28, 1832, and *Gazette,* April 4, 1832.

[13] See *Gazette,* April 4, 1832.

[14] Woodruff, "To the Public," July 21, 1830, *ibid.,* July 21, 1830.

[15] Bertrand, "To the Public. Little Book—Chapter 1st," *Advocate,* July 28, 1830. See also Matthew Cunningham to Editor and "To the Public," *ibid.,* June 30, August 11, 1830; *Gazette,* September 22, 1830.

[16] Diodorus Siculus, "To William E. Woodruff. Chapter II," *Advocate,* September 15, 1830.

[17] Diodorus Siculus, "To William E. Woodruff. Chapter III," *ibid.,* September 29, 1830; Lonnie J. White, "The Election of 1827 and the Conway-Crittenden Duel," *Arkansas Historical Quarterly,* XIX (Winter, 1960), 299–301, 313. For subsequent controversy concerning the Crittenden-Woodruff compromise, see Crittenden, "To the Public," February 28, 1832, *Advocate,* February 29, 1832; "The Recantation of 1828," *ibid.,* March 14, 1832; "Robert Crittenden," *Gazette,* March 7, 1832.

ent's name only if the person offended agreed to say in writing that he wished the name for "personal satisfaction." Woodruff himself thought it an editor's duty to give the name of a correspondent when the person "aggrieved" stated as his object either personal satisfaction or a libel suit. But Woodruff did not plan to call for "Diodorus Siculus's" name because he believed he knew who he was and that he was no gentleman; besides, Woodruff disapproved the practice of duelling.[18]

Bertrand and "Fourche's" remarks precipitating the Bertrand-Woodruff quarrel also presaged a full scale attack on Secretary Fulton. According to Bertrand his "passing remark" relative to Fulton's following in Pope's footsteps by patronizing the *Gazette* cost him a printing job. The court for the adjudication of French and Spanish claims had provided that 158 bills of review should be divided equally between the *Gazette* and *Advocate* for publication. But Bertrand's remark had "excited" Fulton's "ire" and he had, in his capacity as special counsel for the United States, persuaded the court to have all the bills published by the *Gazette.* Fulton's action showed that *"political rottenness* abounds."[19]

The attack on Fulton was continued in the *Advocate* by pseudonymous writers. Noticing that Fulton as acting governor had recently passed over a good Arkansan to appoint William Field, a Kentuckian who was Governor Pope's nephew, to be clerk of the superior court in place of the late David E. McKinney, "Laos" accused Fulton of disregarding the will of the people and allowing himself to be swayed by a powerful faction.[20] Another writer believed this appointment "of a stranger, over the heads of all our citizens," proved Fulton to be unfit to be acting governor.[21] "Fourche" denied a claim said to have been made by the appointee that Fulton had given him the clerkship on the recommendation of Judge Benjamin Johnson.[22]

"Jaw-Bone" defended Fulton in the *Gazette,* asserting that no one had presented any evidence of Fulton's "official misrule" and denying that he was a *"tool"* of Governor Pope and "swayed" by faction. Fulton had selected Field for the clerkship of the superior court be-

[18] *Gazette,* September 22, 1830. See also *Advocate,* September 29, October 13, 1830; Woodruff, "To the Public," October 16, 1830, *Gazette Supplement,* October 20, 1830; *Advocate,* October 27, 1830.

[19] "French and Spanish Claims—Bills of Review," *Advocate,* May 26, 1830.

[20] Laos to Bertrand, *ibid.,* June 16, 1830.

[21] Philo Fourche to Fulton, *ibid.,* June 23, 1830.

[22] Fourche to Editor, *ibid.,* June 30, 1830.

cause, of the two aspirants, he was the more "honest, faithful, and capable."[23] To this the Arkansan replied that if "Jaw-Bone" meant to say that "in point of faithfulness and honesty, I am found wanting, he is a base, unprincipled slanderer, and a foul calumniator." As to qualifications, he had during McKinney's last illness performed the duties of superior court clerk "to the entire satisfaction of the Court." "Jaw-Bone" was trying to convince people that it was better to appoint strangers to office than qualified Arkansans.[24]

In an effort to show that Fulton in appointing Field had been swayed by a faction led by Chester Ashley, "Laos" quoted a private letter written shortly after the election of 1829 by Woodruff to Edwin T. Clark of Phillips County stating that both Governor Pope and Secretary Fulton were "on our side of the question, and zealous in the cause," and that Fulton "will *probably*" receive the returns from Walnut township of Phillips County *"if they should be necessary* in the election for Delegate."[25]

Woodruff claimed that "Laos" had "garbled" the quotations from his letter. He had written Clark that he had seen evidence that the returns from Walnut township would, notwithstanding their rejection by George W. Ferebee, clerk of the Phillips County circuit court, be received by the acting governor in case of a contested election. The "garbled extracts" from the letter used by "Laos" had, according to Woodruff, been made by Ferebee, who was also postmaster at Helena, after Clark had accidently dropped it on a table in the post office.[26]

Evidently hoping to blunt the effect of the charges against Fulton, "Jaw-Bone" strongly censured the conduct of Fulton's predecessor, Crittenden, as secretary. Crittenden had quarrelled with Governor Izard and had while acting governor used the patronage to put his

---

[23] Jaw-Bone to Editor, *Gazette,* June 29, July 7, 1830. Fulton was also defended by "Henry" and "Justice" in *ibid.,* July 28, 1830.

[24] Charles Caldwell to Editor, *ibid.,* July 14, 1830. "Aborigine" doubted that Field was, because of his recent arrival in the Territory, a qualified voter. Aborigine to Fulton, *Advocate,* July 21, 1830. For another attack on Fulton for appointing Field, see Samson to Editor, *ibid.,* July 21, 1830.

[25] Laos to Editor, *ibid.,* July 14, 28, 1830.

[26] "The Stolen Letter," *Gazette,* July 21, 1830. Ferebee claimed, however, that Clark had shown him the letter and that it had for several days lain open on a table in his office. For further controversy over the letter and the election returns, see Laos to Editor, *Advocate,* July 28, 1830; Ferebee, "To the Public," August 7, 1830, *Advocate,* August 18, 1830; Austin Kendrick, "To the Public," September 19, 1830, *Gazette Supplement,* September 29, 1830; Diodorus Siculus, "To William E. Woodruff. Chapter IV," *Advocate,* October 6, 1830.

supporters in office. "Jaw-Bone" considered it paradoxical that Crittenden men should be complaining about Fulton's "utter contempt" for the opinion of the people.[27]

Crittenden immediately issued an address to the people saying that he found it difficult to understand why he had been attacked. He had been away practicing law when the controversy began and had had nothing to do with any of the publications in the *Advocate*. If as secretary, he had been guilty of "many indiscretions" and "injustice[s] to worthy men," he had not "done either *knowingly*." "I can say, with truth, that 'had I served my God with the same fidelity I have *endeavored* to serve you,' the sound of the last trumpet would have no terrors for me."[28]

"Jaw-Bone" noticed that Crittenden had closed his communication in the words of Cardinal Wolsey. This was, he believed, quite appropriate, for Crittenden's and Wolsey's "fortunes" had been

in many respects very much alike. In England, Woolsey [*sic*] had but one superior—and, in Arkansas, Crittenden had but one. The former desired the seat of a *Pope,* in Rome—the latter the seat of a *Pope,* in Arkansas. The former did not obtain his wish, nor did the latter. Both lived in big houses, and both have acknowledged early indiscretions, and the injustice[s] they had done to worthy men. Both have told us, what no one believed, that, if they had served their God as faithfully as they had the people, they would not have dreaded a futurity. The one, after thus speaking, had fallen from a towering height, from which he never rose—and the other is also down, and it is yet to be seen if it be for ever.

Crittenden would, in consequence of "Jaw-Bone's" comparison of his career with Wolsey's, henceforth often be referred to as the "Cardinal."

"Jaw-Bone" also charged Crittenden with being the prime mover and founder of the *Advocate*. In the summer of 1828 Crittenden had, on behalf of himself and seven others, made a secret agreement with a man named Simpson to finance a second paper at Little Rock. When this did not materialize, he backed financially the establishment of the *Advocate,* which would, after Jackson's present term, "hoist the flag" for Henry Clay and support the Crittenden faction against the Sevier faction.[29] Though Bertrand claimed that he alone

[27] Jaw-Bone to Editor, *Gazette,* July 7, 1830.

[28] Crittenden, "To the Citizens of Arkansas," July 9, 1830, *ibid.,* July 14, 1830.

[29] Jaw-Bone to Editor, *ibid.,* July 21, 1830; Jaw-Bone, "A Word to Charley, at Parting," *ibid.,* September 1, 1830. "Jaw-Bone" had alleged in his first communication that the *Advocate* had been established by anti-Jackson men, but he had mentioned no

had been the "prime mover" and "founder" of the *Advocate,* one notices that he never denied that Crittenden had supported monetarily the founding of the paper.[30]

"Jaw-Bone" in his exchanges with Bertrand declared that Bertrand was young, inexperienced, uneducated, lacking in "breeding," and had devoted more time to his toilette and "arts of *dandyism"* than "to books or to the company of the wise and virtuous." (Later in the controversy Bertrand would be given the sobriquet "Beau Charley.")[31] He was, moreover, a hypocrite in that he had, after professing to be persuaded by Pope's dinner speech of October, 1829, to become a Jacksonian, later criticized the speech.[32]

Bertrand denied that Pope's speech had persuaded him to become a Jacksonian. Rather, it had made him understand why Pope, whom he had until that time believed to be a man of ability, had been sent by Jackson "so far in[to] the *back-woods."* "Jaw-Bone's" other accusations he did not deny except to say that while spending considerable time with "Jaw-Bone's" family he had thought himself in the company of "wise" and "virtuous" people. He went on to assert that the publications signed "Jaw-Bone" had been written by Chester Ashley on the basis of information collected by "his jackal and pimp, Wm. E. Woodruff."[33] In a communication in the *Advocate* of the same day, Bertrand's stepfather, Dr. Matthew Cunningham, also identified "Jaw-Bone" as Ashley.[34] Ashley's authorship of "Jaw-Bone" was never challenged.

A native of Massachusetts, born in 1791, Ashley had moved with his parents to New York, graduated from Williams College in Massachusetts, and studied law at Litchfield, Connecticut. After living a short time in Illinois and Missouri, he had come to Little Rock in 1820. He had acquired an interest in New Madrid claims to the townsite of Little Rock, served as attorney for the New Madrid proprietors, presumably played an important role in the removal of the capital from Arkansas Post to Little Rock, and been at one

---

names. Jaw-Bone to Editor, *ibid.,* June 29, 1830. Bertrand had denied the charge. *Advocate,* June 30, 1830. For other charges made by "Jaw-Bone" against Crittenden, see Jaw-Bone to Editor, *Gazette,* August 11, 1830. See also Bertrand, "To the Public," *Advocate,* August 18, 1830; Crittenden, "To the Public," *ibid.,* September 8, 1830; and Aristides to Editor, *ibid.,* August 25, 1830.

[30] Bertrand, "To the Public," *Advocate,* August 18, September 8, 1830.

[31] See Paul Pry, "Dam Jaw-Bone, or the Last Gazette: A Play, or Fiction, In three Acts," *Gazette,* September 22, 1830.

[32] Jaw-Bone, "A Word to Charley, at Parting," *ibid.,* September 1, 1830.

[33] Bertrand, "To the Public," *Advocate,* September 8, 1830. Bertrand had at one time been a Sevier supporter. *Ibid.,* October 31, 1832.

[34] Cunningham to Editor, *ibid.,* September 8, 1830.

time a law-partner of Crittenden.[35] A contemporary described him in 1831 as a great land speculator and an able, "cunning" attorney.[36]

Ashley's role in factional politics is not entirely clear. As a supporter of Conway he seems to have been an important back-stage figure in the election of 1827.[37] Not only was he identified as "Jaw-Bone" in 1830, but he was also charged with being the leader of the faction in power and with having been for several years the "master spirit" controlling the *Gazette*.[38] "Fourche" called Ashley a modern "Tallyrand" (a sobriquet often used in later references to him) because he served as "prime minister" to both Governors Izard and Pope.[39] Evidently he was indeed a most powerful member of the Sevier faction.

Of the newspaper attacks launched in 1830, that by the *Advocate* and its contributors against Governor Pope was undoubtedly the most severe. Pope was first noticed by "Fourche," who criticized him for patronizing the *Gazette,* said by "Fourche" to be an Adams paper.[40] Later "Fourche" detected an "unholy alliance of Little Rock, Governor Pope, & Co." and warned Pope that the people were beginning to become aroused at the "yoke" of "galling despotism."[41]

"A Farmer" observed in a publication in the *Advocate* that

---

[35] *Biographical Directory of the American Congress, 1774–1927* (Washington, 1928), 652; John Hugh Reynolds, *Makers of Arkansas History* (Dallas, 1905), 213–216; U. M. Rose, "Chester Ashley," *Publications of the Arkansas Historical Association,* Vol. III (Fayetteville, 1911), 51–59; Dallas T. Herndon, *Why Little Rock Was Born* (Little Rock, 1933), 111–116; Clarence E. Carter, ed., *Territorial Papers of the United States,* Vol. XIX, *Arkansas Territory, 1819–1825* (Washington, 1953), 370; *Gazette,* January 9, 1827; John Hallum, *Biographical and Pictorial History of Arkansas* (Albany, 1887), I, 121–122.

[36] James Edington to Hugh L. White, August 2, 1831, *Terr. Papers,* XXI, *Arkansas Territory, 1829–1836* (Washington, 1954), 356. David Walker remembered Ashley as "perhaps the most able lawyer" in early Arkansas. Walker to Robert W. Trimble, January 15, 1876, Robert W. Trimble Collection, Arkansas History Commission.

[37] White, "Election of 1827," *Arkansas Historical Quarterly,* XIX, 310, note 83. Bertrand alleged that Ashley was the "chief actor *behind the curtain*" in 1827, causing not only "heart-burnings and bickerings" but also, "by his insiduous machinations," bringing on the Conway-Crittenden duel. Bertrand, "To the Public," *Advocate,* August 18, 1830.

[38] *Ibid.;* Aristides to Editor, *ibid.,* August 11, 1830; Fourche to Editor, *ibid.,* July 14, 1830; Laos to Editor, *ibid.,* July 14, 28, 1830.

[39] Fourche to Editor, *ibid.,* July 14, 1830. According to Pope, his friendship with Ashley derived from the fact that his and Ashley's spouses were "old acquaintances, friends, and relations." Pope, "To the Public," August 2, 1830, *Gazette,* August 4, 1830.

[40] Fourche to Editor, *Advocate,* May 19, June 2, 1830.

[41] Fourche to Editor, *ibid.,* June 30, 1830.

Pope had returned in June from Kentucky and Washington.[42] Understanding that Pope planned to leave again soon for Kentucky, "A Farmer" warned the "Overseer" not to do so, because some of the "hands" on the "plantation" were becoming "very unruly." That President Jackson had refused a request by Pope to come to Washington suggested that all was not well between Pope and Jackson. Pope had gone to Washington to assist Sevier, but whether he actually had no one in Arkansas had been informed.[43]

"Jaw-Bone" claimed that Pope had possessed tacit permission from the President to visit Washington and that Sevier had recently said publicly that Pope had been of considerable help to him in procuring passage of several bills advantageous to the Territory. Even had it been true, as Pope's enemies in Arkansas alleged, that Pope had gone to Washington solely in pursuit of an appointment as minister to a foreign court, the effort would have shown that Pope possessed a "laudable ambition that is common to distinguished men." In answer to criticism of Pope for having said that he was a good governor, and to derisive references to him as an "overseer," "Jaw-Bone" maintained that Pope was indeed a good governor and that his executive position was actually comparable to that of a plantation overseer.[44]

Pope himself discussed his activities in Washington in a communication published by the *Gazette* on August 4. It was untrue that he had attempted while in Washington to have the superior court judges and United States District Attorney Samuel C. Roane removed. His only connection with the recent replacement of Judge Trimble was to "make a statement" about his successor, Edward Cross of Arkansas.[45] He admitted, however, that he had "half in earnest" told Ashley before he left that if it were true that the superior court judges, acting as judges of the court to adjudicate Spanish and French land claims, had decided erroneously against the United States in cases involving a total of 50,000 to 60,000 acres of land, he would, were he President, remove the judges and the district attorney without an investigation. Pope also acknowl-

---

[42] See *Gazette,* June 22, 1830.

[43] A Farmer to Bertrand, *Advocate,* June 30, 1830.

[44] Jaw-Bone to Editor, *Gazette,* July 14, 1830.

[45] Cross was appointed in Trimble's stead in May, 1830. "Appointments by the President," *ibid.,* June 15, 1830; *Terr. Papers,* XXI, 228. A native Tennessean, born in 1798, Cross studied law in Kentucky, practiced his profession in Tennessee, and came in 1826 to Washington County, Arkansas. Fay Hempstead, *A Pictorial History of Arkansas* (St. Louis, 1890), 865–866.

edged that at the time of his departure from Arkansas he had been "well disposed" to have Ashley appointed in Roane's stead because he doubted that Roane had handled the government's part skillfully enough. But he had learned in Washington that the "Spanish business" was an "insuperable barrier," and had concluded that Roane had "discharged his duty."[46]

Pope denied reports of a breach between himself and Sevier. True, he had found upon arriving in Washington that "some artful, designing men had excited" Sevier by telling him that he desired to "control or interfere with him"; but he and Sevier had adjusted their difficulties and thenceforth "acted harmoniously." Having gone to Washington without permission to "settle some private business and to do what I could for the people of the Territory," he had hoped by obtaining passage of a congressional resolution approving his visit to spare President Jackson the embarrassment of sanctioning what he had done. But this plan had failed because Sevier's friends had been "more nice than wise in objecting to a resolution which could have done him [Sevier] no harm, and relieved me from annoyance."[47]

"Laos" conjectured that while there might be no "open rupture" between Pope and Sevier, "a *coolness*" had nevertheless developed. Sevier did not "absolutely" dislike Pope but he "knows him to be an old, broken down, meddling politician, and knows that it is necessary to *checkmate* occasionally, to keep him in order."[48] "Justice" believed, probably correctly, that the publications in the *Advocate* concerning the "supposed" Pope-Sevier "rupture" were designed to cause a permanent separation between them.[49]

Pope was charged with being friendly to Henry Clay. Bertrand published on July 14 a letter from Kentucky stating that in a recent dinner speech at Louisville Pope had used "*certain expressions*" regarding the Jackson administration "which, it is thought, will probably cause the 'reforming' hand of the President, to be extended again to Arkansas." The " 'knowing ones' " in Kentucky believed Pope would soon make "another of his singular changes in politics." A week later Bertrand printed another letter from the

---

[46] Bertrand believed Pope's assertion that he had not attempted to have Roane removed from office to be false, for Sevier had told a gentleman of Little Rock that Pope had worked to have Roane replaced by Ashley, and that he himself had objected to Roane's removal. *Advocate*, August 11, 1830.

[47] Pope, "To the Public," August 2, 1830, *Gazette*, August 4, 1830.

[48] Laos to Editor, *Advocate*, July 28, 1830.

[49] Justice, "Governor Pope, and the Secret Clan who are assailing Private Feelings and Public Character," *Gazette*, July 21, 1830.

same Kentuckian stating that Pope had, before leaving for Arkansas, come out against the Jackson administration and "extolled Mr. Clay's virtues and merits to the skies." Bertrand said also that Pope had recently admitted to several men in Little Rock that he had defected to the Clay camp.[50]

Pope replied that he had no recollection of making the admission Bertrand attributed to him. His remarks about Clay in Louisville had been thrown off "in a convivial moment." He respected Clay, felt no personal animosity toward him, and believed he had squared accounts with him in the presidential election of 1828. Pope thought it "strange" that he should be assailed by "Clay-men" in Kentucky through the *Advocate,* a newspaper professing to be favorable to Jackson.[51]

Several writers in the *Gazette* offered explanations for the attack on Pope. "Justice" and "Henry" considered it an attempt to destroy Pope's popularity "before the period arrives for the distribution of state honors."[52] "Hampden" believed a "few *aspiring* individuals" were, in an effort to "effect their own aggrandizement," trying to divide "the *majority.*"[53]

In a later communication "Henry" concluded that the underlying object of the attacks by the *Advocate* writers on both Pope and Fulton was an attempt "to bring about a change, from a Territorial to a State Government, on the return of the next census, to gratify their own ambitious views." While "Henry" felt considerable "solicitude" for statehood, he believed its advantages and disadvantages should be weighed carefully. The Territory already owed $10,000 in scrip, the annual expense of operating a state government would amount to $26,300, and its organization plus the erection of public buildings would cost $35,000. As a territory, the expenses of her government were borne by the United States, and the money brought into the Territory for this purpose was in itself of much benefit to Arkansans.[54]

"Henry's" comments on the feasibility of state government

[50] "Signs of the Times," *Advocate,* July 14, 21, 1830.

[51] Pope, "To the Public," August 2, 1830, *Gazette,* August 4, 1830. See also *Advocate,* August 11, September 15, 1830; *Gazette,* September 8, October 13, 1830.

[52] Henry, "To the Citizens of Arkansas Territory," *Gazette,* August 18, 1830; Justice, "Governor Pope, and the Secret Clan who are assailing Private Feelings and Public Character," *ibid.,* July 28, 1830.

[53] Communication of Hampden, *ibid.,* August 25, 1830.

[54] Henry, "No. III. To the Citizens of Arkansas Territory," *ibid.* Bertrand believed statehood would enable Arkansas to punish "delinquents at *home*" and demand "our rights *abroad.*" *Advocate,* August 18, 1830.

evoked a retort from "Aristides," who did not believe the people would weigh *"money* against *independence."* The status of Arkansans under territorial government he likened to that of slaves on a plantation. If Arkansas should become a state, population would increase "in a ratio of ten to one" and the state would develop rapidly. "Aristides" believed that "Henry" was Pope and that he opposed statehood because it would end his tenure as governor and his salary.[55]

"Henry" denied both that he was Pope[56] and that statehood would cause an increase in immigration. People would come to Arkansas when they had the means to do so, whatever the type of government. If anything, a change in government would, owing to the factional strife and contention for state offices that would accompany it, keep people away. But "Henry" believed the cost of supporting a state government to be the main objection to statehood.

Writing in the *Advocate* "Aristides" denied what he took to be "Henry's" implication that "Aristides" was Crittenden and asserted that he had never held office in the Territory. To an accusation that the "would-be great men of the Territory" favored statehood, he answered that it was "laudable" to expect to receive offices from the people instead of Washington. Expense was not a valid reason to oppose statehood, for the public debt was decreasing and the formation of a state would encourage immigration and increase Arkansas' wealth. No planter would now "jeopardize his fortune" by removing to Arkansas because he had no way of knowing whether slavery would be permitted under a state constitution.[57]

In September the *Advocate* came out in favor of "going into a State Government, whenever our numbers will justify it, from a firm conviction, that by it, the best interests of the people will be advanced . . ."[58] What were Woodruff's views on the subject?[59]

Shortly thereafter a correspondent in Woodruff's *Gazette* sug-

---

[55] Aristides, "To the Freemen of Arkansas," *ibid.,* September 8, 1830.

[56] "Henry" also denied an accusation by "Aristides" that the writer signing himself "Justice" was Governor Pope. Henry, "No. IV. To the Citizens of Arkansas Territory," *Gazette,* September 15, 1830.

[57] Aristides, "To the Freemen of Arkansas," *Advocate,* September 29, 1830. "Vox Populi" considered "Aristides" a "political demagogue" and his motives suspect because he favored statehood. Vox Populi to Editor, October 21, 1830, *Gazette,* November 3, 1830. Aristides denied the allegations, asserting that he was merely stating his views. Aristides to Editor, *Advocate,* November 10, 1830.

[58] *Advocate,* September 22, 1830. See also *ibid.,* November 17, 1830. From September, 1830, until April, 1831, Bertrand was assisted in publishing the *Advocate* by a partner named William T. Yeomans. *Ibid.,* September 22, 1830, April 27, 1831.

[59] *Ibid.,* October 6, 1830.

gested statehood as a measure to guard against the rumored intention of the Federal government to remove Indians from the East to several of the western counties of Arkansas.[60] Woodruff in reply held that an act recently passed by Congress prohibited the President from removing Indians to any state or organized territory west of the Mississippi,[61] and then went on to argue that Arkansas did not have the necessary population to become a state. A census taken in 1829 had reported less than 25,000 people. Heavy immigration since had increased the number by 5,000 to 10,000, but the population now required for statehood was 40,000, and that number would be increased to 50,000 at the next session of Congress, thus delaying statehood "to a still more distant period." This controversy over the feasibility of forming a state in 1830 presaged a later debate on the matter.

One notices that Sevier escaped the violent shafts of the editors and correspondents in the *Advocate.* This fact was also observed by writers in the *Gazette,* who conjectured that he too would at some time in the near future be attacked. "Hampden" believed that the true object of the "excitement" created by the Crittenden men was to prevent Sevier's reelection to Congress in 1831.[62]

Sevier himself seems to have made an effort to remain aloof from the controversy. After seeing an announcement that as presiding officer at a dinner held July 5 at the country home of Dr. John H. Cocke he had read several toasts "in which the official character of Gov. Pope came directly or indirectly at issue,"[63] Sevier issued a statement in both the *Gazette* and the *Advocate* denying that he had been the actual president of the meeting; he had no part in preparing the toasts and had read them only on account of the temporary absence of the gentleman he considered to be president.[64]

Sevier's statement brought an immediate reply from Cocke to the effect that Sevier, though he had not participated in preparing the toasts, had indeed been president. It was "passing strange" that he should be willing to injure the feelings of a known friend in

[60] Letter from gentleman of Greenock, October 4, 1830, to Editor, *Gazette,* October 13, 1830.

[61] *Ibid.;* 4 *U.S. Stat. at L.* (1846), 411–412. The *Advocate* feared that, notwithstanding this act, Indians might be removed to Arkansas because there was nowhere else for them to be removed to. *Avdocate,* October 20, 1830. See also "The Unnecessary Alarm," *Gazette,* November 10, 1830.

[62] Henry, "To the Citizens of Arkansas Territory," *Gazette,* August 18, 1830; communication of Hampden, *ibid.,* August 25, 1830.

[63] See "Anniversary Celebration," *ibid.,* July 7, 1830.

[64] Sevier to Editor, July 14, 1830, *ibid.,* July 14, 1830; *Advocate,* July 14, 1830.

favor of Governor Pope, a doubtful one. Sevier's "anxiety to screen himself from censure" had placed Cocke "in a very unpleasant situation."[65]

"Justice" forthwith charged that Cocke and James B. Keatts, the latter "a violent enemy" of Jackson, had conspired to widen a supposed breach between Sevier and Pope by inviting to dinner men who were friendly to Pope and then using them to assail Pope's "feelings." Cocke was, moreover, guilty of duplicity in having come to Little Rock and dined in apparent friendship with Pope before Pope had heard about the hostile toasts.[66]

Presumably it was this quarreling in the newspapers that brought about in October a duel between Dr. Cocke and Governor Pope's young nephew and private secretary, William Fontaine Pope. According to Crittenden, Cocke demanded to know the name of the person who had been writing against him under the pseudonym "Justice." Young Pope's name was given by Editor Woodruff (Crittenden believed Governor Pope was the actual author) and Cocke promptly challenged him to a duel.[67] The two men met on the east side of the Mississippi opposite the mouth of White River. Elias Rector served as Pope's second, and James B. Keatts acted for Cocke. After three shots had been exchanged without harm to either man, their friends interceded and the difficulty was adjusted.[68]

In December, 1830, a short piece signed "Devereux" appeared in the *Advocate* charging Governor Pope with degrading the office of governor by "retailing liquor." The "offence" might be less grave if Pope needed money to free himself from debt, but Pope was a wealthy man.[69] Apparently "Devereux" meant to imply that Pope was guilty of avariciousness.

Three weeks later William Fontaine Pope published a card asserting that "Devereux" desired a fight with someone and offering

[65] Cocke to Editor, July 20, 1830, *Gazette*, July 28, 1830; *Advocate*, July 28, 1830.

[66] Justice, "Doct. Cocke and his Aide Camp Keatts," August 2, 1830, *Gazette*, August 11, 1830.

[67] Crittenden to Pope, April 21, 1832, *Advocate*, May 2, 1832. A later member of the Pope family tells us that young Pope, having taken it upon himself to defend the honor of his one-armed and aged uncle, demanded to know the writer of pseudonymous attacks upon Governor Pope appearing in the *Advocate*, and was given Cocke's name. The pseudonymous writer is said to have been "Dinwiddie," but no such name appears in the *Advocate* in 1830. William F. Pope, *Early Days in Arkansas* (Little Rock, 1895), 114–115.

[68] Pope, *Early Days in Arkansas*, 114–115; *Advocate*, October 27, 1830; *Gazette*, October 27, 1830. The *Advocate* reported that Cocke's second shot "broke the skin" of Pope's abdomen, causing him to fall.

[69] Devereux, "Non pudeo quod scio," *Advocate*, December 15, 1830.

to "crown his wishes."[70] After a newspaper exchange,[71] young Pope and "Devereux," who turned out to be Charles F. M. Noland,[72] met in Miller County south of Red River on February 5. At the first fire Pope fell severely wounded in the hip. After a reconciliation Noland and his friends departed and Pope was taken first to the house of Benjamin Milam, then to Washington, Hempstead County, and later to Little Rock.[73]

Noland in a letter to his father on April 2 reported that Pope's recovery was uncertain and that all of Pope's "sunshine friends," including his uncle (Governor Pope), had "deserted him." Noland went on to say that before the duel Crittenden, Bates, Fulton, and Benjamin Desha had joined in an earnest effort to prevent its being fought. Besides that, Crittenden, with whom he had previously been on bad terms, had now befriended him. Noland believed that Crittenden had been "*basely slandered*" in Arkansas Territory and his acts misrepresented; in the last year he had gained rapidly in popularity.[74]

The reconciliation of Pope and Noland was, as it turned out, to be ephemeral. In May Noland addressed a communication to the public asserting that George W. Scott, who had lately been removed as Federal marshal by the President,[75] had lost his place because of a statement by Pope, endorsed by Woodruff, that Scott had caused

---

[70] "A Card," *Gazette Supplement*, January 5, 1831.

[71] Devereux, "A Card," January 12, 1831, *Advocate*, January 12, 1831; Pope, "To the Public," January 8, postscript of January 12, 1831, *Gazette Supplement*, January 12, 1831. Noland assured his father that he had "ample cause" for criticizing the governor. C. F. M. Noland to William Noland, March 21, 1831, Berkeley-Noland Papers, Alderman Library, University of Virginia.

[72] Noland was a Virginian about twenty-one years old who had come to Arkansas after being dismissed from West Point in 1825. His father, William Noland, had served one term as receiver of the Batesville land district. Ted R. Worley, "An Early Arkansas Sportsman: C. F. M. Noland," *Arkansas Historical Quarterly*, XI (Spring, 1952), 25–39; Josiah H. Shinn, "The Life and Public Services of Charles Fenton Mercer Noland," *Publications of the Arkansas Historical Association*, Vol. I (Fayetteville, 1906), 330–343.

[73] *Gazette*, February 16, 1831; *Advocate*, February 16, 1831; Pope, *Early Days in Arkansas*, 118–122; Daniel T. Witter to Woodruff, February 6, 1831, William E. Woodruff Papers, Arkansas History Commission.

[74] C. F. M. Noland to William Noland, April 2, 1831, Berkeley-Noland Papers, Alderman Library, University of Virginia. See also Margaret Smith Ross, ed., "Three Letters of Cephas Washburn," *Arkansas Historical Quarterly*, XVI (Summer, 1957), 176, 178; Thomas P. Eskridge to wife, January 23, 1831, microfilm copies of John Perkins Letters and Papers, Joint University Libraries, Nashville, Tennessee. Governor Pope asserted later that he had attempted to prevent the duel and intimated that Crittenden had promoted it. John Pope to Crittenden, *Gazette Supplement*, March 14, 1832.

[75] See Secretary of State to Judge Bates, March 4, 1831, to Scott, March 4, 1831, and to Rector, March 4, 1831, *Terr. Papers*, XXI, 320–321, note 6.

both duels participated in by Pope. Scott had not, Noland declared emphatically, brought about the duel between himself and Pope. It was also untrue, as rumor had it, that he (Noland) had blamed Scott for the duel.[76]

Pope admitted that he had written the President in the interest of securing Scott's removal, but he denied both that Woodruff had endorsed the letter and that Scott had been accused in it of having been responsible for the two duels. Pope could prove by a witness that Noland himself had blamed Scott for the Pope-Noland duel.[77]

Here the matter rested for the time being, but Pope died of the after effects of his wound. Though he forgave Noland in his last moments the controversy over their duel lived after him.[78]

In looking back upon the events of 1830 we may observe that the appearance of the *Advocate* as spokesman for Crittenden and his friends marked the beginning of intense opposition to the Sevier faction. By attacking Sevier's new allies, Governor Pope and Secretary Fulton, the Crittenden men probably hoped to counteract the additional prestige and influence which Pope and Fulton undoubtedly brought to the Sevier camp, and perhaps, in Pope's case, to drive a wedge in what apparently was a shaky alliance between Pope and Sevier.[79] The fierce assault on Woodruff was presumably designed to injure Woodruff's public standing in the hope of lessening the *Gazette's* influence as spokesman of the Sevier faction. The controversy also brought to light the prominence (but did not make clear the role) of Chester Ashley in the leadership of the Sevier faction. On the eve of the campaign of 1831 the Sevier camp was stronger than ever before but could expect to face an opposition seemingly more determined than in any previous election.

[76] Noland, "To the Public," May 15, 1831, *Advocate,* June 1, 1831.

[77] Pope, "A Card," June 1, 1831, *Gazette,* June 8, 1831.

[78] *Ibid.,* June 22, 1831; *Advocate,* June 22, 1831. For subsequent controversy on the Pope-Noland duel, see Crittenden, "To the Public," February 28, 1832, and to Pope, April 21, 1832, *Advocate,* February 29, May 2, 1832; Pope to Crittenden, March 5, 1832, *Gazette Supplement,* March 14, 1832.

[79] Crittenden asserted in 1834 that the Sevier faction had "never loved Pope" but had *"tolerated* and *partially* sustained him" to injure Crittenden and preserve themselves. Robert Crittenden to John J. Crittenden, May 4, 1834, John J. Crittenden Papers, Duke University Library.

CHAPTER EIGHT

The Election of 1831

THE CAMPAIGN FOR DELEGATE to Congress began on April 6, 1831, with Sevier's announcement that he would be a candidate for reelection.[1] Two weeks later a communication appeared in the *Advocate* from a "large portion of the people" of Crawford County urging Benjamin Desha of Arkansas County to become a candidate and assuring to him the support of the west.[2] Presently the *Gazette* reported a rumor that the Crittenden faction was holding "a *grand Caucus*" at Batesville and warned Sevier's friends to be on the alert for a "secret candidate."[3] On May 4 the *Advocate* proclaimed Desha's candidacy.[4]

Sevier had in the meantime issued a campaign circular that listed not only many beneficial laws that had passed Congress during his recent term but also several measures that had failed through no fault of his. He hoped the people would reelect him in order that he might continue his work for "every public measure deemed by us necessary for the prosperity of Arkansas." In regard to the "excitable question" of statehood, Sevier advised the electorate that until the territorial debt was adjusted, and Arkansas possessed "the population and the means to support a State Government," he would, *"in the absence of your instructions, . . .* feel disposed to oppose" statehood.[5]

---

[1] "August Election, 1831," *Arkansas Gazette* (Little Rock), April 6, 1831.

[2] Communication of The Lovely Boys, March 5, 1831, *Arkansas Advocate* (Little Rock), April 20, 1831. A Sevier supporter did not believe, however, that the west would "desert" Sevier, "an old and tried friend." Nemo to Editor, April 24, 1831, *Gazette,* April 27, 1831.

[3] *Ibid.,* April 27, 1831.

[4] " 'The Bridle's Off'—Desha's a Candidate," *Advocate,* May 4, 1831.

[5] Sevier, "To the Citizens of Arkansas," April 11, 1831, *Gazette,* April 20, 1831.

Desha, born in 1790 in Tennessee, had during his youth been taken to Kentucky where his father, Joseph Desha, became a prominent politician. Benjamin lived in Washington from 1810 to 1813 and served as a captain in the War of 1812. After leaving the army, he farmed in Kentucky and was several times sent to the state legislature. Since 1824 he had been receiver of the Arkansas land district, and though he had entered the race for delegate in the special election of 1827 he had subsequently withdrawn.[6] Albert Pike characterized Desha as "a very large man in every way, intellectually and physically."[7]

In a circular to the freemen of Arkansas, Desha came out for a permanent preemption law; internal improvements; and admission of Arkansas into the Union when the Territory possessed the requisite population. He would not act on the matter of statehood, however, until the people petitioned Congress directly, or through the territorial legislature. Whatever the outcome of the election, he would resign his Federal office sometime during the year and turn to "the cultivation of my farm" for his sole means of support. Though a "zealous supporter" of President Jackson, he was not involved in any "entangling alliances" in the Territory.[8]

Woodruff promptly denied Desha's claim that he was unattached politically, saying that he had actually been brought out by Robert Crittenden. Had Desha been the people's candidate, he would have authorized the announcement of his candidacy in the *Gazette* as well as the *Advocate*.[9]

Woodruff believed Crittenden had found it a difficult task "to bring his candidate to the sticking point" and that he would

find it a still more difficult one to secure his election. However, he has gained one main point in the political game which he has been playing for some time past. By bringing out a candidate, he secures the organization of his party, which may be a matter of considerable importance to him in future campaigns.[10]

---

[6] "Obituary," *Advocate*, December 4, 18, 1835; *Gazette*, December 1, 29, 1835; George Graham to Desha, March 25, 1824, Clarence E. Carter, ed., *Territorial Papers of the United States*, Vol. XIX, *Arkansas Territory, 1819–1825* (Washington, 1953), 629–630; Boyd W. Johnson, "Benjamin Desha," *Arkansas Historical Quarterly*, XIX (Winter, 1960), 348–360.

[7] "Albert Pike's Autobiography," *New Age Magazine*, XXXVIII (February, 1930), 103.

[8] Desha, "To the Freemen of Arkansas," May 7, 1831, *Advocate*, May 11, 1831; *Gazette*, May 18, 1831.

[9] "Col. Desha's Circular," *Gazette*, May 18, 1831.

[10] *Ibid.*, May 4, 1831.

Another Sevier supporter asserted that Crittenden had met Henry Clay in New Orleans, presumably during the winter, and had afterward, on his return to the Territory, begun at Arkansas Post "urging the propriety of Desha's being a candidate."[11]

According to Bertrand, Desha was, contrary to Woodruff's belief, the people's candidate. Notwithstanding considerable urging by the people, he had not decided to enter the race for Congress until Sevier had dared him to by declaring that if the people wanted "to run him . . . pull off the bridle and let him come."[12] A Sevier partisan claimed, however, that Sevier had actually said "if the Cardinal [Crittenden] wants to run, and pack Col. Desha, as he said at Batesville, and beat me, let him take the bridle off, and avow it."[13] This assertion brought, in turn, a denial from "Juste" in the *Advocate* that Crittenden had made such a "foolish or presumptuous" remark. He had actually said that the worst Desha would have to fear during the campaign would be an attempt by the Sevier faction to "pack" Crittenden "and all his sins upon him." That Crittenden, a Clay man, and Desha, a Jackson partisan, should be allies "Juste" explained upon the ground of a friendship between them dating from the War of 1812 when they had served as officers in the same company.[14]

Though some of Sevier's supporters seemed favorably disposed toward Desha himself, they feared that he would, if elected, be controlled by Crittenden and his friends.[15] A Crittenden man believed this apprehension arose from "what Sevier is known to be."[16]

"One of the People" charged early in the canvass, evidently in an attempt to damage Crittenden's reputation and thereby offset his influence in Desha's behalf, that Crittenden had stated recently in a coffee-house of Little Rock that he "would not seek a fight [presumably meaning a duel] with Sevier, but that he [Sevier] could get one out of him." This showed to "One of the People" that Crittenden

---

[11] Communication of One of the People, *ibid.,* May 25, 1831. The writer averred, no doubt with some exaggeration, that Crittenden had "organized his party" while at Arkansas Post.

[12] *Advocate,* May 11, 25, 1831.

[13] One of the People, "To the People of Arkansas," *Gazette,* May 11, 1831. See also *ibid.,* May 18, 25, 1831.

[14] Juste to Editor, *Advocate,* May 18, 1831.

[15] One of the People, "To the People of Arkansas," *Gazette,* May 11, 25, 1831; Amicus, "To the Citizens of Arkansas," *ibid.,* June 1, 1831; XQZ to Editor, *ibid.,* May 18, 1831.

[16] Z, "Number II," *Advocate,* June 22, 1831.

wished to get rid of Sevier in the same way he had disposed of Conway in 1827.[17]

A Crittenden partisan averred in reply that Crittenden's remarks had been deliberately distorted. He had actually said, in discussing some "harsh remarks" made against him by Sevier, that he would "bear much from him, I have great reluctance to enter into another conflict, where even success, will be my ruin, but if forced upon me I will meet it from him . . ."[18] "One of the People" believed this statement was proof of Crittenden's "intentions" toward Sevier. "Every person present" in the "grog-shop" had understood Crittenden's statement "as throwing the battle gage to Sevier."[19]

Crittenden was also accused of being an aristocrat. One of his friends, however, thought this to be

rather a strange charge to be made against a man whom they [Sevier men] have denounced to the public as a bankrupt for the last four years—who came to Arkansas without a dollar—and who owes the limited education he received in his youth to the benevolence of his elder brothers. Him an aristocrat! whose father was a house-joiner by trade, and an enlisted soldier in the revolution! I ask, was it *money* or *family* which made him an aristocrat?[20]

A Sevier partisan nonetheless maintained the truth of the charge, contending that "principle" determined status.[21]

Desha was criticized at the outset of the canvass for neglecting his duties as receiver in favor of electioneering.[22] In a communication printed May 25 a Sevier supporter complained that persons entitled to preemptions were calling daily at the land office in Little Rock to find Desha away with the "Cardinal" on an "electioneering pilgrimage" in the Mississippi counties.[23] Because the time for establishing preemption rights expired on May 29, Woodruff claimed that Desha was more needed at his post than at any other time.[24]

"All of Us" called Desha a "public *pensioner,*" castigated him for not resigning his Federal office, and conjectured that he

[17] One of the People, "To the People of Arkansas," *Gazette,* May 11, 1831.

[18] Juste to Editor, *Advocate,* May 18, 1831. "Juste" said that Crittenden was "*much less* unpopular than formerly." *Ibid.,* June 22, 1831.

[19] Communication of One of the People, *Gazette,* May 25, 1831. "One of the People" believed Crittenden possessed a "restless ambition" politically.

[20] Juste to Editor, *Advocate,* May 18, 1831.

[21] Communication of One of the People, *Gazette,* May 25, 1831.

[22] All of Us to Editor, *ibid.,* May 18, 1831.

[23] Daemon to Editor, *ibid.,* May 25, 1831. Woodruff reported on June 8 that Desha returned to Little Rock on May 25 from his tour of the Mississippi Counties and had left again a week later "on an electioneering tour of the west." *Ibid.,* June 8, 1831.

[24] *Ibid.,* May 25, 1831.

HENRY W. CONWAY

ROBERT CRITTENDEN

AMBROSE H. SEVIER

JAMES MILLER

CHESTER ASHLEY

BENJAMIN JOHNSON

WILLIAM CUMMINS

ABSALOM FOWLER

WILLIAM E. WOODRUFF

CHARLES P. BERTRAND

ANDREW SCOTT

JOHN POPE

GEORGE IZARD

WILLIAM S. FULTON

THE OLD STATE HOUSE (Construction began in 1833)

probably would not have come to Arkansas "had it not been for the commission he had in his pocket."[25] Desha's friends reminded the electorate in reply that Henry W. Conway, whom Sevier had zealously supported for delegate in 1823, had not resigned his post as receiver until after the election.[26]

Woodruff reported in July that Desha's friends around Little Rock were "making great calculations on the *influence* which some of the merchants in the northern counties will have in securing to him the *votes* of their *debtors!*" He hoped the freemen of Arkansas would not permit this "monied aristocracy" to decide their vote.[27] Woodruff was promptly assured by Bertrand that the people of northern Arkansas would "freely and fearlessly" express their opinions at the polls. Bertrand believed "Buck" Woodruff had "been so long in leading strings and bought up by 'treasury pap,' that he judges all others by himself."[28]

Supporters of Sevier argued that his experience was in his favor. He had an admirable record and was held in high esteem not only by his colleagues in Congress but also by the administration.[29] Bertrand considered these arguments to be contrary to the principle of rotation in office,[30] and "Wayne" insisted that even if Sevier had been an excellent delegate, which "Wayne" did not believe to be true, he had "no inalienable right" to the post.[31]

A vigorous campaign was waged against Sevier in the columns of the *Advocate.* Noticing that "Buck" had said Arkansans were indebted to Sevier for the passage of a preemption law,[32] Bertrand asserted that a senator from Alabama had been solely responsible for its success in both houses.[33] Woodruff responded by publishing a letter from Sevier, dated September 23, 1829, stating that the bill had been an outgrowth of "a resolution submitted at my instance."[34]

[25] All of Us, "Out At Last," *ibid.,* May 11, 1831.

[26] Virginius to Editor, *Advocate,* May 18, 1831; One of the Boys, "To the Freemen of Arkansas," *ibid.,* June 8, 1831.

[27] "Ledger Influence," *Gazette,* July 13, 1831.

[28] " 'Le[d]ger Influence,' " *Advocate,* July 20, 1831.

[29] Amicus, "To the Citizens of Arkansas," *Gazette,* May 25, June 1, 1831; One of the People, "To the People of Arkansas," *ibid.,* June 15, 1831; Republican, "No. II, The New Coalition in Arkansas," *ibid.,* July 13, 1831; "What Has Mr. Sevier Done, To Entitle Him To Re-election?," *ibid.,* June 15, 1831.

[30] "Such Republicanism!!," *Advocate,* July 20, 1831.

[31] Wayne to Editor, *ibid.,* June 15, 1831.

[32] See "The Pre-Emption Law," *Gazette,* June 1, 1831.

[33] *Advocate,* June 8, 1831.

[34] "The Pre-Emption Law," *Gazette,* June 15, 1831. Woodruff's position was subsequently reiterated in Republican, "The New Coalition in Arkansas," *ibid.,* July 6, 1831.

Bertrand continued to maintain that Sevier had had nothing to do with the passage of the bill.[35]

Sevier was accused of "tyranny" because he had "caused" Judge Trimble to be removed from the superior court.[36] According to "Arkansas," Sevier himself had admitted in a speech at Batesville that Trimble's "chief or perhaps only sin was that he opposed or voted against" Sevier.[37] "Warren" considered the measures secured by Sevier in Congress to be inadequate compensation for "the loss of an *Independent Judiciary.*"[38]

Desha's friends also assailed Sevier for his stand on statehood. Writing in the *Advocate,* "Arkansas" asked if any man in Arkansas was "so grovelling, so narrow minded in his views, as to weigh for a moment, a dollar against his own political rights." Sevier was endeavoring to influence public opinion by "putting *his own individual* veto" on statehood. The idea of a state government was obnoxious to many prominent Sevier men only because "the salaries of newly formed state governments are not so *comfortable* as those given by Uncle Sam."[39]

A Sevier partisan responded by accusing the Crittenden-Desha "coalition" of trying to force upon the people "the burthens of state government." The Crittenden faction favored statehood solely because they hoped, under a state government, to come to power. Crittenden[40] had several years ago approached "his then bitter opponent" with a proposition that they unite politically so that each might upon the Territory becoming a state "be elevated to a seat in the august Assembly of the Nation."[41]

Bertrand charged in July that Sevier had promised the office of register at Batesville, held by Desha's brother-in-law, Hartwell Boswell, to both William McK. Ball and Caleb S. Manly in return for their support. Ball, who had only recently come to Arkansas, had been sent by Sevier on an electioneering tour of several of the western counties and at last report was making stump speeches in Washington County. Bertrand hoped the people of the west would

---

[35] "The Pre-Emption Law—Again," *Advocate,* June 22, 1831.

[36] Communication of Juste, *ibid.,* June 22, 1831.

[37] Arkansas, "To the Freemen of Arkansas," *ibid.,* May 25, 1831. "Z" believed Sevier's statement at Batesville had "shaken" his popularity with the people. Z, "Number I," *ibid.,* June 8, 1831.

[38] Communication of Warren, *ibid.,* July 13, 1831.

[39] Arkansas to Editors, *ibid.,* April 20, 1831. See also communication of Warren, *ibid.,* June 8, 1831.

[40] Crittenden's name was not called, but the writer left no doubt that he was meant.

[41] Republican, "The New Coalition in Arkansas," *Gazette,* July 6, 1831; Republican, "No. II. The New Coalition in Arkansas," *ibid.,* July 13, 1831.

not "suffer this Eastern Puritan" to *"dictate* and *influence* their votes."[42] Though Ball and Manly later denied they had been promised the registership,[43] one notices that in 1832 Manly was appointed to be receiver at Batesville and Ball to be register at Fayetteville.[44]

Bertrand reported near the end of the campaign that he had been informed by a "poor" and "honest" citizen of Little Rock named Ellitt Bussy that Chester Ashley had threatened to institute a suit against him for the amount due on a note held by Ashley unless Bussy agreed to vote for Sevier.[45] Next day Woodruff printed a deposition purportedly made by Bussy declaring what Bertrand had said to be absolutely false.[46] Bertrand nevertheless maintained the truth of his statement and published a certificate signed by three persons to the effect that Bussy had told them the same thing. According to Bertrand, Ashley had written the deposition printed in the *Gazette,* and Bussy, who was illiterate, had been persuaded to sign it while inebriated.[47]

Presumably in an attempt to win the farmers' vote, a Desha man told the farmers of Arkansas that Desha was "a farmer—so are you"; consequently Desha's "interests are your interests."[48] A Sevier man maintained, however, that Sevier was more a farmer than Desha was, conjecturing that Sevier had rolled more logs and burned more brush during the previous spring than Desha had.[49]

The *Gazette* printed from time to time correspondence purporting to give the relative strength of the candidates in the various counties. A number of letters appearing late in June predicted that Independence, Hempstead, Lawrence, Union, Jackson, Conway, Washington, and St. Francis Counties would go for Sevier. A correspondent in Washington County reported Desha to be "dejected and cast down" and attributed his plight to his "unfortunate selection of a friend [presumably Crittenden] to go with him through the county."[50]

About two weeks before the election Woodruff named fifteen

[42] *Advocate,* July 13, 1831.

[43] Manly to Editor, July 25, 1831, *Gazette,* August 3, 1831; Ball to Editor, *ibid.,* July 20, 1831.

[44] *Terr. Papers,* Vol. XXI, *Arkansas Territory, 1829–1836* (Washington, 1954), 533, note 99, 565, note 94.

[45] "Col. Ashley and his Threats," *Advocate,* July 27, 1831.

[46] *Gazette-Extra,* July 28, 1831.

[47] Bertrand, "To the Public," July 28, 1831, *Advocate,* August 3, 1831.

[48] Old Broad Brim, "To the Farmers of Arkansas," *ibid.,* May 25, June 15, 1831. Earlier Bertrand had referred to Desha as "the Farmer's Candidate." *Ibid.,* May 25, 1831.

[49] One of the People, "To the People of Arkansas," *Gazette,* June 1, 1831.

[50] " 'Signs of the Times,' " *ibid.,* June 29, 1831. For other " 'Signs of the Times' " letters, see *ibid.,* July 6, 13, 20, 27, 1831.

counties which he believed, presumably upon the basis of correspondence, would give majorities to Sevier, and seven which he thought
might go to Desha. He noted that Desha's partisans were trying to
"keep up their spirits, but it is evidently with a good deal of difficulty." None of Sevier's friends expected his majority to be less
than 250 votes.[51]

According to "Civis," writing in the *Advocate,* Sevier himself
claimed that he would win in all sections of the Territory except
the east, where he expected to receive "at least" half the vote.
"Civis," who believed Sevier's calculations to be preposterous,
predicted that Desha would win in all sections except perhaps the
south.[52]

Evidently fearing the effect that "numerous false and injurious
reports" published in the *Gazette* might have on the voters, Bertrand warned his readers not to be deceived.

Many of these communications, we have no doubt, are copied in this town,
and most of them are from lawyers and office hunters, some doubtless, from
honest, but deluded citizens. Some of these puffers, to our knowledge, have
been sent out and are now kept, in the distant counties, for the express
purpose of bragging and boasting Col. Sevier into Congress.[53]

Bertrand's own "conservative" estimate, based upon correspondence
and upon information obtained from persons "daily arriving" in
Little Rock, was that Desha would receive a majority of 540 votes
in the eastern and northern counties plus Jefferson and Pulaski,
and Sevier a majority of 250 in the south and west, leaving Desha
the victor by 290 votes.

One surmises from the evidence in the newspapers that considerable wagering occurred on the outcome of the canvass. A notice
in the *Gazette* by "Incog." offered to make bets with Desha men
totaling $600.[54] Bertrand virtuously doubted that any of Desha's
adherents would respond, for they were "generally of the Farming
and laboring class of society, who do not follow the vicious practice
of gambling, and who unfortunately, *these hard times,* have not
such large sums of money to fool away." No doubt "Incog." was a
Federal officer who *"fed at the public crib."*[55] Woodruff observed

---

[51] " 'Signs of the Times,' " *ibid.,* July 20, 1831.
[52] Civis, "Calculations extraordinary!!," *Advocate,* June 29, 1831.
[53] "The Prospects Before Us," *ibid.,* July 20, 1831. One of the "honest" letters was
presumably from Daniel T. Witter to Woodruff, July 7, 1831, William E. Woodruff
Papers, Arkansas History Commission.
[54] "600 Dollars Cash," *Gazette,* July 13, 1831.
[55] "Betting alias Gambling," *Advocate,* July 20, 1831.

near the end of the campaign that Desha men would not "even *nibble* at a bet" unless Sevier's friends would give them 300 to 500 votes.[56]

Less than a week before the election the *Gazette* reported that Desha had secretly sent a number of circulars to "the distant counties" without permitting a single one to be distributed in Little Rock. Believing that such "unfair *tricks* deserve exposure," Woodruff admonished Arkansans to be on guard and not become "caught in the *snare*."[57]

That same day Desha's circular appeared in the *Advocate*. Bertrand explained that it had not been distributed locally because the people about Little Rock could read it in the *Advocate*.[58] Desha denied recent insinuations by correspondents in the *Gazette*[59] that he had "pursued an unmanly and illiberal course" toward Sevier.

I spurned indignantly, both in my public speeches, and in colloquy, the charge of being influenced in my course by Mr. Crittenden or a Caucus, and I did say that if Col. Sevier had so charged me, he knew it was untrue. I *made no charge*—my course was one of self vindication—a negation of charges made.[60]

In the election, held August 1, Sevier carried twelve of the twenty-three counties, defeating Desha 2,538 to 2,085. Sevier was strong in all sections of the Territory. His large majorities were in Lawrence, Washington, Crittenden, St. Francis, Chicot, Clark, Hempstead, and Union Counties. Desha won Independence, Izard, Phillips, Monroe, Arkansas, and Miller Counties by substantial margins.[61] Bertrand argued that Desha, considering the fact he had been scarcely known outside Arkansas, Jefferson, and Pulaski Counties and had not had time to campaign everywhere, had done quite well. The "season of oppression and misrule" by the Sevier faction was "fast closing."[62]

Several weeks after the election the *Gazette* reprinted a paragraph from the Florence *Gazette,* a Clay paper, calling Desha "the Clay candidate for Delegate."[63] Desha forthwith protested the remark,

[56] *Gazette,* July 27, 1831.

[57] "A Trap to Catch Gulls," *Gazette,* July 27, 1831.

[58] *Advocate,* July 27, 1831.

[59] See " 'Signs of the Times,' " *Gazette,* July 20, 1831.

[60] Desha, "To the Freemen of Arkansas," June 20, 1831, *Advocate,* July 27, 1831.

[61] Election Proclamation, *Gazette,* September 21, 1831. See also "Official Election Returns," *ibid.,* September 7, 1831; "Election Returns—Official," *Advocate,* September 7, 1831.

[62] " 'Glorius News,' " *Advocate,* August 17, 1831.

[63] Paragraph in Florence (Alabama) *Gazette,* reprinted in *Gazette,* August 31, 1831.

blaming the error on the scurrilities of Woodruff's paper "pending the late canvass."[64] Woodruff answered that his only reason for publishing the paragraph was to give Desha "an opportunity of explaining the matter—*if it admitted of a satisfactory explanation.*"[65] Woodruff subsequently denied that he himself had ever accused Desha of being a Clay partisan, though some of his correspondents might have given that "impression."[66]

The campaign for the legislature had also produced considerable excitement. As far back as April 20 an anonymous writer had stated in the *Advocate* that the Sevier faction planned to strain "every nerve" to elect persons to the legislature who would favor giving the public printing to the *Gazette*. In Pulaski County, "Tallyrand" (Ashley) and "Little Billy" (Woodruff) had brought Allen Martin and Peter T. Crutchfield out for the council and house respectively.[67] Another writer reported that Woodruff himself electioneered for certain candidates during a trip to Batesville at the outset of the canvass.[68]

A facetious piece printed in the *Gazette* on April 27 asserted that the Crittenden faction intended making an effort to obtain the election of men who would be friendly to a bid by the *Advocate* for the public printing. In Pulaski County, the Crittendenites were running "Gaunt Toney" (Charles Caldwell)[69] for the council and Absalom Fowler for the house. Fowler had, the writer charged, written the piece printed in the April 20 issue of the *Advocate*.[70] Both Caldwell and Fowler were severely assailed during the campaign by correspondents in the *Gazette*.[71]

Woodruff reported in July that, according to rumor, the Crittenden men were working strenuously "in some of the counties"

[64] Desha to Editor, September 2, 1831, *Advocate*, September 7, 1831.

[65] "A Small Matter," *Gazette*, September 14, 1831.

[66] " 'The Clay Candidate'—again," *ibid.*, October 19, 1831.

[67] One of the People, "The Caucus," *Advocate*, April 20, 1831. Martin denied, however, that he was "a party candidate." Martin, "To the Voters of Pulaski County," June 4, 1831, *Gazette*, June 8, 1831.

[68] Our side, alias Gov. Pope's side, "Buck's Visit to Batesville," *Advocate*, May 11, 1831.

[69] This sobriquet was first applied to Caldwell in the controversy of 1830. See Paul Pry, "Dam Jaw-Bone, or The Last Gazette: A Play, Or Fiction, In three Acts," *Gazette*, September 22, 1830.

[70] Beau Charley, "The Cat out of the Wallet, or the ruminations and plans of the Editor of the Arkansas Advocate with one of his friends," *ibid.*, April 27, 1831. Another unidentified writer accused Crittenden with being the author of the piece. Tally Ho, "The Cardinal Is At His Tricks Again," April 25, 1831, *ibid.*

[71] See communications of Tally Ho, Sphinx, and Q in the corner, *ibid.*, April 27, May 4. Crittenden and Fowler formed a law partnership soon after the election. *Advocate*, August 31, 1831. Fowler was a former Tennessean.

for the election of legislators who would oppose his reelection as public printer. Crittenden himself was "exerting all his skill in the arts and intrigues of electioneering, to defeat us." Obviously worried that the Crittenden men might be successful, Woodruff hoped the people would not elect men pledged to give the public printing to anyone other than the printer submitting the lowest bid.[72]

As it turned out the Crittenden men were successful in securing the election of a majority of their partisans to the legislature.[73] Thus the outcome of the canvass would seem to show that the opposition faction had indeed maintained, if not increased, its relative strength in territorial politics. With the legislature, which had several important problems to consider, in control of Crittenden partisans and the executive in the hands of an ally of Sevier's, the legislative session of 1831 promised to be an unusually stormy one.

[72] "The Public Printing," *Gazette,* July 20, 1831.

[73] "The Public Printing," *ibid.,* October 19, 1831. Elected to the council were Edmund H. Bridges, Crittenden County; Green B. Lincecum, St. Francis County; William Ingram, Monroe County; James H. McKenzie, Phillips County; Terence Farrelly, Arkansas County; William B. Patton, Chicot County; William P. Hackett, Jefferson County; Moses Collins, Clark County; Daniel T. Witter, Hempstead County; Jesse Douglass, Lafayette County; Isaac Pennington, Union County; David Orr, Lawrence County; James Boswell, Independence County; Rowland Tidwell, Jackson County; Jacob Wolf, Izard County; Robert McCamy, Washington County; Robert Sinclair, Crawford County; Isaac Hughes, Pope County; Reuben J. Blount, Conway County; John Wells, Hot Spring County; Charles Caldwell, Pulaski County; Benjamin H. G. Hartfield, Sevier County; and Nathan G. Crittenden, Miller County. Wigton King contested unsuccessfully the election of Hackett. "General Assembly," *ibid.,* October 12, 1831. The candidates chosen to the house were Robert Smith, Jr., and George S. Hudspeth, Lawrence County; Caleb S. Manly and Morgan Magness, Independence and Jackson Counties; Frederick Talbot, Izard County; Abraham Whinnery and James Pope, Washington County; R. C. S. Brown and Charles Wolf, Crawford County; Andrew Scott, Pope County; Nimrod Menefee, Conway and Hot Spring County; Samuel M. Rutherford and Peter T. Crutchfield, Pulaski County; James Livingston, Crittenden County; Samuel Fillingim and John Calvert, St. Francis and Monroe Counties; Fleetwood Hanks, Phillips County; Harold Stillwell, Arkansas County; John Gibson, Chicot County; Nehemiah Holland, Jefferson County; John Wilson, Clark County; Thomas W. Scott and William Trimble, Hempstead County; James S. Conway, Lafayette and Union Counties; and John Clark, Sevier and Miller Counties. "List of members," *ibid.,* August 31, 1831; "Members of the Legislature," *Advocate,* September 7, 1831. Holland's election was contested unsuccessfully by John Palmer. "General Assembly," *Gazette,* October 12, 1831.

CHAPTER NINE

The Legislature of 1831

THE LEGISLATURE MET October 3, organized, and two days later heard the governor's message read by his private secretary, Dr. John T. Fulton. Recent difficulties between the United States and Mexico concerning the location of Arkansas' southwestern boundary had been adjusted. Congress had passed a law, approved March 2, 1831, granting ten sections of land to the Territory for erection of public buildings and making the legislature responsible for selecting the land.[1] Owing to the rapid increase in the population, "improvement," and prosperity of the Territory, Governor Pope thought the time "at hand when the people may rightfully claim to be admitted into the Union as a State."

Pope made several recommendations to the assembly. Congress should be requested to extend the benefits of the preemption law to all persons who had or might in the future settle on unappropriated public land, "provided they enter and pay the Government price within a reasonable time." The tax laws should be amended "so as to redeem the scrip in circulation." Defects in the county court system should be corrected. And, finally, the criminal code should be changed to abolish the "distinction between murder and voluntary manslaughter . . . in all cases where a dirk, pistol, or other deadly weapon is used, except in necessary self-defence."[2]

A few days before the meeting of the legislature an essay signed

---

[1] See 4 *U.S. Stat. at L.* (1846), 473. This law had been passed in response to a memorial of the legislature of 1829. See Clarence E. Carter, ed., *Territorial Papers of the United States,* Vol. XXI, *Arkansas Territory, 1829–1836* (Washington, 1954), 180–181.

[2] "The General Assembly," *Arkansas Gazette* (Little Rock), October 5, 1831; "Governor's Message," *Arkansas Advocate* (Little Rock), October 12, 1831; *Arkansas Legislative Journal,* 1831, pp. 20–25.

"Timothy Catchem" had appeared in the *Gazette* purporting to give an account of a recent conversation the writer had overheard in Little Rock between Crittenden and one of his friends. Crittenden had informed his comrade that Editor Bertrand must, if his *Advocate* were to continue in operation, be elected public printer. The Crittenden men should also work for the election of Charles Caldwell as president of the council. Crittenden had purchased thirty Kentucky hams plus a large supply of spirits for use in persuading members of the assembly to do his bidding.[3]

Bertrand observed facetiously on October 12 that Crittenden's *"canvass hams"* had been quite successful in securing the election of his friends to important posts in the legislature.[4] William Trimble had been chosen speaker of the house and Caldwell president of the council. Absalom Fowler, though defeated for election to the house, had been made secretary of the council. George W. Ferebee of Phillips County had been elected clerk of the house.[5] On October 12, the assembly elected Bertrand to be public printer by a vote of 27 to 19.[6] Woodruff bitterly attributed his defeat to Crittenden's having triumphed over him for the first time in the nearly twelve years they had been at odds.[7]

Since 1821 the meetings of the legislature had been held in a two-room log cabin which Andrew Scott described as a "wretched, decayed, unfinished old frame, too contracted for the purpose, and devoid of a solitary comfort, not even a fire-place, and so open that the smoke almost precluded the use of stoves." Superior Court Judge Edward Cross had on the first day of the 1831 session been "quite drenched in the rain, which fell upon his head and the credentials of the members, while he was administering to them the oaths of office, so damaged was the roof."[8]

On October 4 the assembly appointed a joint committee to consider

[3] Timothy Catchem to Editor, *Gazette,* September 28, 1831.

[4] According to Matthew Cunningham, Woodruff and Governor Pope also entertained members of the assembly. *Advocate,* August 29, 1832.

[5] " 'Timothy Catchem,' " *ibid.,* October 12, 1831; "Arkansas General Assembly," *ibid.,* October 5, 1831. Bertrand said Ferebee's opponent, William McK. Ball, was the writer who called himself "Timothy Catchem."

[6] "General Assembly," *Gazette,* October 19, 1831; *Arkansas Legislative Journal,* 1831, pp. 53–55, 61–62.

[7] "The Public Printing," *Gazette,* October 19, 1831.

[8] Scott to Governor Pope, April 3, 1832, *Advocate,* April 11, 1832. See also Publius to Editor, *ibid.,* April 25, 1832. Scott said the superior court frequently had to sit "in the depth of winter, in wretched hovels, destitute of every comfort, retarding greatly the progress of business . . ." Until Crittenden as secretary "erected permanent and secure buildings, at his own expense," there had been no place to house the executive and legislative records.

the best means of "appropriating" the ten sections which Congress had granted for building a state house.[9] Three proposals were laid before the committee on October 8. Chester Ashley would exchange his house and lots in Little Rock for the ten sections. William McK. Ball would give $10,000 for the ten sections on a credit of eighteen months with Woodruff, Sam C. Roane, Richard C. Byrd, Edward Cross, Joseph Henderson, and Elias Rector as securities. And Robert Crittenden would trade a block containing his brick house and various other buildings for the ten sections. The house was estimated by David G. Eller, carpenter and masterbuilder, to be worth $10,600. In selecting the ten sections Crittenden promised not to locate on improvements.[10]

By the simple process of multiplying the number of acres of the donation (6,400) times the minimum price of public land ($1.25), the committee estimated the grant to be worth $8,000. In the interests of obtaining immediately a "suitable" place for the legislature to meet, avoiding expense and delay in selecting and selling the land, and protecting improvements the committee reported in favor of the Crittenden proposition.[11]

On October 11 the house in committee of the whole sustained the report of the joint committee[12] by a vote of 15 to 9.[13] Two days later the council in committee of the whole reported favorably a bill to exchange the ten sections for Crittenden's house.[14] McCamy forthwith moved to amend the bill to provide that the governor should sell forty land warrants of 160 acres each and that the money from

---

[9] "General Assembly," *Gazette*, October 12, 1831; *Arkansas Legislative Journal*, 1831, pp. 14–15. Councilmen named to the committee were McCamy, Witter, Sinclear, Farrelly, and Blount. Representatives were Manly, Whinnery, Andrew Scott, Menefee, and Smith.

[10] For an excellent description of Crittenden's house and adjoining buildings, see "The Crittenden House," *Advocate*, May 30, 1832.

[11] "General Assembly," *Gazette*, October 12, 1831; *Arkansas Legislative Journal*, 1831, pp. 42–44. Writing in 1833, Secretary Fulton said that $8,000, less the expense of the selection and sale of the lands, had not been considered sufficient to erect a proper state house. Crittenden's house had been considered suitable for use, after the building of a permanent state house, as the governor's residence or as part of a future state university. Fulton to Secretary of State, July 19, 1833, *Terr. Papers*, XXI, 768–770.

[12] A proposal of David G. Eller, submitted by Manly on October 11, to build for $10,000 a two-story state house, forty feet long and sixty-four feet wide, was referred to the joint committee, but it evidently was not seriously considered, for it was never mentioned again either in the legislative journal or in editorials.

[13] Brown, Crutchfield, Fillingim, Hudspeth, Manly, Rutherford, T. W. Scott, Talbot, and Wilson opposed the report; Calvert, Clark, Gibson, Hanks, Holland, Livingston, Magness, Menefee, Pope, A. Scott, Smith, Stillwell, Whinnery, Wolf, and Trimble favored it.

[14] "General Assembly," *Gazette*, October 19, 1831; "The General Assembly," *ibid.*, October 12, 1831; *Arkansas Legislative Journal*, 1831, pp. 55, 58–59.

the sale be used to pay for the building of a state house. The motion was defeated 14 to 8.[15] A motion by McCamy to lay the bill on the table until June 1, 1832, also failed. The next day the council passed the ten-section bill by a vote of 14 to 7, the alignment remaining unchanged except that Hartfield was absent.[16]

In the house on October 17 Manly moved to amend the ten-section bill from an acceptance of Crittenden's proposal into an acceptance of an offer by Chester Ashley to give one town block for the use of the Territory and to build upon it by September 1, 1833, at an estimated cost of $12,000, a two-story state house, 63 feet long and 50 feet wide. The amendment was defeated 15 to 9, the vote being identical with that on October 11 except that Hudspeth and Wolf had changed sides. Preserving the same alignment, the house then voted to approve the bill.[17]

In the meantime, Editor Woodruff had come out with arguments against acceptance of Crittenden's proposal. The house was "about half a mile from the business-part of the town" and some of the buildings would "be of no manner of use to the Territory." Moreover, Eller's estimate of the value of the house was too high because it was based on the cost of labor and material at the time the house was built about 1826. In several years "with judicious management" the house might be worth $15,000 or $20,000, but its present worth was to the Territory not over $5,000.[18] Woodruff believed Crittenden's "canvass hams" had been "one of the principal agents in deciding the State-house question" in his favor.[19] "Our last hope," said Woodruff somewhat forlornly, was for an executive veto.[20]

Bertrand observed that Woodruff had "very *carefully omitted to mention*" that Ball's proposal and Ashley's original proposal had called for locating the ten sections *"without limitation."* Ball was not *"worth a dollar in the world,"* and Ashley's house was not only

---

[15] Bridges, Douglass, Hackett, Hartfield, Lincecum, McCamy, Tidwell, and Witter voted for the measure while Blount, Boswell, Collins, Farrelly, Hughes, Ingram, McKenzie, Orr, Patton, Pennington, Sinclair, Wells, Wolf, and Caldwell balloted against it.

[16] "General Assembly," *Gazette,* October 19, 1831; *Arkansas Legislative Journal,* 1831, pp. 71–73.

[17] "General Assembly," *Gazette,* October 26, 1831; *Arkansas Legislative Journal,* 1831, pp. 104–107.

[18] Note to journal of "General Assembly," and "The General Assembly," *Gazette,* October 12, 1831. Crittenden's house later sold for $6,700. " 'Mr. Crittenden's House,' " *ibid.,* November 20, 1833. See also communication of ".83," *Advocate,* April 3, 1835.

[19] *Gazette,* October 19, 1831.

[20] "The Ten Sections—disposed of," *ibid.*

mortgaged, but also, when compared to Crittenden's, "sinks to the grade of an *'outhouse.'* " Had either Ball's or Ashley's proposals been adopted,

all would have been right. We would not have heard of our honorable Delegate [Sevier], (*who, when Mr. C's.* [Crittenden] *proposition was first talked of, expressed himself in its favor,*) threatening the Members who voted for the bill, with their constituents. Oh, no! *cousin* Chester [Ashley] would then have owned the land [Bertrand evidently meant to imply that Ashley was behind Ball's proposal too], located every *valuable improvement* he could find, and made himself and *others* rich, with the *labor* of the honest and industrious citizen.[21]

In the same issue Bertrand published a speech by Caldwell in the council saying in supporting Crittenden's proposal he was carrying out the will of his constituents. Remarking that Lovely's Purchase claims were selling for less than one dollar an acre, and predicting that the price of government land would be reduced after the national debt was "extinguished," Caldwell argued that the Territory could not realize more than $6,000 from the sale of the ten sections. The opposition to Crittenden's offer he attributed entirely to "the enthusiasm of party zeal."

Governor Pope received the ten-section bill on October 20 and returned it the next day with a veto based mainly upon four points. (1) The act granting the ten sections to the Territory gave the legislature alone the power to select and sell the land, and this authority could not be transferred. (2) The ten sections were worth much more than Crittenden's house and lots; if located "on the choice spots" of the Territory, they would in a few years yield "from twenty to fifty thousand dollars." (3) The bill provided for temporary instead of permanent accommodation of the territorial government. (4) Crittenden's house was not conveniently located for the transaction of the public business or for protection in case of fire "or other casualty."[22]

Woodruff thought Pope would "be sustained in the grounds which he has taken, by at least nine-tenths of his fellow-citizens of this Territory."[23] Bertrand was "not surprised" at the governor's action,

---

[21] "The Ten Sections of Land," *Advocate,* October 22, 1831. The *Advocate* was hampered in reporting the events of the legislature of 1831 by a critical shortage of paper. *Gazette,* October 26, November 23, 1831; *Advocate,* October 22, November 2, December 21, 1831.

[22] "The Governor's Veto, On the Bill disposing of the Ten Sections," *Gazette,* October 26, 1831; "Ten Section Veto," *Advocate,* November 30, 1831; *Arkansas Legislative Journal,* 1831, pp. 139–143.

[23] "The Governor's Veto," *Gazette,* October 26, 1831.

for Delegate Sevier had been "swearing" he "would *defeat* the bill" by having Pope veto it. It was " *'absurd* and *preposterous'* " to believe the ten sections would "in a few years" bring the large sum that Pope estimated. Had Ashley's proposal (presumably the one to exchange his house and lots for the ten sections) been accepted by the legislature instead of Crittenden's, Pope would have approved it.[24] "Publius" charged that Pope vetoed the ten-section bill because he wished to see a state house erected near the river where "his *personal* and *political* friends" owned "the principal part of the property."[25]

On October 22 an attempt was made in the council to muster a two-thirds majority to override the veto. The fourteen who had originally supported the bill voted to override, but the return of Hartfield raised the nayes to eight and barely defeated the attempt.[26]

Two days later Farrelly moved to reconsider. Ruled out of order by the chair (Caldwell), he appealed the decision to the council, was sustained 12 to 9, and then moved to lay the ten-section bill on the table. A proposal by Lincecum to amend the motion to have the bill laid on the table until July 4, 1832, was defeated 14 to 8. The alignment on this vote was the same as that on the attempt to override the governor's veto. Farrelly's motion was then approved and the bill laid on the table.

A resolution by McCamy on October 26 looking toward a bill to authorize the governor to employ agents to select and sell the ten sections was defeated 14 to 7.[27] On November 7 several last minute attempts to make disposition of the ten sections failed, and the legislature adjourned without taking further action.[28]

The day that Governor Pope returned the ten-section bill to the

[24] *Advocate,* October 26, 1831. Bertrand later accused Ashley of being behind the veto. "The Ten Sections of Land," *ibid.,* November 30, 1831.

[25] Publius to Editor, *ibid.,* June 20, 1832.

[26] "General Assembly," *Gazette,* October 26, 1831. Woodruff considered Pope's veto to be "to all intents and purposes" beyond the "reach and control" of the legislators "unless they commence anew, and pass it through all its various stages in both Houses." "The Governor's Veto," *ibid.*

[27] "General Assembly," *ibid.,* November 2, 1831; *Arkansas Legislative Journal,* 1831, pp. 154–155. Bridges, who had previously voted with the minority, voted with the majority on this vote and McKenzie, who also had previously voted with the minority, did not vote.

[28] "The General Assembly," *Gazette,* November 9, 1831; *Arkansas Legislative Journal,* 1831, p. 320; Boswell to Bertrand, November 14, 1831, printed in *Gazette,* November 23, 1831. Andrew Scott said later that the legislature had made no other disposition of the ten sections because it lacked confidence in the ability of Pope—who had shown himself completely ignorant "of the *value* of the grant, as well as the cost of the building"—to "manage" the matter properly. Scott to Pope, *Advocate,* April 11, 1832.

legislature Nimrod Menefee had during a speech in the house denounced Woodruff in what Woodruff described as "abusive" language that might secure Menefee "the smiles of a few *black-guards*"
but must make honorable men "look upon him with pity and contempt."[29] The next week Woodruff reported that on October 29 during a recess of the house he had been copying from the legislative
journal at the clerk's table when Menefee approached him with a
"heavy cane in his hand." According to Woodruff, he stood up, drew
his pistol, and warned Menefee to keep away, whereupon Menefee
pulled a dirk, and he raised his pistol, but the pistol accidently discharged into the floor. Then Menefee struck him with a cane, they
grappled, and were separated by members of the assembly. Woodruff pronounced himself "surrounded by danger" but resolved not
to "swerve from our duty."[30]

The governor vetoed a bill to prohibit non-residents of one-
fourth or more Indian blood from giving evidence against whites
in any territorial tribunal. Pope's main objection was that such a
prohibition would allow whites to commit crimes with "impunity"
in Indian country.[31] The house voted 20 to 4 to override Pope's
veto,[32] but the council apparently took no parallel action.

Pope also vetoed a measure providing for a board of eight doctors
to regulate the practice of medicine and surgery in Arkansas. Pope
thought the bill gave the board too much power over the medical
profession.[33] The house endeavored to override Pope's veto, but
failed by one vote of a two-thirds majority.[34] According to Woodruff, Pope's veto of the "Medical Aristocracy Bill" was "very popular
among the people."[35] Bertrand believed that the "Quack's Bill"
would have prevented *mere pretenders* and *steam manufactured
doctors,* from imposing themselves on the public, as qualified prac-
titioners of medicine." The governor had disapproved of the bill

[29] *Gazette,* October 26, 1831.

[30] "High-Handed Legislation," *ibid.,* November 2, 1831. See also *Advocate,* November 2, 1831.

[31] "General Assembly," *Gazette,* November 2, 1831; *Arkansas Legislative Journal,*
1831, pp. 222–223. See also Pope to Secretary of War, November 24, 1831, *Terr.
Papers,* XXI, 431–432.

[32] "General Assembly," *Gazette,* November 2, 1831; *Arkansas Legislative Journal,*
1831, pp. 303–304.

[33] Veto message, November 3, 1831, *Gazette,* November 9, 1831, January 4, 1832;
Arkansas Legislative Journal, 1831, pp. 288–291.

[34] "General Assembly," *Gazette,* November 9, 1831; *Arkansas Legislative Journal,*
1831, pp. 303–304.

[35] *Gazette,* November 16, 1831. Woodruff said the only persons disappointed by
the veto were doctors who expected promotion in the profession "by the establishment
of a *Medical aristocracy.*"

because Ashley, urged by Woodruff and many of Woodruff's unqualified doctor friends, had persuaded him to.[36]

Andrew Scott had on October 26 introduced a memorial asking
Congress to pass a law permitting Arkansas to elect the territorial
governor. The next day the memorial passed the house by an overwhelming vote of 18 to 5. Though it was probably prompted in part
by the governor's veto of the ten-section bill, it drew the support of
several opponents. On October 28 the council amended the memorial
to ask that the territorial secretary also be elected. The amended
memorial passed the council by a vote of 16 to 6.[37]

On November 2 the legislature passed a joint resolution to place
the amended memorial in the hands of a joint committee for trans-
mission to Delegate Sevier. The next day Andrew Scott of the joint
committee reported that Chairman Brown of the committee on en-
rolments had, notwithstanding the joint resolution, given the memorial to the governor.[38] Two days later Scott proposed that Speaker
Trimble be requested to send a message to "John Pope" asking Pope
to return the memorial. A motion by Hudspeth to substitute the
word "governor" for "John Pope" failed 13 to 9, and the resolution passed 15 to 6, Crutchfield, Manly, T. W. Scott, Talbot, Whinnery, and Wilson dissenting. When the speaker's message reached
Pope, he refused to receive it on the ground that it was not addressed
to him in his official capacity. Returning the memorial through
proper channels without signature, he asserted that he would have
approved the memorial, had it not contained "some innuendoes and
insinuations" against his official conduct.[39]

Andrew Scott moved on November 5 that the house postpone
consideration of Pope's message until January 1, 1832. Scott's motion succeeded, and two others, that the message be read to the house
and that it be printed in the house journal, were rejected by close

[36] *Advocate*, February 22, 1832.

[37] "General Assembly," *Gazette*, November 2, 1831. See also *ibid.*, November 9,
1831; *Arkansas Legislative Journal*, 1831, pp. 198, 207–208, 213.

[38] Scott moved on November 4 that Brown be expelled from the house for having
"knowingly violated his privilege" as a member. The resolution was submitted to a
select committee but no further action seems to have been taken. "General Assembly,"
Gazette, November 9, 1831; *Arkansas Legislative Journal*, 1831, pp. 306–307.

[39] See Pope to legislature, November 5, 1831, *Gazette*, November 9, 1831; *Arkansas
Legislative Journal*, 1831, pp. 265, 284–286, 301, 305–307. Pope evidently believed,
probably correctly, that the legislature had him in mind in stating "there remains
amongst the people [of Arkansas], a power and an influence, derogatory to liberty, and
free institutions; greatly retarding their prosperity, checking their independence,
mar[r]ing their wisest plans, and thwarting their dearest interests." See *Terr. Papers*,
XXI, 437–438; *Gazette*, April 18, 1832.

votes. The memorial was then placed in possession of the joint committee appointed to give it to Delegate Sevier. Scott reported that Sevier received the memorial "with alacrity, and assured your committee that he would pay to it every attention, as he admired the principles upon which it was founded."[40]

Other work of the legislature consisted of locating permanent seats of justice for Chicot, Crittenden, Conway, Sevier, Jackson, and Miller Counties; amending the tax laws; adjusting boundaries between certain counties; providing that, beginning in 1833, all elective officials be chosen in the month of August; incorporating the town of Little Rock; amending the land laws pertaining to military bounty lands; revising the militia laws; calling in the territorial scrip; making appropriations for 1832 and 1833; and amending the county court system.[41] Nearly two dozen memorials to Congress dealt with matters such as internal improvements, land, frontier defense, and Indians.[42]

During the fall and winter the *Gazette* printed, under the heading of "Public Sentiment," correspondence from persons over the Territory purporting to show the ten-section bill had been quite unpopular. A gentleman of Phillips County had heard nothing but "maledictions" against the legislators who supported it. A letter from Greenock in Crittenden County said that Pope's veto had been "announced in our little town by the discharge of muskets, rifles, fusees, &c."[43]

The *Advocate* charged cynically that Woodruff was an "expert" at "procuring letters approbatory of any measure he espouses," and alleged that he and other Sevier men had been strong advocates of Crittenden's offer

until it was suggested to them, that should the Legislature accede to Crittenden's intended proposition, it would enable Crittenden to free himself from all his [financial] embarrasments [*sic*], and foil those choice, though

[40] "General Assembly," *Gazette,* November 9, 1831; *Arkansas Legislative Journal,* 1831, pp. 314, 316–318. Sevier subsequently presented the memorial to Congress with the statement that "he himself entirely dissented" from "sundry charges of misconduct and mal-administrations [insinuated] against" Governor Pope. "Congressional Summary," *Gazette,* January 18, 1832.

[41] *Arkansas Acts,* 1831, pp. 3–9, 19–29, 37–40, 42–44, 65–66, 67–69, 71–75, 76–79, 80–82, 87–89, 92–95.

[42] "Memorials," *Gazette,* November 16, 1831; *Terr. Papers,* XXI, 400–409, 411–427, 437–438, 451–452. Woodruff complained that the legislature passed so many memorials that he despaired "even of their being listened to."

[43] "Public Sentiment," *Gazette,* November 23, 30, December 7, 1831, January 4, 1832.

evil spirits, in their schemes to sacrifice him, to the malignity of their diabolical passions.[44]

Woodruff replied that the *Advocate's* assertion was, in his case, *"totally destitute of truth."* He had "from the first" believed the object of the majority of the legislature in accepting Crittenden's proposal to be to extricate Crittenden from his financial discomfiture.[45]

In February, 1832, Woodruff reprinted from the *Kentucky Gazette* an editorial by George J. Trotter, Pope's nephew, giving an account of the ten-section bill highly favorable to Pope and uncomplimentary to Crittenden. According to Trotter, "a band of desperadoes headed by Robert Crittenden are clubbed together [in Arkansas], to blackguard and browbeat every man who has sufficient self-respect, to hold himself aloof from *their interests."* They had been trying to "blackguard" Pope out of the Territory ever since his accession to the governorship.[46]

In a letter to the *Advocate* Crittenden responded that it was entirely false to claim that he had been the leader of the majority in the legislature; they were men of "character" and "high intelligence" who had "dared to resist the powers that be." The suggestion of exchanging his house for the ten sections had originated with Acting Governor Fulton in September, 1831. At that time he himself had been unfavorable to the idea, but need of money later changed his mind. Crittenden went on to aver that Superior Court Clerk William Field[47] and Superior Court Judges Cross, Johnson, Eskridge, and Bates had been favorable to his proposal, though all except Bates were friendly to Pope; and that Representative Manly, a vigorous opponent of the offer in the legislature, had, before the meeting of the assembly, also given it his endorsement. In refer-

[44] "The Ten Sections of Land," *Advocate,* November 30, 1831. Crittenden later wrote his brother that his enemies had seized upon his financial "embarrassments" as "a certain means of ascertaining my ruin." Robert Crittenden to John J. Crittenden, May 4, 1834, John J. Crittenden Papers, Duke University Library.

[45] *Gazette,* December 7, 1831.

[46] Editorial in *Kentucky Gazette* (Lexington), January 21, 1832, reprinted in *Arkansas Gazette,* February 15, 1832, and in Crittenden, "To the Public," February 28, 1832, *Advocate,* February 29, 1832. This editorial was an answer to a statement in the *National Journal* that Pope had, by his vetoes, made himself unpopular in Arkansas.

[47] Field had in January, 1832, defeated Crittenden's candidate, Henry L. Biscoe, for the clerkship by a vote of 1,901 to 1,549. See *Gazette,* November 9, December 14, 21, 1831, February 8, 15, 22, 1832; *Advocate,* December 28, 1831, February 1, 15, 1832; Wm. B. Wooddy to Woodruff, December 15, 1831, William E. Woodruff Papers, Arkansas History Commission.

ence to the memorial pertaining to the election of the governor and secretary, Crittenden denied having had anything to do with it. Crittenden believed Pope had not only prompted Trotter's editorial but had also persuaded Woodruff to reprint it.[48]

Crittenden's communication brought replies from Field and Pope. Field admitted having at one time favored Crittenden's proposal, but he had, upon reflection, changed his mind. He now believed that the land would sell for at least $12,000; and that Congress had granted it for "the express purpose" of erecting a "splendid" state house. Ashley's offer to donate six lots worth $3,000 to the Territory on condition that a state house be built upon them should have been accepted by the legislature.[49] When it was rejected, Field had concluded, "as most men did," that Crittenden's friends in the legislature "had determined to make the exchange with him, and him alone—and the result is with the public."[50]

Pope denied any connection with Trotter's editorial. In regard to the memorial, he contended that Brown had, in giving it to him, been complying with a joint rule of both houses. He would have returned it to the house had a committee been sent to him in his capacity as governor. Did not Crittenden know that the message to "John Pope" was to have been followed, "if necessary," by a legislative order for the arrest of "John Pope," and that a *"posse"* was to have been summoned to execute it? Had such action been taken, Pope would have been "constrained" to call out the militia, "read to your friends the Rioting Act," and suppress "the posse, alias mob, by force." Pope intimated that the Crittenden men had hoped he would fall "in the contest" in order that Secretary Fulton might become acting governor and approve the ten-section measure. Pope doubted, however, that Fulton would have obliged them, for he believed Fulton had suggested the exchange to Crittenden "without much reflection or information."[51]

[48] Crittenden, "To the Public," February 28, 1832, *Advocate,* February 29, 1832. For another criticism of Trotter's editorial, see Cassius to Editor, *ibid.,* February 22, 1832.

[49] Bertrand asserted that Ashley had "not even a *shadow of title"* to these lots and did not believe they would bring him an "average [of] $200 a-piece." "Ashley's liberal offer," *ibid.,* April 18, 1832.

[50] Field, "To the Public," March 6, 1832, *Gazette,* March 7, 1832.

[51] Pope, "To Robert Crittenden," *Gazette Supplement,* March 14, 1832. Caldwell had stated in a speech before the council that Fulton "was a strong advocate" of Crittenden's proposal. *Advocate,* October 22, 1831. Fulton himself said later that he had during the meeting of the legislature changed his mind upon learning from members about the existence of valuable land in the southern and western sections of the Territory. Fulton to Secretary of State, July 19, 1833, *Terr. Papers,* XXI, 768–770.

Pope's communication provoked responses from Crittenden, Menefee, and Scott. Crittenden said that Pope's attempt to show him to have been an "active auxiliary" in the matter of the memorial was based on "assumed facts," and that during the meeting of the legislature Pope had decided deliberately to provoke a "quarrel" with him as a means of gaining favor with the Sevier faction.[52] Menefee disavowed an insinuation by Pope that Crittenden had been behind his attack on Woodruff during the recess of the house. And he called Pope's story about a mob to take the memorial from Pope a gross "fabrication."[53] Scott also denied Pope's statements concerning a mob, and claimed that Crittenden had had nothing to do with the "leading measures" passed by the recent legislature.[54]

Woodruff subsequently alleged that Crittenden had planned to locate a part of the ten sections "below" and adjoining Little Rock where 2,000 acres would now command $10,000 and in five years a mere 100 acres of it laid out in town lots would bring even more than that amount.[55] Bertrand replied that Ashley could inform Woodruff that Crittenden would have been unable to locate a single *"foot* of land within four miles of town" because it had all been improved.[56]

During the spring and summer of 1832 Bertrand printed correspondence from persons over the Territory purporting to give public opinion on the ten-section affair. If one might believe these letters, opinion was, presumably in consequence of the communications printed in the *Advocate,* becoming more favorable toward the action of the majority of the legislature.[57] Woodruff, claiming that the correspondence in the *Advocate* had been written *"for effect,"* pub-

[52] Crittenden to Pope, April 21, 1832, *Advocate,* May 2, 1832. See also Crittenden to Pope, March 14, 1832, *ibid.,* March 28, 1832; Pope to Crittenden, April 3, 1832, *Gazette,* April 4, 1832.

[53] Menefee, "To the Citizens of Conway and Hot Spring Counties," March 28, 1832, *Advocate,* April 4, 1832. Noticing that Field had estimated the value of the six lots offered by Ashley to be $3,000, Menefee pointed out that had Crittenden's twelve lots been figured in the estimate of the value of his offer, the estimated worth of Crittenden's property would have been $13,600. Woodruff, however, did not believe Crittenden's lots to be worth over "$20 or $25 a-piece." *Gazette,* April 11, 1832.

[54] Scott to Pope, April 3, 1832, *Advocate,* April 11, 1832. For another defense of the majority of the legislature in passing the ten-section bill, see Caldwell, "To the Public," March 20, 1832, *ibid.,* March 21, 1832.

[55] *Gazette,* April 18, 1832.

[56] *Advocate,* April 25, 1832. Bertrand alleged that Ball's securities, whom Ball's proposal had been designed to benefit, had planned not only to locate an improved tract of land "below" Little Rock but also "every valuable *improvement* in Washington County."

[57] See *ibid.,* April 18, 25, May 2, 30, July 11, 1832.

lished communications from various persons in the Territory to show that Pope's veto was still popular.[58]

In April, 1832, Delegate Sevier submitted to Congress a petition signed by 110 Arkansans, including Woodruff, William Field, Chester Ashley, Benjamin Johnson, and William McK. Ball, complaining of the failure of the territorial legislature to make any disposition of the ten sections and asking that Congress authorize the governor to select the land.[59] Presumably in compliance with this petition, Congress passed a measure placing the disposal of the ten sections in the hands of the governor.[60]

Governor Pope gave notice in October that the ten sections, or whatever part remained unsold in February, 1833, would then be offered for sale to the highest bidder at a minimum price of $5.00 an acre with six per cent off for cash and a reduction of $1,000 to anyone buying five sections. Settlers living on lands selected to be a part of the donation would have until the third Monday in January, 1833, the opportunity of buying at the minimum price the land on which they resided.[61] As it turned out, the governor had by January sold over eight of the ten sections—five for $15,000 and the rest at $5.00 an acre—and decided not to hold a public sale of the remaining land.[62] What Pope's critics thought of his conduct will be considered in the next chapter.

In August, 1832, the *Advocate,* edited temporarily by Dr. Matthew Cunningham,[63] Bertrand's step-father, called President Jackson's recent veto of the bill to recharter the National Bank of the United States "high-handed" because it ran counter to "the will of a large majority of the representatives of the people."[64] Forthwith Woodruff asserted that the *Advocate* had "thrown off" its "mask" and come out openly against Jackson.[65] This Cunningham denied, pointing out that he had not said the veto was "unjust" or "impolitic." The Jackson administration had "our approbation in its general course," though some of its acts were objectionable. Only "such

---

[58] See *Gazette,* May 9, June 20, July 4, August 1, 1832.
[59] *Terr. Papers,* XXI, 493–494; *House Journal,* 22 Cong., 1 sess., 560, 568, 597.
[60] Act approved July 4, 1832, 4 *U.S. Stat. at L.* (1846), 563.
[61] Executive Proclamation, October 30, 1832, *Gazette,* October 31, 1832.
[62] "The Ten Sections," *ibid.,* January 23, 1833.
[63] Editor Bertrand left Little Rock in July, 1832, to travel over parts of the Territory for his health, and did not return until late September. Editor, "To the Patrons of the Advocate," *Advocate,* July 18, 1832, October 3, 1832; *Gazette,* October 3, 1832.
[64] "The President's Veto," *Advocate,* August 15, 1832.
[65] "The Mask Thrown Off," *Gazette,* August 22, 1832.

soulless reptiles" as Woodruff applauded "measures which in their hearts they execrate, for the purpose of *begging* patronage."[66] Woodruff accused "old Matthew" of crawfishing without even offering " 'King's excuse.' "[67]

Woodruff announced in December that President Jackson had won reelection to a second term "by a triumphant majority, over the combined influence of Clayites, high-toned Tariffites, Calhounites, Nullifiers, Anti-masons, Money-changers, and the *Apostate Editors of the Arkansas Advocate.*" So confident had the Crittenden men been of a Clay victory that they had thrown *"off the mask"* in favor of Clay. The Crittendenites no longer had sufficient support in Arkansas to make henceforth "even a respectable show." What stand they would now take it was "difficult to determine."[68]

Other squabbling in 1832 occurred between the Sevier and Crittenden factions over whether Sevier had been responsible for Bates's not being reappointed to a second term on the superior court. The Sevier men attributed his removal to his intemperance, while the Crittendenites ascribed it to his opposition to Sevier in the election of 1831.[69]

Sevier's enemies accused him of gambling, intemperance, abusing the franking privilege, and leaving Washington without paying his debts.[70] Sevier denied he had left Washington "dodging" his creditors. Woodruff denied that Sevier was intemperate,[71] and also denied an assertion by the *Advocate* that Sevier, Ashley, and Fulton managed and edited the *Gazette.*[72]

In looking back upon the events of 1831 and 1832 one surmises that both factions had at the outset of the legislative session favored the exchange of the ten sections for Crittenden's house. The Sevier faction came, however, to believe that the Territory had more to

[66] *Advocate,* August 29, 1832. Cunningham later stated that he objected to "certain doctrines" in the veto message. *Ibid.,* September 19, 1832.

[67] "Crawfishing—Or Backing Out," *Gazette,* September 5, 1832. For other exchanges relative to the sincerity of the *Advocate's* Jacksonianism, see *Gazette,* September 26, October 24, 1832; *Advocate,* October 17, 24, 1832.

[68] "The Presidential Election," *Gazette,* December 12, 1832.

[69] See *Terr. Papers,* XXI, 474, note 35; *Advocate,* April 18, July 4, 18, August 1, September 19, 1832; *Gazette,* April 25, June 27, July 18, August 15, September 26, 1832. Bates was replaced by Charles S. Bibb of Kentucky, son of Senator George M. Bibb. Charles died of cholera less than five months after taking office, and was succeeded by Alexander M. Clayton of Tennessee. *Gazette,* November 7, 1832; *Advocate,* November 7, 1832; *Terr. Papers,* XXI, 578–579.

[70] See *Advocate,* January 25, February 8, 29, August 22, October 3, 1832.

[71] See *Gazette,* May 2, September 5, October 3, 10, 31, 1832.

[72] *Advocate,* October 10, 17, 31, 1832; *Gazette,* October 24, 1832.

gain by selling the land and building a state house. The Crittenden men responded by a resolute support of the proposed exchange.[73] Governor Pope's veto of the bill made his alliance with the Sevier faction more secure, and his success in selling a part of the ten sections by January, 1833, at an amount far above the government price of public land seemed to vindicate not only his veto but also the action of the members of the legislature who had steadfastly opposed the bill. Jackson's defeat of Henry Clay in the presidential election of 1832 was another blow to the Crittendenites. The events of 1831 and 1832 clearly left the Crittenden faction weaker than ever before.

[73] Secretary Fulton later said that they had been "blinded . . . by prejudice . . . and heated by opposition." He did not believe, as some of the Sevier men charged, that they had been "corrupted." Fulton to Secretary of State, July 19, 1833, *Terr. Papers,* XXI, 769.

CHAPTER TEN

The Election of 1833

THOUGH Bertrand intimated in August, 1832, that Benjamin Desha would again be a candidate for Congress in the forthcoming election,[1] Desha declined to run.[2] Late that year the *Advocate* announced that a large number of citizens of Crawford County had recently met and requested Crittenden to become a candidate.[3] In March, 1833, Crittenden actually gave notice that he would be a candidate. The same day Sevier announced that he would seek a fourth term.[4]

Crittenden's public statement to the freemen of Arkansas called attention to his long service as territorial secretary. He promised to work for internal improvements and for a preemption law giving each settler the right to enter forty acres of land. He favored statehood when the Territory had the requisite population, but would take no action on the matter until a majority of the people requested him to. He had participated in "the strifes and contests of the day . . . with reluctance, and when I thought" that only by so doing "I could protect my rights as a man, or my character as a gentleman." The "party feuds and conflicts which have since [Governor Izard's administration] distracted us at home, and sunk us in the estimation of the good and virtuous abroad" he attributed to Woodruff without mentioning his name. In an obvious dig at Sevier, he declared that he had no relatives in Arkansas to "sustain me or re-

[1] Bertrand to Editor, August 6, 1832, *Arkansas Advocate* (Little Rock), August 22, 1832.

[2] *Arkansas Gazette* (Little Rock), December 12, 1832.

[3] "Movements of the People," *Advocate,* December 12, 1832. See also "Public Sentiment," *Gazette,* January 2, 1833. According to Woodruff, the Crittenden movement was gotten up by his friends after he said that he would run if "his *party*" made "a *public call* on him." "A Trap to Catch Gulls," *ibid.,* December 12, 1832. See also *ibid.,* December 19, 1832.

[4] *Gazette,* March 27, 1833; *Advocate,* March 27, 1833.

ceive office at my hands—no powerful family combination is around
me to yield me support, and in requital, receive the crumbs of the
Treasury—my dependence is and shall remain solely upon the
people . . ."[5]

Sevier's circular to the people referred to his many accomplishments since his first election to Congress. Recently he had secured
(1) two new land offices; (2) a separate surveyor general's office;[6]
and (3) appropriations for removing snags from the Arkansas, surveying the White and St. Francis Rivers, completing a road from
Jackson to Washington, and finishing repairs on the Memphis–
Little Rock road. He had been responsible for a law extending the
suffrage to all free white adult males who had resided six months in
Arkansas, and for an act granting one thousand acres of land adjoining Little Rock to be selected by the governor for use in erecting
a territorial court house and jail. He had obtained passage of a number of other measures and had worked for several that had failed
through no fault of his own. He would continue pursuing Henry W.
Conway's "example" of looking after the people's interests even if
"by doing so, my life shall terminate as tragically as his."[7]

The campaign was preceded by an attempt on the part of William
Cummins, a Pulaski County attorney and former Kentuckian,[8] to
have Superior Court Judge Benjamin Johnson, Sevier's father-in-law,
impeached. In October, 1832, Cummins had informed Johnson in
the *Advocate* that he intended preferring to the President and Senate
charges of misconduct against him.[9] According to Cummins, Johnson

[5] Crittenden, "To the Freemen of Arkansas," April 6, 1833, *Advocate*, April 17,
1833; *Gazette*, April 24, 1833.

[6] Sevier's cousin, James S. Conway, had been made surveyor general. Clarence E.
Carter, ed., *Territorial Papers of the United States*, Vol. XXI, *Arkansas Territory, 1829–
1836* (Washington, 1954), 514–515.

[7] Sevier, "To the Citizens of Arkansas," March 25, 1833, *Gazette*, April 3, 1833. A
charge by Bertrand that Sevier's "flaming Address" was the production of Pope and
Ashley was emphatically denied by Woodruff. "The Circular," *Advocate*, April 3, 17,
1833; *Gazette*, April 10, 24, 1833.

[8] Fay Hempstead, *A Pictorial History of Arkansas* (St. Louis, 1890), 769–770.
Cummins, who had come to Arkansas in 1824, was now thirty-two years old.

[9] Cummins to Johnson, *Advocate*, October 24, 1832; *Terr. Papers*, XXI, 632–638.
Cummins had preferred charges of misconduct against Johnson in the winter of 1828–
1829, but because he had not known the proper "method of proceeding" he had submitted no evidence to sustain them. The charges had been referred to Superior Court
Judge William Trimble, a Crittenden supporter, who had testified that Johnson was
"a gentleman of strict honor and integrity, and withal an able, impartial and popular
Judge." Sevier to Editor, *Advocate*, October 31, 1832. Trimble refused in 1832–1833
to testify for either Johnson or Cummins. Trimble to Editor, October 29, 1832, *ibid.*,
November 14, 1832; *Gazette*, November 14, 1832; Cummins to Editor, November 19,
1832, *Advocate*, November 28, 1832; *Gazette*, November 28, 1832; Trimble to Editor,
December 31, 1832; *Advocate*, January 2, 1833.

was guilty of (1) showing "strong partiality" toward the offenders in a certain case before the Pulaski circuit court in 1829, (2) threatening to cut the throat of a citizen of Pulaski County at the polls in 1829, (3) drinking excessively on the bench, (4) giving on occasion an opinion in court before the submission of cause, (5) rendering "inconsistent, vascillating [*sic*], and contradictory" decisions, (6) inducing a fellow judge who was in an "unguarded situation" to bet at faro "in order to win his money, and divide it between yourself and the [faro] bank," (7) violating in a case tried in the Jefferson circuit court a "decision of the Superior Court, and the laws you were bound to administer," and (8) failing to punish a man who twice attempted to kill another on the porch of the Pulaski circuit court over which Johnson was presiding.

In January, 1833, Cummins submitted, through an agent, Egbert Harris, the charges with supporting testimony in the form of an impeachment to the Speaker of the House of Representatives.[10] When the Speaker brought the matter before the House on January 14, Delegate Sevier moved that the charges and testimony be referred to the Judiciary Committee and made a long, eloquent speech defending "my constituent, my relative and friend" who had for many years served as "a mere *Territorial* Judge." He endeavored to refute or explain the charges against Johnson and offered supporting statements by Governor Pope, Secretary Fulton, Superior Court Judges Edward Cross and Thomas P. Eskridge, District Attorney Samuel C. Roane, and others.[11] According to Sevier, several of Cummins's fourteen witnesses—they included Absalom Fowler, O. V. Howell, and Andrew Scott—had been guilty of various things for which they criticized Johnson, and only one of them was a "worthy" and truthful man. The charges, said Sevier, "would never have found their way to this House, if it were not that Judge Johnson is my relative, and that that relative is the Delegate from Arkansas." The effort "to transfer our local feuds to this Hall for settlement" was intended "purely for political effect" in Arkansas. He was expected to "endeavor to defeat this investigation," but instead he welcomed it.[12]

---

[10] See *Terr. Papers*, XXI, 593–638.

[11] Many letters favorable to Johnson had been sent during the fall and winter from Johnson's friends in Arkansas to the President or Sevier. See *ibid.*, 641–668.

[12] "Mr. Sevier's Speech," *Gazette*, February 27, 1833; *Advocate*, March 6, 1833; *House Journal*, 22 Cong., 2 sess., 179. Woodruff reprinted Sevier's speech from the *National Intelligencer* (see *Gazette*, February 20, 1833), and Bertrand probably republished it from the *Gazette*. It did not appear in *Register of Debates*.

On February 8 the Judiciary Committee reported that it doubted whether a territorial judge was "a proper subject of trial by impeachment" but had nevertheless examined the testimony offered for and against the charges and decided in favor of Johnson. The House disposed of the matter by laying the report upon the table.[13]

In a public letter, dated March 25, Cummins denied that he and his witnesses had entertained any motive other than "a hope that some reform of the gross abuses practised by Judge Johnson, in his courts, and which extended their effects to the whole community, could be effected by his removal." He had been compelled to bring charges against Johnson in the House of Representatives because Johnson's renomination for a fourth term had been "hurried" through the Senate nearly two months before his commission expired and before the testimony against him could reach Washington.[14]

In May "Jaw-Bone" reported in the *Gazette* that Cummins had admitted having earlier written a friend in Hempstead County that Johnson's removal would have "great political effect." "Jaw-Bone" claimed that Crittenden had been behind Cummins's attempt to have Johnson impeached and averred that on the occasion of Cummins's "confession" Crittenden was so "thunderstruck" that his face went through a rapid change of colors.[15]

Cummins acknowledged in the *Advocate* having stated in a letter that the Johnson matter would affect the election, but denied that he had preferred charges merely "to injure Sevier's election." "Jaw-Bone's" communication was designed "to divert the public attention from the grossly improper conduct of A. H. Sevier" in defending Johnson in the House of Representatives.[16]

Cummins subsequently noticed that Sevier had not answered his communication of March 25. Sevier's speech in Congress had, he said, "grossly" slandered a number of Arkansans for "no excuse or reason" except the "*pecuniary* effect upon the pocket of his friend

---

[13] "Case of Judge Johnson," *Gazette*, March 20, 1833; "Congressional," *Advocate*, March 20, 1833; Committee Report, *Terr. Papers*, XXI, 669–671; *House Journal*, 22 Cong., 2 sess., 290.

[14] Cummins to Editor, March 25, 1833, *Advocate*, March 27, 1833. Johnson was nominated December 11, 1832, and confirmed the next day. His commission expired January 23, 1833. *Terr. Papers*, Vol. XX, *Arkansas Territory, 1825–1829* (Washington, 1954), 825, XXI, 578, note 18.

[15] Jaw-Bone, "Sevier, Crittenden, and Cummins," *Gazette*, May 22, 1833. Lafayette believed Governor Pope to be "Jaw-Bone." "No. III," *Advocate*, May 22, 1833.

[16] Cummins to Editor, *ibid.*, June 12, 1833.

and relation Judge Johnson."[17] No one in Arkansas had been "bold enough" to disavow the charges Cummins had preferred; even Sevier in Congress "could only intimate" that they were false. It was completely untrue that, as Sevier men had asserted, Cummins had brought charges "from personal dislike or hate, in me towards Sevier."[18]

Sevier responded late in July to Cummins's prodding. He denied any "unnecessary haste" in Johnson's renomination and confirmation. They had been obtained early in the session in order that his commission might have ample time to reach him before the expiration of his term, thus preventing the possibility of a temporary vacancy on the bench. President Jackson, who had received Cummins's charges (though evidently not the testimony)[19] before nominating Johnson, considered them to be "futile, contemptible, and unworthy of notice." Sevier denied that he had slandered Arkansans or that he had had a "pecuniary" motive in defending Johnson. He believed that Cummins as a candidate for the territorial house and security for a large bet on the outcome of the congressional election had his own reasons for behaving as he did, but that his main purpose was to promote the election of "his master," Robert Crittenden.[20]

In bringing charges against Johnson, Cummins may have been prompted by a sincere desire to correct what he and others considered to be misconduct on the part of the judge, but the fact that the charges and testimony had not been submitted at the previous Congress, when no election was approaching, strongly suggests that Cummins hoped his action might injure Sevier's chances in the election of 1833. That the impeachment attempt was a partisan affair may also be evidenced by the fact that, in as far as political affilia-

[17] O. V. Howell, one of Cummins's witnesses, took exception to what Sevier said about him. *Advocate,* April 10, May 15, July 17, 1833; *Gazette,* May 1, 1833. So also did Egbert Harris, whom Sevier had called a "hired menial" and a "Swiss carrier." *Gazette,* March 13, 1833; *Advocate,* March 13, 20, 1833.

[18] Cummins to Editor, *Advocate,* July 17, 1833.

[19] Cummins doubted whether Jackson or the Senate had seen the charges, much less the testimony. The testimony, which was carried to Washington by Secretary Fulton, arrived there nearly a month after Johnson's renomination had been confirmed. The charges had been sent several weeks earlier. Cummins to Editor, July 23, 1833, *ibid.,* July 24, 1833. There is no evidence in *Senate Executive Journal,* IV (December 11, 12, 1832), 280, 286, that the Senate at the time of Johnson's confirmation was aware of Cummins's charges.

[20] Sevier to Editor, July 20, 27, 1833, *Gazette,* July 31, 1833. See also Cummins to Editor, July 23, 1833, *Advocate,* July 24, 1833; Cummins, "To the Voters of Pulaski County," August 1, 1833, *ibid.,* August 7, 1833.

tions can be determined, Cummins's witnesses seem to have been Crittenden partisans while Johnson's defenders were supporters of Sevier.[21]

Undoubtedly the most important issue of the campaign was Governor Pope's handling of the ten-section grant for a state house. As early as February, 1833, Bertrand had complained that Pope was locating ten-section claims on improvements. Settlers near the Mississippi had by removing landmarks and erasing "from the corner trees, the blazes and brands made by the public Surveyors," attempted to prevent speculators from "obtaining a knowledge of the quarter sections on which improvements were made, until the lands should be in the market." But Pope was authorizing purchasers of ten-section land "to re-survey the public domain; and by this measure, [they] ascertain the metes and bounds of any improvement" they "may wish to possess." Sevier should be held responsible for "the iniquity of every transaction" of this sort.[22]

In May a resident of Arkansas County reported in the *Advocate* that Pope had located upon some improvements in neighboring Chicot County.[23] Benjamin L. Miles of Chicot County admitted in the *Gazette* that "some *small* and *late improvements* have been entered," but he had "not heard of any to which any law of Congress has yet extended the right of Pre-emption."[24] Miles evidently meant to say that the improvements in question had been made since the expiration of the time allowed to enter preemptions under the acts of 1830 and 1832.[25]

In early June William Cummins published in the *Advocate* a letter from Elijah Hayward, Commissioner of the General Land Office, to Register Bernard Smith at Little Rock, stating that two of Pope's locations under the law granting to the Territory one thousand acres adjoining Little Rock for use in building a court house and jail were

[21] For the names of Cummins's witnesses, see James Woodson Bates to Cummins, December 11, 1832, *Terr. Papers*, XXI, 631, and for names of men who testified for Johnson, see *ibid.*, 641–668.

[22] *Advocate*, February 27, 1833. See also Virgil to Editor, *Gazette*, May 29, 1833. Noticing "rumors" that he had committed outrages against poor settlers, Pope declared in April that he had no "individual interest" in locating the ten sections and promised to redress the "grievances" of anyone whom he had "wronged." Pope, "To the People of Arkansas," April 8, 1833, *ibid.*, April 10, 1833.

[23] "Editor's Correspondence," *Advocate*, May 8, 1833. See also "The Ten Sections," *ibid.*, May 15, 1833.

[24] "The Location of the Ten Sections on Improvements," *Gazette*, May 15, 1833; Miles, "To the Public," May 24, 1832[3], *ibid.*, June 5, 1833.

[25] See 4 *U.S. Stat. at L.* (1846), 420–421, 503, 603; Henry Ford White, "The Economic and Social Development of Arkansas Prior to 1836" (unpublished Ph.D. dissertation, University of Texas, 1931), 187–189.

invalid because they conflicted with preemption claims proved under the act of May 29, 1830.[26] Cummins believed the Commissioner's decision with respect to the thousand-acre claims applied "with equal force to locations made by virtue of the *Ten Section Claims.*" Sevier had succeeded in having the disposal of the ten sections placed under Pope's supervision because Sevier had known the territorial legislature would object to locating upon improvements and wished to enable himself, Pope, and others to make a speculation.[27]

"Jaw-Bone" answered in the *Gazette* that Pope considered that the preemption claims upon which he had located thousand-acre claims were invalid. Cummins was trying to make Pope's acts "odious and unpopular with the people; and then by a legerdemain in which his partizan coadjutors profess great skill, he so shuffles his cards as to turn up Mr. Sevier as the prime mover of every act of Gov. Pope which he wishes the people to view."[28]

Cummins also published a letter from the Commissioner to Pope advising the governor that Secretary of the Treasury Louis McLane had ruled that Pope did not possess authority to locate ten-section claims, as Pope had done in one instance, on fractions of quarter-sections.[29] "Duane" did not agree with McLane's opinion and conjectured that it would be reversed by the new Secretary of the Treasury, William J. Duane.[30]

Bertrand printed on June 12 letters from Daniel W. Hampton, Henry Latting, John T. White, and James P. Collinsworth to William H. Gaines complaining that Silas Craig, who had purchased and selected five sections of the ten-section donation in Chicot County,[31] had located upon their improvements.[32] A reply signed by the "most respectable" men in Chicot County, published

[26] Hayward to Smith, May 7, 1833, *Advocate,* June 5, 1833; 4 *U.S. Stat. at L.* (1846), 420–421.

[27] "Important to Pre-emption claimants," *Advocate,* June 5, 1833. See also Watchman of the Neighborhood and O'Connell to Editor, *ibid.,* June 19, 1833.

[28] "Jaw-Bone's Reply to Wm. Cummins' Publication," *Gazette,* June 12, 1833. Pope had located upon three preemption claims which he thought invalid. See Pope to Secretary of Treasury, July 8, 1833, *Terr. Papers,* XXI, 754–755.

[29] Hayward to Pope, March 2, 1833, *Advocate,* June 5, 1833. See also Hayward to Secretary of Treasury, April 10, 1833, and to Pope, May 2, 20, 1833, *Terr. Papers,* XXI, 708–709, 712–713, 728.

[30] Duane to Editor, *Gazette,* June 12, 1833.

[31] "The Locations of the Ten Sections on Improvements," *ibid.,* May 15, 1833. Pope evidently allowed the purchasers of ten-section land to select, subject to his approval, the land they desired.

[32] "Location of the Ten Sections on Improvements," *Advocate,* June 12, 1833. See also Gaines to Bertrand, May 30, 1833, *ibid.,* June 26, 1833; "Mr. Wm. H. Gaines, of Ky.," *Gazette,* July 10, 1833; "Mr. Wm. H. Gaines—Again," *ibid.,* July 24, 1833.

in the *Gazette,* averred that none of the four men resided on their improvements.[33]

Governor Pope had left Arkansas early in May for his usual summer vacation in Kentucky.[34] In July he wrote from Shelbyville that he had in selecting the ten sections

located no improvements, without the consent, and on special application of the owner, except with regard to some small improvements, which it is said are included within the location of Silas Craig, worth perhaps ten dollars per acre. They had no right of pre-emption, no right to the land—and their only possible or colorable claim is to an equivalent for the labor expended. This I am persuaded Craig has paid or offered to do; what injury then has been done?

Notwithstanding the "machinations" of "the enemies of the Territory," Pope expected his ten-section locations and at least 840 acres of his locations under the thousand-acre grant to be "maintained."[35] He would have more to say about his ten-section and thousand-acre locations during the meeting of the legislature.

Pope's selection of a site for a state house between "the steam-mill and Mr. [Joseph] Henderson's block" was also criticized during the campaign.[36] Pope explained before leaving for Kentucky that a better site would have taken too much money from the building fund and that two other possible sites had possessed certain disadvantages.[37] The site chosen was in

a commanding situation, on the river, with a street on every side, and the view from the river, or the town, can never be obscured by other buildings. It is equal, if not superior, to any place on the river. I have procured an indisputable title.[38]

[33] "Location of the Ten Sections," *Gazette,* July 24, 1833. In connection with the White claim, see " 'Much Ado About Nothing!,' " *ibid.,* June 15, 1833; *Advocate,* June 12, 1833.

[34] *Gazette,* May 8, 1833.

[35] "Gov. Pope, On the Ten Sections, and 1000 Acre Donation," *ibid.,* July 31, 1833. Pope had been unable to locate the entire thousand-acre grant on lands adjoining Little Rock to the east and had consequently located 160 acres south of town upon a New Madrid claim. See Pope to Secretary of Treasury, July 8, 1833, *Terr. Papers,* XXI, 750.

[36] "Lafayette" complained that Pope had purchased a site when the Territory already owned one "in a much more eligible situation" meaning presumably the site on which the capitol had been since 1821. "Lafayette" intimated that Pope's motive lay in the fact that the old site was "near *Crittenden's,*" the new one, near property belonging to Chester Ashley. Lafayette to Pope, "No. III," *Advocate,* May 22, 1833.

[37] One of them—Ashley's block of lots—was "too remote from the business-part of town," while the title to the other—the square on which the old state house stood—was not clear.

[38] Pope related later that Ashley, David G. Eller, and William Russell had given a part of the site, and that he had purchased the remainder from Russell for $800, half of which was advanced by Ashley, Henderson, Richard C. Byrd, Woodruff, and Sevier. "The State-house Fund," *Gazette,* November 20, 1833. Some years later it turned out

Pope stated further that he had retained George Weigart, a "sober, steady, and skilful" architect from Kentucky, to plan and supervise the building of the state house, and that laborers were already at work on the foundation.[39] During his sojourn to Kentucky, Pope designated Chester Ashley his agent to supervise the state house fund.

Presently several Crittendenites asserted in the *Advocate* that work on the state house had stopped owing to lack of funds.[40] Bertrand wondered if the ten-section fund had not "been *divided* among hands, and the people left to *whistle* for a State-house."[41] Woodruff promptly denied that work had been arrested and asserted that forty to sixty hands and six or eight teams were "constantly at work on and about it." Crittenden's friends were trying to secure Crittenden's election by "fabricating the most idle and palpable falsehoods, and disseminating them among the People, under the faint hope of working the ruin of Col. Sevier."[42] The Crittenden men continued to maintain the truth of their allegations. Bertrand printed letters of John H. Cocke and B. W. Lee, who lived near the site, saying that work had been halted for several weeks. According to Bertrand, Ashley himself had given lack of funds as the reason for the cessation of operations.[43] Ashley was, another Crittenden man averred, using "for his own *private purposes*" brick that had been made for the state house walls.[44] Woodruff flatly denied the truth of these assertions as well as of "insinuations" that he, Pope, Ashley, Sevier, and others had divided the state house funds among themselves. He admitted, however, that work on the foundation had ceased owing to a late flood which had prevented the masons from obtaining a supply of sand from bars in the Arkansas. Though the foundations of the main building and one of the wings had been completed, brick could not be laid until lum-

that Pope was totally wrong in thinking he had obtained an unquestionable title. See Myra McAlmont Vaughan, "A History of the Old State House," *Publications of the Arkansas Historical Association,* Vol. III (Fayetteville, 1911), 254–255.

[39] Pope, "To the People of Arkansas," April 8, 1833, *Gazette,* April 10, 1833. See also "The State-house Fund," *ibid.,* November 20, 1833. Pope's first choice for an architect had been Gideon Shryock who had designed Kentucky's capitol. Though Shryock declined the offer he prepared a plan for Arkansas' state house which Pope and Weigart "abridged."

[40] Lafayette and O'Connell to Pope, *Advocate,* June 19, 1833.

[41] "Just As We Expected," *ibid.,* June 26, 1833.

[42] "The State-House," *Gazette,* June 26, 1833; "The State-House-Not Stopped," *ibid.,* July 3, 1833.

[43] "The Magnificent State-house," *Advocate,* July 3, 1833; "The State-House—Again," *ibid.,* July 10, 1833.

[44] W, "To the Independent Voters of Arkansas," *ibid.,* July 3, 1833.

ber with which to build frames arrived. In the meantime, the hands had been making brick, procuring limestone, and cutting wood. In support of his story, Woodruff printed a letter from Weigart saying that progress on the state house had not stopped, and one from Thorn and Cook, contractors for the stone and brick work, stating that the hands were making brick.[45]

Bertrand responded that no one had said the hands were not making brick, only that progress on the building itself had been discontinued. Thorn and Cook could be selling the brick they were making. Bertrand then printed a certificate with forty-eight signatures asserting that no stone or brick work had been done on the state house for nearly a month.[46]

Woodruff could not say positively that the bricks Thorn and Cook were making would be used in the state house, but they, who were "honest" and "industrious" men, had so asserted. The Gazette carried a statement signed by over one hundred persons to the effect that work was progressing on the state house and money was not wanting.[47] Bertrand believed Ashley had written the statement and obtained signatures through "deception and misrepresentation."[48]

About a week before the election Bertrand promised to "show, in the course of a week or two, that we had good authority for saying that the State-house had *stopped for want of funds.*"[49] But his promise was not carried out, and the furor over the building of the state house subsided after the election. Clearly it had been a device whereby the Crittenden men sought to place the Sevier faction in a bad light.

According to correspondents in the newspapers, Crittenden's main attack in his stump speeches was directed against Governor Pope.[50] Pope himself later stated that he "was [in 1833] made the burthen of the electioneering song, not only in the opposition paper, but [also on] every stump in the country, and the whole artillery of

---

[45] "The State-House—again," *Gazette,* July 10, 1833. See also "The State-house—once more," *ibid.,* July 17, 1833.

[46] "The State-house—again," *Advocate,* July 17, 1833.

[47] "Another Certificate," "The State-house—not stopped," *Gazette,* July 24, 1833.

[48] "The State-House," *Advocate,* July 24, 1833.

[49] "The brick-Yard," *ibid.,* July 31, 1833.

[50] See Jaw-Bone to Robert Crittenden, *Gazette,* April 17, 1833; *ibid.,* June 5, 1833; Republican, "To the Citizens of Arkansas Territory," *ibid.,* July 3, 1833; A Looker-On, " 'The Campaign Opened,' " *Advocate,* March 27, 1833. Crittenden also assailed Woodruff and Ashley.

the opposition, was levelled at me."[51] Though Crittenden seems to have assailed Pope mainly for his part in the management of the ten-section grant, he also criticized him for letting privately to personal and political friends a lucrative contract for repair of the Memphis–Little Rock road.[52]

Crittenden's attack led two Sevier men to conjecture that Crittenden was not campaigning to win election as delegate but to destroy Pope's popularity and thereby remove Pope as a future opponent for a seat in the United States Senate.[53] But Woodruff reported Crittenden himself as saying in essence during a speech in Little Rock that "his object in opposing Col. Sevier was not so much for the *honor* of a seat in Congress, as to *prove* to the world that he had been calumniated and slandered, and that the People do not believe him to be as bad a man as he has been represented."[54] One infers from this statement, if true, that Crittenden wished the people to elect him delegate as a means of vindicating his conduct in the ten-section controversy of 1831–1832.

Sevier's supporters argued during the campaign that Crittenden's attachment to Clayism in national politics would prevent him from being a successful delegate.[55] One Crittenden supporter maintained that the national politics of the candidates made no difference in "our local politics,"[56] and another averred that the anti-Jackson dele-

---

[51] Pope, "To the Public," September 23, 1834, *Terr. Papers,* XXI, 986. This address was in *Political Intelligencer* (Little Rock), September 26, 1834, of which no file is known.

[52] "Election for Delegate," *Advocate,* April 17, 1833; *ibid.,* May 22, 1833; "The Location of the Ten Sections on Improvements," *Gazette,* May 15, 1833; "Public Sentiment," *ibid.,* April 17, 1833. For additional information on Pope's management of the fund for repair of the Memphis–Little Rock road, see *Advocate,* November 28, December 19, 1832, January 23, 30, February 6, 13, April 17, May 8, 1833; *Gazette,* December 5, 1832, January 16, February 6, April 24, 1833.

[53] A Looker On, [not in Venice, but] in Arkansas, "No. I. To Robert Crittenden, Esquire," *Gazette,* April 3, 1833; Jaw-Bone, "No. II. To Robert Crittenden, Esquire," *ibid.,* April 17, 1833.

[54] *Ibid.,* May 15, 1833. A citizen of Washington County reported Crittenden's saying there that he did not expect to win in 1833 but was looking ahead to 1835. "Public Sentiment," *ibid.,* July 10, 1833.

[55] "Public Sentiment," *ibid.,* July 10, 1833; "A Looker-On, [not in Venice, but] in Arkansas, "No. I. To Robert Crittenden, Esquire," *ibid.,* April 3, 1833; Republican, "To the Citizens of Arkansas Territory," *ibid.,* July 3, 1833. Hiram A. Whittington, a zealous Sevier man, believed Arkansans were interested in "men and not measures" and that they cared "very little" about a candidate's national politics. Hiram A. Whittington to Granville Whittington, August 3, 1833, in Margaret Smith Ross, ed., "Letters of Hiram Abiff Whittington, 1827–1834," *Pulaski County Historical Society Bulletin,* No. 3 (December, 1956), 39–40.

[56] Capitol Hill, "No. I," *Advocate,* April 24, 1833.

gate from Florida Territory had accomplished much more for his constituents than Sevier had.[57] A citizen of Washington County recalled that Sevier had favored William H. Crawford of Georgia over Jackson in the presidential election of 1824 and asserted that Sevier's present advisers, Woodruff, Ashley, "and others," were, despite their Jacksonian professions, actually Clay men in principle.[58]

Crittenden was also accused of being "an aristocrat of the deepest dye" whose "principles" and "example" were "dangerous."[59] Bertrand responded by representing Crittenden as the candidate of the common people and Sevier as the candidate of the officeholders.[60]

A Sevier man blamed Crittenden for "feuds and broils in keeping our Territory in a continual state of warfare" and for causing "either directly or indirectly" all the duels that had occurred in Arkansas.[61] Crittenden himself commented near the end of the campaign that "in the distant parts of the Territory" he had found "the most absurd calumnies circulating" in relation to his duel with Conway.

I was charged with having my clothes made impenetrable to a ball—with having shot him after he had missed me, and was in my power—and in one neighborhood, I was assailed for having followed him to Kentucky and there killed him, because he had [in 1827] beat *me* for Congress. These stories were circulated among the new emigrants, and believed . . .

Crittenden denied a report that he had said on the stump that Conway had been the challenger. Rather, he had challenged Conway, but he had done so only because Conway gave him no alternative "between absolute dishonor and a conflict."[62]

James Woodson Bates's support of Crittenden brought from a Sevier man a reminder to the people of what Bates had said against Crittenden in 1827. But Crittenden would join "Old Nick himself to accomplish his purposes," and Bates on his part was no doubt moved by "One of the currents so common in politics."[63]

---

[57] Looker-On, "Information for the People," *ibid.*, May 1, 1833; "The Indefatigable Delegate," *ibid.*, May 8, 1833.

[58] "Editor's Correspondence," *ibid.*, May 1, 1833. See also A Voter to Editor, May 19, 1833, *ibid.*, May 29, 1833.

[59] One of the People, "To the Voters of Arkansas.—No. III," *Gazette*, June 12, 1833.

[60] *Advocate*, July 3, 1833.

[61] Many Voters, "To the Citizens of Arkansas," *Gazette*, July 10, 1833.

[62] Crittenden, "To the People of Arkansas," July 23, 1833, *Advocate*, July 24, 1833; "Public Sentiment," *Gazette*, July 17, 1833; "Review of 'Public Sentiment,'" *Advocate*, April 24, 1833.

[63] "Judge Bates' Opinion of Mr. Crittenden," *Gazette*, May 15, 1833. Bates's return to the Crittenden camp may have been a consequence of the Noland-Crittenden

Crittenden was criticized for having broken off relations with Dr. William P. Reyburn and the Reverend William W. Stevenson, a Presbyterian minister, because they had voted for Sevier in 1831.[64] He replied that their voting for Sevier amounted to a betrayal of friendship, both having professed to him before the election that they were friendly to Sevier's opponent, Desha.[65] A citizen of Washington County believed Crittenden's attitude toward Stevenson, who was popular in that county, would hurt Crittenden in the election.[66]

Crittenden was also accused of having speculated in Spanish Bowie and Lovely's Purchase claims.[67] He denied speculation in Lovely claims, and one of his friends noticed that in the matter of the Bowie claims no one had ever responded to a challenge by Crittenden to investigate his conduct.[68]

The fact that Desha had lost his place as receiver at Little Rock entered the campaign when Woodruff reported that Crittenden had stated that Sevier had caused Desha's removal. Actually Desha had been removed because he had defaulted for $6,434.62.[69] Crittenden denied having asserted specifically that Sevier had caused Desha's removal, though he had said that Desha had been removed shortly after the election of 1831, and that he did not believe that Desha had actually defaulted. At the instance of Governor Pope, who had wished to pay the legislature of 1831, Desha had withheld government money longer than the law authorized him to do, and while he was waiting for a check from Washington to cover the amount used to pay the legislators, he had been removed.[70] According to

friendship which had, as noticed in a previous chapter, developed early in 1831. Noland read law with Bates and lived at his house. In the election of 1831 Bates had supported Desha and had subsequently been removed from office for that reason, or so the Crittenden men said. *Advocate,* April 18, July 4, 18, August 1, September 19, 1832; William Noland to Catherine Noland, January 22, 1827, Berkeley-Noland Papers, Alderman Library, University of Virginia; Ted R. Worley, "An Early Arkansas Sportsman: C. F. M. Noland," *Arkansas Historical Quarterly,* XI (Spring, 1952), 26; Lonnie J. White, "The Arkansas Territorial Election of 1823," *ibid.,* XVIII (Winter, 1959), 337, note 38.

[64] "Mr. Crittenden's Letter to Mr. Stevenson," *Gazette,* May 8, 1833.

[65] Crittenden to Bertrand, May 22, 1833, *Advocate,* June 5, 1833. According to "Z," Crittenden had befriended Stevenson when he was still a travelling preacher, taken him into his home, and given him his first broadcloth suit. Z, "To William W. Stevenson, Bishop of Little Rock," *ibid.,* May 22, 1833.

[66] "Public Sentiment," *Gazette,* June 26, 1833. For additional information on the Crittenden-Stevenson matter, see *Advocate,* May 15, 22, 29, June 26, 1833; *Gazette,* May 22, June 5, 12, 1833.

[67] *Gazette,* May 15, April 24, 1833.

[68] Crittenden to Bertrand, May 22, 1833, *Advocate,* June 5, 1833; "More Slander," *ibid.,* July 3, 1833; Lafayette to Pope, "No. II," *ibid.,* May 1, 1833.

[69] "The Removal of Col. Desha," *Gazette,* July 17, 1833.

[70] Crittenden, "To the People of Arkansas," July 23, 1833, *Advocate,* July 24, 1833.

Bertrand, all the money for which Desha had been held in default had been in his office when the government called for it except some $2,000 or $3,000 which had, unknown to Desha, been taken by Joseph Henderson, Chester Ashley's brother-in-law and Desha's deputy. Desha had been compelled to make up what Henderson had stolen. A suit against Henderson for recovery of the money was before the superior court.[71]

Sevier's friends argued that Sevier's experience was in his favor. He had been an excellent delegate and was popular with Congress and the administration.[72] Bertrand conceded that Sevier was a man of "respectable attainments," but maintained that Crittenden was the abler.

There is no man, who is acquainted with Mr. Crittenden, let him be friend or foe, but will do him the justice to accord him talents of the first order. To say nothing of the opinion of his friends, he has violent enemies, who have repeatedly said of him, that he was by far the most talented man in Arkansas.[73]

Most of the campaigning by Crittenden and Sevier on the stump was done in the western and northern sections where the larger part of the population of the Territory resided.[74] The two candidates travelled through the country together and spoke at the same places until about mid-June, when Sevier left Crittenden in Washington County and returned to Little Rock.[75] Woodruff observed that while the candidates were in Little Rock in May that they treated each other with "that courtesy that is always due from one gentleman toward another." A speech of Sevier's had, however, been interrupted several times by Bertrand, who had swaggered about the room with a pistol prominently exposed.[76] Bertrand denied that he had swaggered and claimed that he had interrupted Sevier only once when his name was used "improperly." He had been carrying a pistol to

---

[71] "Col. Desha's Removal," *ibid.,* July 31, 1833. Woodruff charged also that Desha had, by failing to deposit the government money in his possession at the time of his removal, defaulted for an additional $5,216.15. "The Removal of Col. Desha," *Gazette,* July 17, 1833. Bertrand answered that Desha had, knowing the government would send someone for it, merely held the money to save himself the trouble and expense of depositing it. "Col. Desha's Removal," *Advocate,* July 31, 1833. See also *Terr. Papers,* XXI, 429–430, 704–705, 965.

[72] "Col. Sevier at Washington," *Gazette,* May 8, 1833; Aristides to Editor, *ibid.,* June 5, 1833; "Public Sentiment," *ibid.,* June 26, 1835.

[73] "Crittenden and Sevier," *Advocate,* July 3, 1833.

[74] Orville W. Taylor, *Negro Slavery in Arkansas* (Durham, 1958), 26–29.

[75] See *Advocate,* April 17, May 1, June 12, 26, July 10, 1833; *Gazette,* May 15, 29, June 5, 26, July 10, 17, 1833.

[76] *Gazette,* May 15, 1833.

redress any "personal indignity" by Sevier, who had, he understood, called him in previous speeches "the *damndest liar* in Arkansas." Sevier himself had had two pistols, both cocked.[77]

Crittenden campaigned longer in populous Washington County, which seems to have been a Sevier stronghold,[78] than in any other. His opponents alleged that Crittenden's crowds were so small on two occasions that he did not speak.[79] According to Bertrand, Crittenden found upon arriving in War Eagle township that only a few people had gathered at the place he was scheduled to speak because several of Sevier's friends had sent runners through the township telling people that whiskey would be served at a Sevier rally nearby. Crittenden had then gone over to address the crowd gathered for Sevier. But he had been only "partially successful" because many of the audience were drunk and part had been lured away by Receiver Matthew Leeper of the Fayetteville land office and others who had waved a handkerchief and shouted that those who were thirsty should follow them for free whiskey.[80] Woodruff branded Bertrand's story a fabrication employed to vent Crittenden's rage on citizens of Washington County who favored Sevier.[81]

One of Sevier's zealous supporters in 1833 was Superior Court Judge Thomas P. Eskridge. In a public address to the people, published July 24 in the *Advocate,* Crittenden asserted that Eskridge had been at one time or another "the servile tool of all and every party" in the Territory. During the present campaign he had "dishonored the judgment seat, by his low contemptible political juggling, passing from the bench to the crowd, and there uttering deliberate falsehoods, to serve his present master."[82] The same day the *Gazette* carried a piece by Eskridge accusing Crittenden of having been "the *curse* and *scourge*" of Arkansas. Crittenden could not converse twenty minutes without "indulging in the grossest personal abuse of some one." He had

kept the country in a commotion for years . . . [having been] the agitator of faction, the instigator of crime, the promoter of duels, the corrupter of

[77] Bertrand, "To the Public," May 21, 1833, *Advocate,* May 22, 1833.
[78] See "Col. Sevier and Mr. Crittenden in Washington County," *Gazette,* July 3, 1833.
[79] "Mr. Crittenden's reception in Washington County," *ibid.,* July 10, 1833.
[80] Bertrand, "To the Freemen of Arkansas," *Advocate,* July 10, 1833. See also Washington, "To the People of Arkansas" and "Correction," *ibid.*
[81] "Unparalleled Effrontery," *Gazette,* July 24, 1833.
[82] Crittenden, "To the People of Arkansas," July 23, 1833, *Advocate,* July 24, 1833. For other attacks on Eskridge by Crittenden men, see Arkansas to Eskridge, *ibid.,* June 26, 1833; Absalom Fowler to Editor, July 26, 1833, *ibid.,* July 31, 1833.

morals, the open and shameless gambler, [and] the inmate of the vilest and most debasing associations of profligacy . . ."[83]

Both the *Advocate* and the *Gazette* published correspondence from people over the Territory purporting to give public sentiment. Writers in the *Gazette* invariably prophesied that Sevier would win in their counties or localities; those in the *Advocate* forecasted success for Crittenden. One notices, however, that the letters foretelling a Sevier victory exhibited on the whole much more confidence than did those favoring Crittenden.[84] Woodruff predicted on three separate occasions, presumably upon the basis of correspondence received, that Sevier would win by a majority of 1,500 or 2,000 votes.[85]

In the last issue of the *Advocate* prior to the election, "A Citizen of Little Rock" reported that Sevier had on the afternoon of July 15 been involved in a fracas in Little Rock. He and some friends had, after dining and drinking champagne at Bissell's Globe Tavern, appeared upon the street, where several of them had provoked fights with Crittenden men, of whom one was William Cummins. When Sheriff John K. Taylor attempted to arrest one of the rioters, he was seized by Sevier, who had been encouraging his friends "to acts of violence." Sevier brandished a knife and advised Taylor that he should not take his friend before a magistrate. Several of Sevier's "more *sober* and prudent" partisans had separated them. En route to the jail the sheriff's prisoner twice tried to shoot him, and during one of the attempts Sevier shouted to his friend to " 'SHOOT THE DAMN'D RASCAL.' "[86] Bertrand, who claimed to have been an eye witness to part of what happened, stated that "A Citizen of Little Rock" *"challenges, he dares* a call for the *proof* in a *legal* manner."[87]

Woodruff, who also printed the story by "A Citizen of Little Rock," said that Crittendenites had secretly sent it in handbill form to distant counties "just on the eve of the election, with the intention of imposing it on the people for truth, without affording Mr. Sevier and his friends an opportunity of rebutting it, which they can easily do . . ." Woodruff admitted, however, that Sevier and his

---

[83] Eskridge to Editor, July 13, 1833, *Gazette*, July 24, 1833.

[84] *Advocate*, April 3, 24, May 1, 8, 29, June 12, 26, July 3, 10, 17, 24, 31, 1833; *Gazette*, January 23, February 27, April 10, 24, May 8, 22, 29, June 5, 19, July 3, 10, 17, 24, 1833.

[85] "The Campaign Opened," *Gazette*, March 20, 1833; *ibid.*, May 8, 1833; "Col. Sevier and Mr. Crittenden in Washington County," *ibid.*, July 3, 1833.

[86] A Citizen of Little Rock, "Outrageous Conduct of A. H. Sevier, At Little Rock," *Advocate*, July 31, 1833. See also Jno. Fisher to Editor, *Gazette*, July 17, 1833; Taylor, "To the Public," *Advocate*, July 24, 1833.

[87] "Col. Sevier at Little Rock," *Advocate*, July 31, 1833.

friends had while drinking "become tolerably merry" and that several fights had occurred during which pistols, knives, "and other weapons" had been "exhibited." But no one had been hurt and Sevier had taken no active part in the affair.[88]

At the polls on August 5 Sevier received 4,476 votes to Crittenden's 2,520. The vote showed Sevier to be strong in all sections of the Territory. He carried eighteen of the twenty-three counties, winning all but Monroe and Arkansas Counties in the east and Lafayette, Sevier, and Miller Counties in the southwest. The vote was quite close in Crawford, Conway, Phillips, Monroe, Hot Spring, Lafayette, and Sevier Counties and moderately close in Pulaski, Chicot, Jefferson, and Independence Counties. Sevier's greatest support came from Washington County where he received 877 votes to 187 for Crittenden.[89]

In the election of members to the legislature[90] the voters selected a majority of Sevier men.[91] In the contest for superior court clerk, William Field defeated Mynheer Schweppenheizer, the Crittenden candidate, by a vote of 4,476 to 534.[92]

The election was followed by difficulties between Crittenden and

[88] *Gazette,* July 31, 1833.

[89] Election Proclamation, September 17, 1833, *ibid.,* September 18, 1833.

[90] Elected to the council were Thompson H. Ficklin, Lawrence County; James Boswell, Independence County; Jacob Wolf, Izard County; Mark Bean, Washington County; Robert Sinclear, Crawford County; John Williamson, Pope County; Amos Kuykendall, Conway County; Allen Martin, Pulaski County; Rowland Tidwell, Jackson County; Lafayette Jones, Monroe County; C. H. Alexander, St. Francis County; Wright W. Elliott, Crittenden County; William F. Moore, Phillips County; Terence Farrelly, Arkansas County; Samuel Anderson, Chicot County; Hiram Smith, Union County; James H. Caldwell, Jefferson County; Asa Thompson, Clark County; James W. Judkins, Hempstead County; George G. Duty, Lafayette County; James Clark, Miller County; Joseph W. McCane, Sevier County; and John S. T. Callaway, Hot Spring County. Sinclear died while the legislature was in session and was not replaced. "General Assembly," *ibid.,* November 27, 1833. Chosen to be representatives were George S. Hudspeth and John Hammond, Lawrence County; Peyton Tucker and Morgan Magness, Independence County; Frederick Talbot and Hugh Tinnen, Izard County; John B. Dixon, John Ragan, John Alexander, and James Byrnside, Washington County; William Whitson and Bennett H. Martin, Crawford County; Westley Garrett, Pope County; Jesse C. Roberts, Conway County; Samuel M. Rutherford and Richard C. Byrd, Pulaski County; John C. Saylors and John Hill, St. Francis, Jackson, and Monroe Counties; Peter G. Rives, Crittenden County; Millinder Hanks, Phillips County; Harold Stillwell, Arkansas County; Thomas J. Thurmond, Chicot and Union Counties; Ignace Bogy, Jefferson County; John Wilson, Clark County; William Shaw and Hewett Burt, Hempstead County; Jacob Buzzard, Lafayette and Miller Counties; and John Clark, Sevier and Hot Spring Counties. "List of Members," *ibid.,* September 11, 1833; *Advocate,* September 18, 1833.

[91] Substantiative of this statement is the fact that both branches chose Sevier men as presiding officers. The house elected John Wilson speaker, the council, John Williamson president. "General Assembly," *Gazette,* October 16, 1833; *ibid.,* October 23, 1833; "Arkansas Legislature," *Advocate,* October 9, 1833.

[92] *Gazette,* September 18, 1833.

Eskridge and between Cummins and Sevier. Crittenden challenged Eskridge to a duel because of Eskridge's remarks against him in the *Gazette* (above). But Eskridge refused the call, according to Crittenden, on the grounds of religion.[93] Cummins challenged Sevier because of the "tenor" of Sevier's recent publications against him and the "expressions and insinuations against my character" in Sevier's congressional speech defending Judge Johnson. Sevier refused the call on the ground that his obligations to the people as delegate precluded an immediate meeting and because he doubted whether Cummins's *"assigned* reasons" for challenging him were his *"true* and *only* reasons." If, however, Cummins chose to "renew" the call after Sevier had left office Sevier would "then occupy different grounds, and be left to act according to the then state of the case."[94]

Owing to the dilapidated condition of the old state house, the legislature convened October 7 in two rooms of "the long row of frame buildings" belonging to Charles Caldwell. Two days later the assembly met in joint session to hear the governor's message read by his private secretary, John P. Field. Governor Pope predicted that population and wealth of the Territory would in a few years "authorize an application to Congress for admission into the Union . . ." Meantime the legislature should apply to Congress for "ample appropriations" for roads.

Pope reported that he had, under a congressional act of March 2, 1833,[95] advertised for sale twenty sections from the two townships of land selected under an act of March 2, 1827,[96] for a seminary of learning. But since some of the land advertised had been "injured" by a recent overflow of the Arkansas River, he thought it best to postpone temporarily the sale of a considerable portion. After paying the cost of selecting the two townships, the money from the sale of the twenty sections should be used "to commence a literary establishment." Many people with large families had not migrated to Arkansas because of the lack of educational facilities.

The President had recently upheld the opinion of former Secretary of the Treasury McLane that the ten sections granted for use

[93] Crittenden, "To the Public," August 24, 1833, "To the Public," October 22, 1833, "To the Hon. T. P. Eskridge," November 5, 1833, *Advocate,* August 28, October 23, November 13, 1833. See also "T. P. Eskridge," *ibid.,* February 21, 1834; William Trimble to Crittenden, November 8, 1833, *ibid.,* December 4, 1833; Robert Crittenden to John J. Crittenden, May 4, 1834, John J. Crittenden Papers, Duke University Library.

[94] "Correspondence," *Advocate,* September 18, 1833; *Gazette,* September 18, 1833.

[95] 4 *U.S. Stat. at L.* (1846), 661.

[96] *Ibid.,* 235.

in building a state house could not be located in fractions of quarter-sections;[97] consequently one of the locations Pope had made would have to be changed. But in the case of the thousand-acre grant the President had decided that this restriction did not apply. The 840 acres that Pope had located would be sold at public sale later in the month.[98]

During the session a difference between Governor Pope and Secretary Fulton over Pope's authority to supervise the building of the state house came to light. Fulton had been offended when Pope during his absence in Kentucky left the management of the ten-section fund in the hands of an agent rather than to him as acting governor.[99] Then he had discovered in the acts of Congress that the governor did not, without the authorization of the territorial legislature, possess the power to select a capitol site "or to plan or to build the public building . . . or appropriate the ten section fund." He had forthwith protested to Chester Ashley, Pope's agent, "against the appropriation of the ten section fund." He had not, however, thought it proper to make public his findings until after the election for fear they might be "improperly used."

Fulton reported his views in a letter to the legislature early in November. Since neither of the ten-section acts made provision for the appropriation of money, Fulton argued that the legislature alone could, under Arkansas' organic law, control the fund.[100] Fulton's communication was referred to select committees in both house and council. The house committee reasoned that if Congress had intended the territorial legislature to appropriate the ten-section fund it would have required the governor to pay the proceeds from the sale of the land into the treasury. Moreover, if the legislature possessed the power under the first ten-section act to dispose of the land and build the state house, then the governor "must have the same power by the express words of the second act." By a vote of 16 to 9 the house

[97] See Attorney General Roger B. Taney to Jackson, August 30, 1833, microfilm copies of Jackson Papers, University of Texas Library; Memorandum by President, September 2, 1833, *Terr. Papers,* XXI, 787–788.

[98] "The General Assembly," *Gazette,* October 9, 1833; "General Assembly," *ibid.,* October 16, 1833. See also "Sale of the 1000 acres," *ibid.,* October 23, 1833.

[99] Acting Governor Fulton to Secretary of State, July 31, 1833, *Terr. Papers,* XXI, 779–780. Pope's only public explanation of his course was that he had not wished to "impose" "trouble and responsibility" on Fulton and "expose" him to the attacks of the *Advocate.* "Gov. Pope's reply to Mr. Cummins," *Gazette,* July 31, 1833. Fulton regarded Pope's course in this matter as only the latest of "various acts of indignity" which he had suffered at Pope's hands over a period of eighteen months.

[100] Fulton to Williamson and Wilson, "General Assembly," *Gazette,* November 13, 1833; "Arkansas Legislature," *Advocate,* November 6, 1833.

approved a resolution submitted by the committee that Pope had not transcended his authority. The council committee, however, thought that if Congress had intended in the ten-section acts to give the power in question to the governor it would have done so as clearly as it had in the thousand-acre act. Though concurring in the committee report, the council rejected by a vote of 11 to 7 a resolution that "farther enactments appear necessary."[101]

In a special message to the legislature, Governor Pope, who resented Fulton's actions, sharply criticized him for having, without first advising Pope of his views, protested the governor's authority to appropriate the ten-section fund to Ashley. Had Fulton's protest caused Ashley to stop work on the state house

a majority of members would probably have been returned to the General Assembly politically hostile to the Governor, and Col. Sevier's election might have been defeated. The undertakers of the building would have been ruined, and must have been indemnified for their losses out of my private fortune, or the Public Treasury.

Though Pope understood that Fulton had threatened to issue a proclamation stopping work on the state house "the moment my back is turned," he hoped that "the late admonition given to the Secretary, by the General Assembly . . . will free me from farther embarrassment from that quarter."[102]

Fulton soon denied in a public address that he had threatened to issue a proclamation such as Pope had mentioned. It was to prevent the necessity of one that he had made known his views to the legislature. Notwithstanding the assembly's decision, he still believed his interpretation of the ten-section acts to be correct. As to

the course I have taken in relation to this business, I have been influenced alone by a sense of public duty; and, although a hope has been expressed, that I will profit from the admonitions I have received, yet, as I do not acknowledge either the justice or the truth of those admonitions, I fear I shall continue to be as obstinate an asserter of the rights of the people hereafter, as I have endeavored heretofore to be.[103]

Evidently fearing that his trouble with Pope might prevent his reappointment to a second term as secretary, Fulton sent to President Jackson in November a letter of recommendation (he also sent a copy to Sevier) signed by all but two of the members of the

[101] *Gazette*, November 13, 1833; "Arkansas Legislature," *Advocate*, November 20, 1833; Martin and Clark, "Report," *ibid.*, December 4, 1830.

[102] "The State-house Fund," *Gazette*, November 20, 1833.

[103] Fulton, "To the Public," *ibid.*, November 20, 1833; *Advocate*, December 11, 1833.

legislature.[104] In December Fulton wrote Representative James K. Polk of Tennessee to request that he "see the President" on his behalf. Governor Pope was "about to resign, and quit the Territory" and had said that he intended, upon doing so, to have Fulton "dismissed from office." Fulton had "faithfully attended" to all the governor's duties during Pope's "long and repeated absences from the Territory" and had been friendly to Pope as long as Pope "would permit." Pope's "effort against me, is certainly the most unholy act."[105] In the event Pope did not resign, nor did he, as far as the evidence shows, attempt either to prevent Fulton's reappointment or to have him removed.[106]

The legislature's election of Woodruff (by a vote of 26 to 23) to be public printer caused a difficulty between the *Gazette* and the *Advocate*. Bertrand claimed that the *Advocate's* bid had been *"nine and one-quarter per cent."* lower than Woodruff's and that "partizan feelings" had influenced the legislature to select Woodruff.[107] Woodruff promptly denied Bertrand's assertion, claiming that his bid was five per cent lower than Bertrand's.[108] Bertrand and a new assistant editor, Albert Pike, continued, however, to maintain that the *Advocate's* bid was the lower, averring that Woodruff had deliberately made his bid ambiguous so the legislature could not detect that it was actually the higher.[109]

The legislature of 1833 repealed the act of 1831 amending the county court system; divided the militia into six brigades; altered the southern boundary of Izard County; created Mississippi, Carroll, Pike, Green, Van Buren, Johnson, and Scott Counties; authorized the territorial treasurer to loan the surplus in the seminary-land fund; dissolved several marriages; repealed an act of 1823 prohibiting the sale of liquor to soldiers; authorized Jefferson and Jackson Counties to levy property taxes to pay for building jails; incorporated the town of Helena; amended the election laws; ap-

---

[104] See Secretary Fulton to Sevier, November 21, 1833, *Terr. Papers*, XXI, 864–865. Sevier, who regretted the "misunderstanding" between Pope and Fulton, and believed they had "quarrelled *literally* about nothing," recommended Fulton for another term. Sevier to President, December 12, 1833, *ibid.*, 863.

[105] Fulton to Polk, December 11, 1833, Polk Papers, Library of Congress.

[106] Fulton was renominated December 16, 1833, confirmed December 24, and commissioned February 17, 1834, effective March 17. *Terr. Papers*, XXI, 907, note 63.

[107] "Public Printer," *Advocate*, October 16, 1833.

[108] *Gazette*, October 16, 1833; "The Public Printing," *ibid.*, October 23, 1833; "The Public Printing—Again," *ibid.*, October 30, 1833; *ibid.*, November 6, 1833.

[109] "The Public Printing," *Advocate*, October 23, 30, November 13, 1833; Walter L. Brown, "Albert Pike, Arkansas Editor," *Arkansas Historical Quarterly*, X (Winter, 1951), 394–395.

propriated money for 1834–1835; and authorized the territorial auditor to sell military bounty lands that had for five years been "struck off" to the Territory for non-payment of taxes.[110] Thirty-two memorials to the President or Congress dealt largely with internal improvements and land.[111] William Pelham was chosen territorial auditor, and Samuel M. Rutherford treasurer.[112]

The question of Pope's location of ten-section claims on improvements came up again when Thurmond of Chicot County tried unsuccessfully to obtain approval of a memorial asking Congress to void Pope's locations not only upon lands that had been improved prior to a preemption act of July, 1832, but also on surveyed land. The *Advocate* thought the memorial, which had been killed by Sevier men, showed "conclusively" that improvements had been located upon.[113] Woodruff, however, disagreed, and asserted that Thurmond's memorial was designed solely to stop the sales of ten-section claims and thereby prevent progress on the state house.[114] Evidence in the *Territorial Papers* shows that Pope did locate a part of the ten sections upon land claimed by preemptioners.[115]

Though President Jackson had, as noticed above, decided that Pope's location of ten-section claims in fractions of quarter-sections was illegal, he subsequently modified his decision to accept locations in fractions if made "in legal subdivisions" and on condition that they be "taken in satisfaction" of full quarter-sections.[116] Presumably to alleviate difficulty arising from Pope's having selected and sold more than the number of fractions (forty) he was entitled to under the modified decision, Congress in 1838 passed a measure confirming all Pope's ten-section selections.[117]

[110] *Arkansas Acts,* 1833, pp. 7–11, 13–19, 24, 26–29, 30–32, 33–35, 36, 39, 41–42, 44, 45, 47, 53–54, 57–59, 70, 74–79, 84–94, 98–104, 114–117.

[111] "The General Assembly," *Gazette,* November 20, 1833; *Terr. Papers,* XXI, 807–809, 813–844, 845, note 64, 847–848, 853–854.

[112] *Advocate,* November 13, 1833. The *Advocate* alleged that James Scull, treasurer since 1819, had been replaced solely because he "was not a *Sevier-man."*

[113] "The Ten Sections, &c.," *ibid.,* November 27, 1833.

[114] "The Ten Sections," *Gazette,* December 4, 1833.

[115] The preemption claimants were permitted either to withdraw the money they had invested or to continue payments and take the matter to court. See Hayward to Secretary of Treasury, October 28, 1833, *Terr. Papers,* XXI, 809–811; Secretary of Treasury to Hayward, October 31, 1833, May 21, 1834, *ibid.,* 813, 944; Secretary of Treasury to Ethan A. Brown, October 8, 1835, *ibid.,* 1102–1103; .83 to Editor, "No. VII," *Advocate,* April 24, 1835.

[116] Secretary of Treasury to Hayward and to Governor Pope, January 20, 1834, February 13, 1835, *Terr. Papers,* XXI, 906, 1021; *Gazette,* February 11, 1834.

[117] 5 *U.S. Stat. at L.* (1850), 208–209; Secretary of Treasury to President, November 3, 1835, *Terr. Papers,* XXI, 1119–1121; Brown to Governor Fulton, November 5, 1835, *ibid.,* 1125–1126; Attorney General to Secretary of Treasury, August 8, 1836, *ibid.,* 1244–1245.

In a special report to the legislature of 1833 Pope stated that he had received $6,854 in cash and $17,650 in notes for the four-fifths of the ten-section grant that he had sold. A state house consisting of a center building and a west wing would cost some $30,-000; an east wing, to comprise the territorial court house, would be paid for out of the thousand-acre fund.[118] As it turned out, the state house cost considerably more than Pope anticipated. In December, 1834, Sevier sought unsuccessfully to obtain from Congress an additional grant of ten sections with which to complete the building.[119] In 1835 the territorial legislature requested a further appropriation of ten sections,[120] and in 1836 Congress granted five.[121] Albert Pike, hardly a disinterested witness, wrote early in 1836 that the main building was "partly covered with *tin;* and is commonly called 'Pope's folly.'"[122] In 1840 the state legislature was compelled to appropriate the money to finish construction. When finally completed that year the state house had cost a total of $123,379. Of this amount $31,722 came from the sale of the ten sections; $38,-000 from the sale of the five sections; $16,657 from the sale of the thousand acres; and $37,000 from legislative appropriation.[123]

It would seem, in retrospect, that Robert Crittenden could not have chosen a more inopportune time to run for high office than in 1833. Aside from the handicap of his own dubious personal popularity among the plain people, he had to face what seems to have been a widespread antipathy against him and his faction for having offered and unyieldingly supported the ten-section bill of 1831. The outcome of the election showed the Sevier faction to be completely dominant in territorial politics. The difficulty between Governor Pope and Secretary Fulton, however, foreshadowed trouble in the Sevier camp.

[118] "The State-house Fund," *Gazette,* November 20, 1833.

[119] "Congressional Summary," *ibid.,* February 3, 1835; *Advocate,* March 13, 1835.

[120] *Terr. Papers,* XXI, 1123–1124.

[121] 5 *U.S. Stat. at L.* (1850), 58–59. See also Clara B. Kennan, "Arkansas's Old State House," *Arkansas Historical Quarterly,* IX (Spring, 1950), 36.

[122] Pike, "Letters from Arkansas," *American Monthly Magazine,* I (January, 1836), 25–30.

[123] Hempstead, *Pictorial History of Arkansas,* 239–240; Vaughan, "A History of the Old State House," *Publications of the Arkansas Historical Association,* III, 253–254; Clara B. Eno, "Old and New Capitols of Arkansas," *Arkansas Historical Quarterly,* IV (Autumn, 1945), 243–244.

CHAPTER ELEVEN

The Statehood Movement

THOUGH HE HAD NOT MENTIONED statehood in the campaign of 1833, Delegate Sevier took it upon himself to offer in the House of Representatives on December 17, 1833, a resolution that the Committee on Territories be instructed to inquire into the expediency of permitting the people of Arkansas to form a constitution preparatory to admission into the Union.[1]

Sevier explained his unexpected action in a long letter to the *Gazette*. Since Michigan Territory would come in as a free state, the balance of political power in the Senate would be destroyed unless a slave state was admitted at the same time.[2] If the delegate from Florida Territory, who was absent, were to press Florida successfully, then Arkansas' admission would probably be delayed until Wisconsin Territory should be ready "a quarter of a century" hence. The time was now propitious for admission not only because Arkansas might come in "without trammels upon the subject of slavery," but also because she should be able "to obtain liberal grants of per centage upon the sales of our public lands, together with absolute grants to all the salines within our limits."

Against the objection that statehood could mean the end of internal improvements at Federal expense, Sevier hoped that "during the necessary delay to our admission" provision would be made "for many of our most important works." As to the expense of statehood, Sevier pointed out that (1) grants would be "made us to meet such a contingency," (2) that an increase in population in consequence of statehood would bring an increase in revenue, (3) and that "additional objects of taxation are daily multiplying."

[1] *House Journal*, 23 Cong., 1 sess., 83–84.
[2] There were in 1833 twelve free states and twelve slave states.

He himself had "hitherto" opposed statehood on account of the insufficiency of Arkansas' population and her embarrassed financial condition, and would still favor delaying a few years were it not for Michigan's application for admission.[3]

Editor Woodruff, who had consistently argued against statehood, thought Sevier's reasons for acting "without the co-operation of the Legislature, or any instructions from his constitutents" would "carry conviction to the minds of many who now doubt the expediency of our applying for admission."[4] Woodruff himself took no stand one way or another, but writers in the *Gazette* gave statehood their unqualified endorsement. "Seventy-Six" believed Arkansas would "never have a stable and respectable community, so much to be desired, unless we cease to be a mere province, or distant plantation, of the empire."[5] "Old Times" thought Arkansas

had better go into a slave State Government, while we have an opportunity: for, if ever those humane philanthrophists [*sic*]—as the anti-slavery men call themselves—get the ascendency [*sic*] in Congress, they will sound their tocsin of alarm, and agitate the question of emancipation. And then, what will the probable result be? Why, a total abolition of slavery, and, as a consequence growing out of it, a dissolution of the Union.[6]

The *Advocate* also favored statehood. Arkansas' debt would continue to increase so long as she remained a Territory but once a state, the natural increase of population would "by increasing our revenue, soon relieve us from debt." Also, "freedom is better than any vassalage." Observing that it had always supported statehood, the *Advocate* did not believe that Sevier deserved all the merit for the action he had taken.[7] A subsequent editorial questioned the motives of Sevier's *"sudden* change" in favor of statehood. Arkansas' "situation" was no better at present than it had been in 1831 when he strongly opposed admission. At that time he had promised not to propose statehood without instructions from Arkansas. As for the action of Michigan Territory, she had announced her intention to apply for admission prior to the last session of Congress, but Sevier did not then come out for statehood. The real reason for his change

---

[3] Sevier to Editor, December 18, 1833, *Arkansas Gazette* (Little Rock), January 21, 1834.

[4] "State Government," *ibid.*

[5] Seventy-Six, "A State Government, or Not: That is the Question," January 15, 1834, *ibid.,* January 28, 1834.

[6] Old Times to Editor, *ibid.,* February 4, 1834. See also comments of "Hickory," "Hempstead" and "Spring Hill," *ibid..* January 28, July 15, September 2, 9, 1834.

[7] "The Editor's Table," *Arkansas Advocate* (Little Rock), January 24, 1834.

was a desire to secure to his uncle, Richard M. Johnson of Kentucky, "the *vote* of Arkansas" in the presidential election of 1836.[8]

Another newspaper, the Helena *Herald* (established in July, 1833),[9] supported Sevier, arguing as he did that it would be better to remain a Territory "for some years yet to come" were it not "a matter of great importance" to "keep up a happy balance of power in the Senate."[10]

Though Sevier's resolution was approved by the House and referred to the Committee on Territories, no bill seems to have been reported out by the committee. Instead John Tipton of Indiana, acting "at the request of individuals interested," introduced into the Senate in late January bills to permit Michigan and Arkansas to form state constitutions. Both bills were referred to a select committee composed of Tipton, Felix Grundy of Tennessee, Alexander Porter of Louisiana, Arnold Naudain of Delaware, and Thomas Ewing of Ohio.[11]

Tipton reported the bills with amendments on May 2,[12] and they were brought forward for discussion on May 9. Tipton explained that they had not been reported earlier because the committee had "for months" been unable to come to an agreement. Finally a majority had decided to strike out the enabling clauses and to authorize the taking of censuses. Tipton was opposed to these changes because they would delay for a year a decision on admission. He now proposed amendments under which the marshals of each Territory would be required to take a census, and if such census reported the requisite population of 47,700 the territorial governor would order the election of a constitutional convention. But the Michigan bill was laid on the table, and consideration of the Arkansas bill was postponed.[13]

---

[8] "To the Hon. A. H. Sevier," *ibid.,* March 21, 1834.

[9] See "Prospectus," June 28, 1833, *Gazette,* July 10, 1833. Though Woodruff had previously announced that the *Herald* would be established by John Steele (*Gazette,* October 3, 1832), the prospectus stated that the paper would be edited by J. E. Graham and published by C. S. Smith and James Lindsay. Steele was, however, if not the editor of the *Herald* at the time of its establishment, soon to become editor. *Gazette,* February 11, 1834; *Advocate,* February 28, 1834. No file of the *Herald* is known to be extant.

[10] "State Government," *Herald,* reprinted in *Gazette,* February 18, 1834.

[11] *Senate Journal,* 23 Cong., 1 sess., 118, 121; "Congressional Summary," *Gazette,* February 25, 1834; communication of A Friend of the West, June 30, 1834, Washington *Globe,* reprinted in *Gazette,* July 29, 1834. Tipton introduced the Michigan bill on January 27 and the Arkansas bill two days later.

[12] *Senate Journal,* 23 Cong., 1 sess., 241–242.

[13] *Ibid.,* 257; *Congressional Globe,* 23 Cong., 1 sess., I (May 9, 1834), 374–375; *Register of Debates in Congress,* 23 Cong., 1 sess., X (May 9, 1834), 1719–1721; "Congressional Summary," *Gazette,* June 3, 10, 1834; "Remarks of Mr. Tipton," *Advocate,* June 6, 1834. See also communication of A Friend of the West, June 30, 1834, Washington *Globe,* reprinted in *Gazette,* July 29, 1834.

On May 12 the Arkansas bill was again brought forward, but a motion by Ewing to lay it on the table prevailed by a vote of 22 to 20. Tabulation of the vote by states shows that the vote was not sectional.[14]

Sevier wrote Woodruff the next day that the admission of Arkansas and Michigan was "considered pretty much a party question in the Senate, as you will see from the votes." He was confident that "a law will pass to authorize" the taking of a census, "and, in the event of our population amounting to forty-seven thousand seven hundred, that the people will be authorized to form a constitution, if they choose to do so." A question, likely to be soon settled, about the boundary between Michigan and Ohio had delayed action on the Arkansas and Michigan bills.[15]

On June 26 Tipton moved to take up the Arkansas bill, "intimating his intention [also] to move [later] to take up" the Michigan bill. His only object, he said, was to authorize Arkansas to take a census preparatory to final admission. By a non-sectional vote of 17 to 16, the Senate sustained Tipton's motion. An ensuing motion by Daniel Webster of Massachusetts to lay the bill on the table failed, 16 to 15, but a similar one by Peleg Sprague of Maine succeeded, 17 to 14.[16] Congress subsequently adjourned without taking action on either the Arkansas or the Michigan bill.

Significant events had in the meantime been taking place in territorial politics. In January, 1834, the *Gazette* reprinted an article from a newspaper of Gallatin, Tennessee, Secretary Fulton's former home town, calling Governor Pope a "dictatorial 'Overseer' " because he had assumed "unauthorized" power to supervise the building of the state house.[17] Editor Woodruff had kept out of the Pope-Fulton quarrel of the previous fall, but he now took sides in an editorial denying that Pope had attempted a "usurption" of powers.[18] The same issue of the *Gazette* carried a communication by "Investigator" questioning Fulton's motives in the state house matter.[19] Fulton in replying a fortnight later noticed that Woodruff had said

[14] *Senate Journal,* 23 Cong., 1 sess., 262. Both *Congressional Globe* and *Register of Debates* give the vote as 22 to 19, George M. Bibb of Kentucky not voting.

[15] Sevier to Editor, May 13, 1834, *Gazette,* June 3, 1834.

[16] *Senate Journal,* 23 Cong., 1 sess., 358–359; *Congressional Globe,* 23 Cong., 1 sess., I (June 26, 1834), 473; *Register of Debates,* 23 Cong., 1 sess., X (June 26, 1834), 2078; "Congressional Summary," *Gazette,* July 22, 1834. The *Senate Journal* reports the vote on Tipton's motion as 17 to 15, George M. Bibb of Kentucky not voting. The details of the votes on Webster's and Sprague's motions are not given.

[17] Gallatin *Union,* reprinted in *Gazette,* January 1, 1834; *Advocate,* January 1, 1834.

[18] "The State-House Fund," *Gazette,* January 1, 1834. See also A Jacksonian to Editor, *ibid.,* January 15, 1834.

[19] Investigator to Fulton, *ibid.,* January 1, 1834.

nothing to defend him against the "imputations" of "Investigator" and concluded that Woodruff had joined Pope in an "unholy effort to destroy me."[20] Sevier managed to remain aloof from the Woodruff-Fulton squabble and retain the friendship of both men.

In late March, 1834, President Jackson appointed Thomas J. Lacy of Tennessee to be superior court judge in place of Alexander M. Clayton, who had resigned.[21] Sevier complained that Jackson had "disregarded" his recommendation of an Arkansan in favor of a non-resident who was a friend and former law student of Governor Pope.[22] The *Advocate* then challenged Sevier to "reconcile" Jackson's appointment of a Pope man "with the loud cry raised" in the campaign of 1833 about Sevier's great influence with the President. The *Advocate* believed the Sevierites were "about dismounting from the hobby of *Jacksonism,* which has served their purpose so well, and mounting that of *Johnsonism* [Richard M. Johnson of Kentucky]." They were also suffering heartburnings because Pope had "determined to cast aside his slough of dependence, and to live or die on his own bottom."[23]

Sevier replied facetiously that he had recently learned that Lacy was not only "much tinctured" with "Sevierism" but also with "Johnsonism." Actually there was, Sevier intimated, no difference between Johnsonism and Jacksonism, for Johnson was a Jackson man and either he or Van Buren would be nominated for President in 1836.[24] Later, after Lacy's arrival in the Territory, the *Advocate* averred that he was *"determined"* to take no part in territorial politics and cited the Nashville (Tennessee) *Banner* for a statement that Lacy was "tinctured with no *isms* of any kind."[25]

In July, 1834, John Steele,[26] former editor of the Helena *Herald,* began at Little Rock a new paper called the *Political Intelligencer.*[27] Governor Pope who had recently been entrusted by Congress with

[20] Fulton to Editor, *ibid.,* January 15, 1834. See also *ibid.,* February 25, 1834.

[21] Clarence E. Carter, ed., *Territorial Papers of the United States,* Vol. XXI, *Arkansas Territory, 1829–1836* (Washington, 1954), 913–914, 920–921, 929, 930–931. Clayton gave poor health and low salary as his reasons for resigning.

[22] Sevier to Woodruff, March 17, 1834, *Gazette,* April 15, 1834.

[23] *Advocate,* April 18, 1834.

[24] Sevier to Editor, May 13, 1834, *Gazette,* June 3, 1834.

[25] *Advocate,* June 6, July 11, 1834.

[26] Steele, a lawyer and a native of the Mississippi Valley, came to Arkansas from Missouri. See "Gov. Pope and His Man Steele," *Gazette,* September 16, 1834; Steele, "To the People of Arkansas," September 9, 1834, *Political Intelligencer Extra,* reprinted in *Advocate,* September 12, 1834; *Gazette,* September 30, 1834.

[27] See prospectus in *Advocate,* February 28, 1834; *Gazette,* February 25, 1834; "Construction of the Ten Section Act," *ibid.,* February 11, 1834; Pope, "To the Public," September 23, 1834, *Political Intelligencer,* September 26, 1834, reprinted in *Terr. Papers,* XXI, 983. No file of the *Intelligencer* is known.

an appropriation of $3,000 for digesting and printing the territorial statutes[28] engaged Steele to do both jobs. Woodruff promptly protested Pope's action. There were in Arkansas lawyers and judges at least as competent as Steele whose experience and time in the Territory gave them stronger claims than his to the work of digesting the laws. As to the printing, Woodruff thought his own experience and long residence in Arkansas gave him some claim to the job, "the only really good one in our line of business that has ever [been] offered in the Territory."[29]

A week later Woodruff noticed that Pope had been "making sad complaints" because the *Gazette* had carried the proceedings of a public meeting at Jonesboro, Miller County, castigating him for disregarding the wishes of the people in the appointment of a county judge.[30] If Pope thought that Woodruff should in courtesy have shown the proceedings to him in advance of publication, he should remember that he had not treated Woodruff with courtesy in giving "a *three-thousand-dollar-job,* in our line, to a competitor . . ."[31]

In reply Steele informed the public that the digesting and printing work had been given him by Pope on condition that it be done under Pope's direction and with his help. Steele had obtained to assist him a lawyer from Jackson County, James McCampbell, who had for several years been preparing a digest of the territorial statutes. Woodruff had received the "public patronage" for so long that he thought he had a monopoly on it.[32]

Woodruff responded that Steele's publication was "the joint production of Gov. Pope and his man Steele," and alleged that Steele had, in order to obtain the printing job, been required by Pope to assume the digesting work so that Pope might retain the money due the compiler. In the past Pope had been not "unmindful of his *pecuniary* interest in wrongfully appropriating to himself, on the score of commissions, a portion of the public funds placed under his *'direction'* and *'superintendence'* for public purposes." And he had been "chiefly instrumental" in the establishment of the *Political Intelligencer.*[33]

[28] Act approved June 27, 1834, 4 *U.S. Stat. at L.* (1846), 695.

[29] "The Digest," *Gazette,* August 26, 1834.

[30] See "Public Meeting at Jonesboro," *ibid.,* August 19, 1834.

[31] *Ibid.,* September 2, 1834.

[32] Steele, "To the People of Arkansas," September 9, 1834, *Political Intelligencer Extra,* reprinted in *Advocate,* September 12, 1834. The digest was published in 1835. See J. Steele and J. M'Campbell, eds., *Laws of Arkansas Territory* (Little Rock, 1835).

[33] "Gov. Pope and His Man Steele," *Gazette,* September 16, 1834. Crittenden also believed that Pope was behind the establishment of the *Intelligencer.* Robert Crittenden to John J. Crittenden, May 4, 1834, John J. Crittenden Papers, Duke University Library.

Denying all of Woodruff's assertions, Pope charged that Woodruff was trying "to produce a rupture between Col. Sevier and myself, in order to secure the patronage of Col. Sevier and his friends."

> If Col. Sevier wishes our political and social relations to remain unimpaired, it seems to me that he owes it to himself and his *real* friends, to make a public disavowal and condemnation of Woodruff's conduct, and to cast from him, or reform, the mischievous pack who are aiding and abetting in this warfare on me, and whose main object is, to sever us to answer their selfish purposes. He owes me this—I have been a heart christian in his support, and made common cause with him against all his opponents. He cannot expect to keep a corps of troops marauding on my feelings and character. Sooner than submit to this our political connection must be dissolved—I speak with frankness.[34]

Woodruff replied that Sevier would not abandon an old friend for "a *pretended* one."[35]

The difficulty in the Sevier camp was undoubtedly welcomed by the Crittenden men. Robert Crittenden himself wrote his brother, John J. Crittenden, in May, 1834, that Pope had recently proposed through an agent that he (Robert) "might be one of the *senators* in Congress in conjunction with Pope" if he would join Pope against Sevier. But Robert, completely despising Pope, had "spurned" the offer. He had also "had indications that Sevier and his friends would now be glad to conciliate." Either Pope would be "driven back" to the Sevier faction or the Sevier men would "throw him off and tender the hand of fellow ship to *us.*" According to Robert, Richard M. Johnson of Kentucky controlled the Sevier faction in Arkansas; and from Robert's letter one may infer that John J. Crittenden directed the Crittenden faction in the Territory. If Johnson and John J. Crittenden united in Kentucky, as Robert understood was likely (presumably in the event Johnson was nominated for President), then Robert and Sevier would probably act together in Arkansas at the organization of the state government. Robert made it clear, however, that he would not support Van Buren for President.[36] Whatever hopes the Crittenden faction may have had were shattered by Crittenden's untimely death on December 18, 1834.[37]

[34] Pope, "To the Public," September 23, 1834, *Political Intelligencer,* September 26, 1834, reprinted in *Terr. Papers,* XXI, 977–991.

[35] "Gov. Pope," *Gazette,* September 30, 1834. For further bickering, see *ibid.,* October 7, 14, 21, 1834.

[36] Robert Crittenden to John J. Crittenden, May 4, 1834, John J. Crittenden Papers, Duke University Library.

[37] *Advocate,* January 2, 9, 23, 1835; *Gazette,* January 6, 1835; Farrar Newberry, "Some Notes on Robert Crittenden," *Arkansas Historical Quarterly,* XVI (Autumn, 1957), 254–256. Crittenden died of an attack of pleurisy at Vicksburg, Mississippi,

On December 17, the day before Crittenden's death, Secretary Fulton wrote President Jackson that in "fierce discussions" on the national bank he had sustained Jackson "almost single handed" against the arguments of Pope and Crittenden men. If Pope and Crittenden united to support each other for the senatorships and won (Fulton believed Crittenden could win without help from anyone), then both senators from Arkansas would oppose the administration. But Pope's ambition could be thwarted, Fulton believed, if Jackson declined to renominate him for another term.[38]

To Jackson's close friend and adviser, William B. Lewis of Tennessee, Fulton wrote that Pope was opposed not only to Jackson but also to Van Buren. If Pope was reappointed, he and his nephew, William Field, would "exert a powerful influence on our elections."[39] Lewis enclosed Fulton's letter in one of his own to Van Buren stating that he doubted "the propriety" of Pope's reappointment "as it will enable him to keep up the deception as to his Jacksonism, and to delude a portion at least of the friends of the Administration." If Jackson dropped Pope, Lewis thought that he could not do better than nominate Fulton to be governor, and that in time Fulton might be elected senator, "which would be a very important consideration, as relates to the Administration."[40]

Though Pope had stated in his message to the territorial legislature of 1833 that he did not expect to seek reappointment,[41] he wrote the Secretary of State early in February, 1835, that he was "willing to continue" as governor in order that he might finish important business entrusted to him and settle his public accounts.[42] But Jackson had in the meantime nominated Fulton[43] for the governorship and Lewis Randolph of Virginia for the secretaryship.[44]

where he was practicing law. He had advised his brother, John J. Crittenden, in May, 1834, that he might move to Mississippi in the winter of 1834. Robert Crittenden to John J. Crittenden, May 4, 1834, John J. Crittenden Papers, Duke University Library. There is, however, no evidence in the *Gazette* or *Advocate* to indicate that Crittenden had become a permanent resident in Mississippi at the time of his death.

[38] Fulton to President, December 17, 1834, microfilm copies of Jackson Papers, University of Texas Library; *Terr. Papers,* XXI, 1002–1006.

[39] Fulton to Lewis, December 19, 1834, Van Buren Papers, Library of Congress (microfilm copies in University of Texas Library); *Terr. Papers,* XXI, 1006–1008.

[40] Lewis to Van Buren, January 15, 1835, Van Buren Papers, Library of Congress; *Terr. Papers,* XXI, 1013. Lewis's suggestion that Fulton be nominated in Pope's stead has evidently been edited out of the letter in *Terr. Papers.*

[41] "General Assembly," *Gazette,* October 16, 1833.

[42] Pope to Secretary of State, February 2, 1835, *Terr. Papers,* XXI, 1017–1018.

[43] *Ibid.,* 1029, note 1; Sevier to Woodruff, January 28, 1835, *Gazette,* March 10, 1835.

[44] *Terr. Papers,* XXI, 1024–1026, note 76, 1029. Fulton's commission was dated February 27, effective March 9. Randolph, a grandson of Thomas Jefferson, was a clerk

Pope had been left out of consideration, Jackson said, because he had written earlier that he would not be a candidate (Pope soon denied having so written).[45]

Extremely disappointed over his failure to obtain reappointment, Pope blamed his mistreatment on Sevier. According to Pope, Sevier had called upon him before departing for Washington late in 1834, "solemnly disclaimed any agency . . . in Woodruff's villainy, and tendered, in strong terms, a continuation of his friendship." But he had subsequently failed to give Pope the "slightest notice" of Jackson's "intended outrage" until it was too late for Pope to do anything about it.[46] Woodruff defended Sevier, maintaining that he had had "no agency in the matter; and, had the President consulted *his* wish, we are disposed to think Gov. Pope would have been reappointed."[47] Whatever Sevier's part in the affair, Pope evidently considered his aspirations in Arkansas defeated, and he returned to Kentucky.[48]

Congress having done nothing further toward statehood for Arkansas,[49] Sevier on March 31, 1835, issued a circular informing the people that the Michigan territorial council had of its own volition passed a law calling an election for delegates to a constitutional convention, that Michigan would consequently submit a constitution to Congress at the next session, and that "she is imploring us to take a similar step, and stand by her in her hour of trial." If Michigan should be admitted without Arkansas, Sevier declared, Arkansas would be left "completely at the mercy of both Houses of Congress" in the matter of slavery.[50]

Sevier strongly implied that he favored taking action similar to that of Michigan, and Woodruff at the same time came out flatly

in the State Department at the time of his appointment on February 23. Endorsement to letter of Randolph to Secretary of State, March 7, 1835, *ibid.*, 1030; "Postscript," *Gazette,* March 3, 1835; Fay Hempstead, *Historical Review of Arkansas* (3 vols., Chicago, 1911), I, 126.

[45] Secretary of State to Pope, February 28, 1835, *Terr. Papers,* XXI, 1029–1030; Pope, "To the Public," March 13, 1835, *Times* (Little Rock), March 14, 1835.

[46] Pope, "To the Public," March 7, 1835, *Times,* March 7, 1835, reprinted in *Gazette,* March 10, 1835.

[47] "Governor Pope's Expiring Groans," *Gazette,* March 10, 1835. For further controversy over Pope's not being reappointed, see Pope, "To the Public," March 13, 1835, *Times,* March 14, 1835; "Ex-Gov. Pope—Again," *Gazette,* March 17, 1835; "Ex-Gov. Pope—Once More," *ibid.,* March 24, 1835; "His Fallen Majesty, Ex-Gov. Pope," *ibid.,* March 31, 1835; *Advocate,* March 20, 1835.

[48] Orval W. Baylor, *John Pope, Kentuckian: His Life and Times, 1770–1845* (Cynthiana, Kentucky, 1943), 400–479. Pope later served in Congress.

[49] See Orville W. Taylor, *Negro Slavery in Arkansas* (Durham, 1958), 36.

[50] Sevier, "To the People of Arkansas," March 31, 1835, *Gazette,* April 7, 1835.

for "admission *immediately.*" The abolitionists were growing stronger in the East. Recently a petition "from certain fanatics" had been presented asking Congress to abolish slavery not only in the District of Columbia but also in the territories. If a territorial census then in progress showed Arkansas to have the necessary population, would it

not be advisable and proper for the Governor—since Congress has failed to act on the subject during the late session—to convene the Legislature immediately, and recommend to them the passage of a law authorizing the calling of a Convention to form a CONSTITUTION, to be submitted to Congress at the next session, and that our admission be demanded simultaneously with that of Michigan.[51]

The *Advocate,* owned and edited since January, 1835, by Albert Pike (1809–1891),[52] chortled at the inconsistency of Sevier and Woodruff in changing from opposing to favoring statehood, but endorsed their views.[53]

The *Times,* successor to the *Political Intelligencer,* opposed immediate admission both editorially and through the correspondence it chose to print. Editor Andrew J. Hunt thought the additional expense of state government would result in "heavy taxes" and thereby reduce immigration.[54] "St. Francis" objected on grounds of expense and because internal improvements would cease.[55]

"Arkansas" did not believe that northern "fanatics," unpopular as they were at home, could cause a slavery restriction to be imposed on Arkansas.[56] In another communication, "Arkansas" averred that Arkansas need not hurry into state government on ac-

[51] "State Government, and the Slave Question," *ibid.,* March 31, 1835.

[52] After having taught school in his native Massachusetts, Pike had in 1831 accompanied a trading expedition to Mexico. Coming thence to Arkansas the next year, he taught school in Crawford and Pope Counties. Robert Crittenden in 1833 persuaded Editor Bertrand to bring Pike, whose literary ability had already been demonstrated, to Little Rock to work on the *Advocate.* Pike was admitted to the bar in 1834. He subsequently purchased the *Advocate* from Bertrand, who was in poor health. Pike was for a time associated in publishing the *Advocate* with C. E. Rice. Walter Lee Brown, "Albert Pike, 1809–1891" (unpublished Ph.D. dissertation, University of Texas, 1955), 4, 12–13, 16–25, 27–67, 72, 76–80, 94–95; Brown, "Albert Pike, Arkansas Editor," *Arkansas Historical Quarterly,* X (Winter, 1951), 392–401; *Advocate,* January 23, November 20, 1835. See also Fred W. Allsopp, *Albert Pike; A Biography* (Little Rock, 1928), 1–68.

[53] *Advocate,* January 23, May 8, 29, June 12, July 3, 1835. See also "Remarks," *ibid.,* June 26, 1835; "Col. Fowler's Speech," *Gazette,* June 30, 1835.

[54] *Times,* May 16, 23, 1835. The first issue of the *Times* appeared January 30, 1835. *Ibid.,* January 30, 1835. Hunt, a native Ohioan, twenty-one years old, was a recent immigrant. *Ibid.,* September 19, 1835.

[55] St. Francis, "State Government. No. I," *ibid.,* May 16, 1835.

[56] Arkansas, "No. II," *ibid.,* May 30, 1835.

count of the slavery problem because the Missouri Compromise of 1820 gave states in the Louisiana Purchase below 36°30′ the right to hold slaves.[57]

Another writer objected to immediate state government for two reasons,

first, we are in such a state of vassalage to a few men, that a Constitution made now would be exclusively of a party character, and shaped to suit the views of the ambitious partizan—secondly, we should have all our officers, state and federal, saddled upon us from one family [presumably meaning the Sevier-Conway-Johnson family] . . .[58]

Notwithstanding a certain amount of opposition, the people generally seemed to be overwhelmingly favorable to immediate statehood. During the spring and summer, public meetings in Jackson, Hot Spring, Pulaski, Pope, Arkansas, St. Francis, Independence, Crittenden, Lawrence, and Washington Counties requested the governor to convene the legislature in special session after the August election in order that it might provide for an election of delegates to a constitutional convention.[59] At Woodruff's suggestion the ballots used in the August election asked voters whether they were for or against statehood.[60] The result was overwhelming in favor of immediate statehood.[61] A large vote (5,764) for Sevier, though he was unopposed, also seemed to imply popular confidence in his course in the matter of immediate statehood.[62] The census taken during the summer showed Arkansas to possess a population of 52,240, an increase in excess of 20,000 since 1830, and more than the required number for statehood.[63]

[57] Arkansas, "State Government. No. III," *ibid.*, June 13, 1835.

[58] Americus, "State Government," *ibid.*, May 9, 1835.

[59] *Gazette*, May 26, June 9, 16, 23, 30, July 7, 21, 28, August 25, 1835; *Advocate*, June 19, July 17, 24, August 28, 1835. See also Jesse Turner, "The Constitution of 1836," *Publications of the Arkansas Historical Association*, Vol. III (Fayetteville, 1911), 82–86; Taylor, *Negro Slavery in Arkansas*, 36–39; Brown, "Albert Pike, Arkansas Editor," *Arkansas Historical Quarterly*, X, 401–402.

[60] "State Government," *Gazette*, May 26, 1835; *Advocate*, May 29, 1835. The *Times* complained because the ballot forms, which Woodruff printed, posed the question for or against statehood instead of for or against *"immediate* admission." *Times*, July 4, 1835. Actually Woodruff's reason for suggesting the inclusion of the question on the ballots was to determine popular attitude toward "pressing the admission of Arkansas . . . at the ensuing session of Congress." "Form of Election Returns," *Gazette*, June 30, 1835.

[61] *Gazette*, September 29, 1835; *Times*, August 29, 1835.

[62] Election Proclamation, September 26, 1835, *Gazette*, September 29, 1835. William Field, Wharton Rector, Mark Bean, and others were mentioned in the newspapers prior to the election as possible contenders for Sevier's post. *Advocate*, May 15, 29, 1835; *Times*, May 16, 23, 1835; *Gazette*, September 30, October 7, 1834, June 2, 1835.

[63] Abstract of Territorial Census, January 4, 1836, *Terr. Papers*, XXI, 1144–1145. Woodruff reported the number in August, 1835, as 51,809, including 9,838 Negroes, but his figures were based on incomplete returns. *Gazette*, August 25, 1835.

Governor Fulton refused to call a special session of the legislature, arguing that Arkansas did not have the "power" to form a constitution and state government without a congressional enabling act. Even if the treaty of 1803 with France gave such power—and Fulton denied that it did—Fulton did not see how it "fixes a rule which Congress is bound to obey, and establishes a right in favor of the citizens of this Territory, when the constitution itself leaves the power to admit new States entirely to the sense of justice and expediency of the Congress." A constitution "can only be made by the people of a State, in their sovereign capacity. So long as they are bound by the organic law of a superior government, they are dependent upon her" and can do nothing to destroy "the government which the superior has established over them." Thus the territorial legislature had no power to alter the government established by Congress.[64]

Editors Woodruff and Pike were both disappointed at Fulton's stand.[65] Pike thought that the governor could have called the territorial lawmakers into special session

without alluding in any way to their action on the question of State government. If they saw fit, after coming together, to act on that matter, the Governor could have vetoed it—and he would have given no aid to "this unlawful proceeding."

The legislature might then have overridden Fulton's veto, freeing Fulton from any responsibility in the matter. Editor Hunt also disapproved Fulton's course because it ran counter to the wishes of a majority of the people.[66] Only the Helena *Herald* came out in support of the governor's position.[67]

Fulton reported to the Secretary of State that his address had produced "no change of determination whatever," and requested that, should the legislature during the regular October meeting pass a "disorganizing" act, the matter be laid before the President.[68] Nearly two weeks later Fulton wrote directly to the President asking for instructions. Though he was "exceedingly anxious that Arkansas may vote in the Presidential contest," he did not "wish the people

---

[64] Fulton, "To the Public," August 4, 1835, *Gazette*, August 4, 1835; *Times*, August 8, 1835; *Advocate*, August 14, 1835. See also Fulton to Woodruff, *Gazette*, September 1, 1835.

[65] "Gov. Fulton, and the State Government Question," *Gazette*, August 25, 1835; *Advocate*, August 14, 1835.

[66] *Times*, August 8, 1835.

[67] "Governor Fulton's Address," *Herald*, reprinted in *Times*, August 29, 1835, and *Gazette*, September 8, 1835.

[68] Governor Fulton to Secretary of State, August 10, 1835, enclosing a copy of his address to the public. *Terr. Papers*, XXI, 1064–1073.

to commit themselves, until next summer." His reluctance stemmed from a belief that Chester Ashley and other friends of Hugh Lawson White, presidential candidate from Tennessee,[69] would, "under the influence of the existing excitement"—presumably excitement against Jackson for his attitude toward the national bank—be able in the congressional and state elections to obtain the election of anti-Jackson men. There was

something of *Bankism,* as well as Whiteism, at the bottom of this violent struggle here [on the matter of immediate statehood]. Ashley, who completely controls a powerful party, is a violent Bank man; and *must* have obtained loans from *some quarter,* to the amount of $100,000 within the last two years.—During the Bank panic, he publicly wished "all the dollars of the Bank were in your belly."[70]

Fulton's letter moved President Jackson to ask Attorney General Benjamin F. Butler whether the people of Arkansas could lawfully form a constitution and state government without first obtaining congressional authority.[71] Butler's opinion, forwarded on October 3 to Fulton, concurred in Fulton's views "so far as they indicate an intention not to sanction . . . any legislative or other procedings [*sic*] towards the formation of a state Government, until Congress shall have authorized it." But the people had a right to meet together peaceably in primary assemblies, "or in conventions chosen by such assemblies, for the purpose of petitioning Congress" for admission into the Union. If Arkansans thought it "proper to accompany their petition by a written constitution" framed by delegates "chosen by such assemblies," Butler could "perceive no legal objection to their power to do so."[72]

The legislature met and organized on October 5.[73] In his biennial message the governor defined his position with respect to statehood:

[69] "Hon. Hugh L. White," *Advocate,* April 17, 1835.

[70] Governor Fulton to President, August 22, 1835, *Terr. Papers,* XXI, 1074. A correspondent in the *Times* also believed that the national bank was involved in "the sudden change" in favor of immediate state government. Communication of A Citizen, *Times,* September 12, 1835.

[71] Secretary of State to Attorney General, August 31, 1835, *Terr. Papers,* XXI, 1077.

[72] Attorney General to Secretary of State, September 21, 1835, and Acting Secretary of State to Governor Fulton, October 3, 1835, *Terr. Papers,* XXI, 1082–1087, 1097; "The Governor's Message, and Opinion of the Attorney General," *Gazette,* November 10, 1835; *Times,* November 16, 1835.

[73] The council convened in the Baptist Meeting House, the house, in the Presbyterian Meeting House. "The General Assembly," *Gazette,* October 6, 1835. Councilmen were James Smith, Arkansas County; John Clark, Chicot County; Amos Kuykendall, Conway County; Richard C. S. Brown, Crawford County; Abner E. Thornton, Clark County; Thomas H. Clark, Carroll County; George B. Croft, Greene County; Wright W. Elliott, Crittenden County; James W. Judkins, Hempstead County; Hiram A. Whitting-

Considering the pecuniary sacrifices and the increase of burthens which a change of government was calculated to produce, I have doubted the expediency of too sudden a change, but I have felt no desire to check the tide of popular opinion in favor of a State Government; and, as the people have willed it, I now feel it to be my duty to forward this important object, by all the means competent to be used by the Executive power of this Territory.[74]

Woodruff was "highly pleased to perceive" that Fulton "recedes from the grounds heretofore [*sic*] taken by him, against State Government."[75] But if Woodruff thought, as he seemed to, that Fulton no longer considered an enabling act necessary, he was mistaken, for the governor's message nowhere said that he would support the calling of a constitutional convention in the absence of congressional authority.[76]

On October 7 each house appointed seven members to a joint committee to consider that part of the governor's message pertaining to statehood.[77] A resolution submitted a week later that the assembly prescribe the time and mode for organizing a convention to frame a constitution was approved by overwhelming votes in both

---

ton, Hot Spring County; Jacob Wolf, Izard County; John Ringgold, Independence County; Rowland Tidwell, Jackson County; Richard H. Young, Jefferson County; John W. Patrick, Johnson County; Peyton R. Pitman, Lawrence County; Jacob Buzzard, Lafayette County; Thomas J. Mills, Mississippi County; Isaac Taylor, Monroe County; James Lattermore, Miller County; William F. Moore, Phillips County; Elijah Kelly, Pike County; John Williamson, Pope County; Charles Caldwell, Pulaski County; Mark W. Izard, St. Francis County; Joseph W. McKean, Sevier County; Hugh Bradley, Union County; John L. Lafferty, Van Buren County; and Mark Bean, Washington County. House members were Bushrod W. Lee and Charles H. Seay, Arkansas and Union Counties; Hedgeman Triplett, Chicot County; Thomas Mathers, Conway and Van Buren Counties; James Logan and Andrew Morton, Crawford County; John Wilson, Clark and Hot Spring Counties; John Troy, Crittenden and Mississippi Counties; John E. Stallings, Carroll County; William Shaw and James H. Walker, Hempstead County; William Moore and Morgan Magness, Independence County; Brown C. Roberts, Izard County; John Hill and E. D. W. Scruggs, Jackson, St. Francis, and Monroe Counties; M. R. T. Outlaw, Jefferson County; John Ward, Johnson County; Joseph Porter, William Jarrett, and A. Henderson, Lawrence and Greene Counties; Thomas J. Peel, Lafayette County; N. Dandrige Ellis, Miller County; John J. Bowie, Phillips County; Laban Howell, Pope County; William Cummins and Absalom Fowler, Pulaski County; James Holman, Sevier and Pike Counties; and Abraham Whinnery, David Walker, Francis Dunn, Thomas H. Tennant, and Onesimus Evans, Washington County. "General Assembly," *Gazette,* October 6, 1835; *Advocate,* October 9, 1835; *Times,* October 10, 1835.

[74] "Governor's Message," October 6, 1835, *Gazette,* October 6, 1835; *Advocate,* October 9, 1835; *Times,* October 10, 1835.

[75] "The General Assembly," *Gazette,* October 6, 1835.

[76] On this matter, see communications of Subscriber and Justicia, *ibid.,* February 16, 1836.

[77] "General Assembly," *ibid.,* October 13, 1835; *Times,* October 10, 1835. The council appointed Ringgold, Bean, John Clark, Moore, Williamson, Brown, and McKean; the house, Fowler, Cummins, Mathers, James H. Walker, David Walker, Evans, and Ellis.

houses.[78] On October 19 Chairman Fowler of the joint committee introduced a bill providing for the election of forty-two delegates to a constitutional convention to meet the first Monday of January, 1836, at Little Rock.[79]

In the joint committee Fowler had proposed, according to his own account written some weeks later, that the convention be either identical in number (sixty-two) and apportionment with the territorial assembly or that it consist of sixty members apportioned according to white population. A majority of the committee favored a smaller body, and someone suggested forty-five delegates to be apportioned equally among the white population. Ellis of Miller County objected to the proposed method of apportionment, contending that three-fifths of the slaves should be counted. But he "then expressed himself satisfied with the proposition of some other member of the committee that each county should have one representative, and the residue be apportioned among the larger counties" according to the number of whites. This proposition was approved and a bill was drafted providing for the election of forty-two delegates, half of them to come from the south and east.[80]

On the very day the bill was introduced, Woodruff noticed considerable objection to it among the members from the south and east on the matter of representation and predicted that unless the north and west made some concession the bill might be rejected.[81] The difficulty rose from Arkansas' being divided geographically into two major regions—the highlands of the north and west and the lowlands of the south and east. In 1835 about 46 per cent of the total population and about 66 per cent of the slaves lived in the seventeen lowland counties of the south and east, the remainder in the seventeen highland counties of the north and west.[82] This disparity in total and slave populations between the two regions is also evident in later censuses.[83]

When on October 20 the convention bill came up for considera-

[78] "General Assembly," *Gazette,* October 20, 1835; *Times,* October 26, 1835.

[79] "General Assembly," *Gazette,* October 27, 1835; *Times,* October 26, 1835.

[80] Fowler, "To the Freemen of the Counties of White, Saline, & Pulaski," December 3, 1835, *Advocate,* December 4, 1835.

[81] *Gazette,* October 20, 1835.

[82] These percentages are derived from the territorial census of 1835. *Terr. Papers,* XXI, 1144–1145; *Gazette,* August 25, 1835.

[83] See Taylor, *Negro Slavery in Arkansas,* 27, 49; Robert B. Walz, "Arkansas Slaveholdings and Slaveholders in 1850," *Arkansas Historical Quarterly,* XII (Spring, 1953), 38–51. My percentages and Taylor's are not, owing evidently to our having used different dividing lines between the sections, entirely compatible. For excellent maps showing the regional divisions of Arkansas, see Robert Bradshaw Walz, "Migration into Arkansas, 1834–1880" (unpublished Ph.D. dissertation, University of Texas, 1958), 36, 40.

tion in the house, James H. Walker of Hempstead County moved an amendment providing that each county send to the convention delegates equal in number to its representatives and councilmen in the territorial legislature.[84] According to Editor Pike, Walker "defended his position of property representation, by the argument that were it not for the slaves in the Territory, we have not the requisite population to entitle us to admission into the Union."[85]

Speaking in favor of the amendment, Cummins of Pulaski County asserted (as reported by Woodruff) that

it would create a *balance of power,* and check the *sectional feelings* which had unfortunately sprung up in the Legislature, and which would most probably be imparted to the people, and would again influence the Convention in forming the Constitution. He [Cummins] urged, that, since sectional interests seemed to exist in the Territory, it was the duty of the Legislature to guard against their having any improper influence, by giving a district representation, which was the mode adopted in the formation of the Federal Constitution, to balance and unite the different districts . . .[86]

Cummins later told his constituents that he had supported the measure because it would have made his county, located in the center of the Territory, the balance of power between the north and west and the south and east whereas under the committee bill Pulaski "did not so fully hold the balance in her hands."[87]

After a motion by Whinnery of Washington County to lay the bill on the table had failed, Walker's amendment was voted on and passed 18 to 15, the south and east supporting it, the north and west opposing. The house then went into committee of the whole on the convention bill and reported it back without amendment. At this point David Walker of Washington County moved to commit the bill to a select committee with instructions to amend it so as to give "to every five hundred free white male inhabitants the right to send one Representative" to the convention. James H. Walker and Cummins objected strongly to such an amendment on the grounds that it would destroy "the county representation, and gave the entire control of the destinies of the country to a few of the populous counties."[88]

[84] Fowler said that Walker's amendment called for twenty-nine delegates from the north and west and thirty-three from the south and east (including Pulaski County). Fowler, "To the Freemen of the Counties of White, Saline, & Pulaski," December 3, 1835, *Advocate,* December 4, 1835.

[85] *Ibid.,* October 30, 1835.

[86] "The Convention Bill," *Gazette,* October 27, 1835.

[87] Cummins, "To the Voters of Pulaski, Saline, and White Counties," *Advocate,* November 20, 1835.

[88] See "The Convention Bill," *Gazette,* October 27, 1835.

By a vote of 17 to 16 the south and east succeeded in defeating Walker's motion. The convention bill was then engrossed for a third reading.[89]

The next day the house defeated a motion by Fowler to reconsider the order to engross the bill and one by Howell of Pope County to reconsider the vote on Walker's motion to commit the bill to a select committee. Another motion by David Walker, this one to commit the bill to a select committee with instructions to report a clause making provision for the election of one delegate for every five hundred free white males, "provided that each county should have one delegate," carried 17 to 15. The voting alignment was almost identical with that on David Walker's previous motion except that Howell voted this time with the north and west and Roberts, who had been supporting the south and east, apparently did not vote.[90]

On October 22 David Walker of the select committee reported the bill as instructed, and the house approved the report by a vote of 17 to 16. The alignment on this division was identical with that on the previous one except Roberts was now present and voting with the south and east. The house rules were on motion of Whinnery dispensed with and the bill read for a third time. Cummins promptly offered an amendment "giving every county one member, and then dividing the whole number of free white males into divisions of five hundred, and giving each division one member," but he subsequently withdrew his motion. The convention bill was then voted on and passed by an overwhelming vote.

Taking up the bill on October 23, the council after some consideration referred it to the committee of the whole. The next day the committee reported an amendment that the convention consist of the same number of delegates as the territorial legislature and that representation be apportioned in the same manner.[91] The council voted 15 to 13 to concur in the report, the north and west voting against. After a third reading the amended bill was returned to the house.

In the house on October 26 a compromise proposal by David Walker to amend the council's amendment passed 27 to 6. The same day the council concurred, 25 to 4, in the action of the house.[92] As finally amended, the bill provided for fifty-two delegates, twenty-

[89] "General Assembly," *ibid.; Times,* November 2, 1835.

[90] "General Assembly," *Gazette,* October 27, 1835; *Times,* November 2, 1835. The journal gives the vote as 17 to 16 but actually lists only 15 members voting "no."

[91] See *Advocate,* October 30, 1835.

[92] "General Assembly," *Gazette,* October 27, 1835; *Times,* November 2, 9, 1835.

seven to come from the north and west and twenty-five from the south and east.[93]

After the adjournment David Walker stated in the *Gazette* that the representatives of the southern and eastern counties had

insisted, as of right, that they should have an additional representation equal to three-fifths of their slave population; while other gentleman on the same side, towards the close of the debate, very *modestly* insisted that districts of country should have votes in Convention, independent of population.[94]

"Senex" denied that all southern and eastern representatives had, as Walker implied, insisted upon counting three-fifths of the slaves in apportioning representatives; actually only a small minority had spoken "in favor of this, even in private conversation, and only one spoke of it on the floor . . ." The reason a majority of the southern and eastern members opposed an apportionment based solely on free white population was that they feared the south and east would be dominated by the more populous north and west.[95]

When the convention bill reached Governor Fulton he declined to sign it because he did not believe he had the "power to sanction" a measure which the legislature had no "power" to pass in the first place. Considering it useless, however, to return it for reconsideration, he allowed it to become law without his signature. In support of his views he included the opinion of the Attorney General (referred to above) in his message informing the legislature of his action.[96]

Other work of the legislature consisted of creating White, Randolph, Saline, and Searcy Counties; graduating the land tax according to quality of land; calling in scrip issued by Crawford County; offering a bounty to persons killing wolves; incorporating the town of

[93] "The Convention Bill," *Gazette*, November 3, 1835; *Times*, November 9, 1835; Fowler, "To the Freemen of the Counties of White, Saline, & Pulaski," December 3, 1835, *Advocate*, December 4, 1835; *Times*, November 2, 1835; *Arkansas Acts*, 1835, pp. 96–99. The sectional distribution of delegates is mine.

[94] Walker, "To the People of Washington County," November 3, 1835, *Gazette*, November 3, 1835. See also *Times*, November 9, 1835; communication by Walker published in *ibid.*, November 30, 1835; *Gazette*, November 24, 1835; and Jack B. Scroggs, "Arkansas Statehood: A Study in State and National Political Schism," *Arkansas Historical Quarterly*, XX (Autumn, 1961), 239.

[95] Senex, "Mr. Walker's Circular," *Gazette*, November 10, 1835. Two of Albert Pike's editorials support this assertion. *Advocate*, October 30, November 6, 1835. See also communications of "A.B.C.," *Times*, November 23, 30, 1835, and Brown, "Albert Pike, Arkansas Editor," *Arkansas Historical Quarterly*, X, 404–405.

[96] "The Convention Bill," *Gazette*, November 3, 1835; "The Governor's Message, and Opinion of the Attorney General," *ibid.*, November 10, 1835; *Advocate*, November 13, 1835; *Times*, November 9, 16, 1835.

Fayetteville; dissolving a marriage; and appropriating money for part of 1835, 1836, and 1837.[97] A bill to charter a bank passed the council but in the house was laid on the table until January 1, 1836.[98] Several memorials to Congress dealt mainly with land and internal improvements.[99] The publishers of the *Times,* John H. Reed and Jefferson Smith,[100] were elected public printers.[101] Elias N. Conway was chosen to be auditor and Charles P. Bertrand to be territorial treasurer.[102]

With the passage of the convention bill of 1835 the initial phase of the statehood movement may be considered to have terminated. So great was the desire of a majority of the people and their representatives for immediate statehood that the legislature had followed Michigan in the anomalous action of calling a constitutional convention without prior authorization by Congress.[103] The final steps toward statehood would be taken the next year.

[97] *Arkansas Acts,* 1835, pp. 9–13, 14–16, 26–31, 33–34, 36–39, 42–44, 50–55, 67–68, 84–87, 100–103.

[98] *Times,* November 9, 1835.

[99] *Terr. Papers,* XXI, 1105, 1110–1113, 1114–1117, 1121–1125.

[100] Smith had in June, 1835, become a partner of Andrew J. Hunt. But Hunt had continued to be sole editor until his death in September. John H. Reed succeeded Hunt as both partner and sole editor. *Times,* June 20, September 19, October 3, 10, 1835.

[101] *Advocate,* October 16, 1835. Woodruff complained that the legislature did not decide the election of a printer "on the merits or competency of the candidates to execute the public printing with neatness and despatch, but on the *proposals* made by them." "Joint Elections by the Legislature," *Gazette,* October 13, 1835.

[102] *Advocate,* October 16, 1835.

[103] Tennessee had in 1796 framed a constitution without an enabling act. William Alphonso Walker, Jr., "Tennessee, 1796–1821" (unpublished Ph.D. dissertation, University of Texas, 1959), 24–85; Philip M. Hamer, ed., *Tennessee, A History, 1673–1932* (4 vols., New York, 1933), I, 169–182. Vermont, Kentucky, and Maine had also framed state constitutions without the prior authorization of Congress, but none of these had been a territory before its admission as a state. See Dallas T. Herndon, *Centennial History of Arkansas* (3 vols., Little Rock, 1922), I, 225–226.

CHAPTER TWELVE

The Territory Becomes a State

DURING THE PERIOD between the meeting of the assembly of 1835 and the convening of the constitutional convention, the *Times* and *Advocate* debated the question of apportioning representation in the future state legislature. Pike favored a lower house with membership apportioned according to the number of free white males and a senate with membership based on district representation. The house would be the people's *"agent"* and the senate would serve as a check on the house and protect the minority in the south and east from oppression by the majority in the north and west. "If," Pike reasoned, "the principle that the majority shall rule is not to be taken with some reservation and allowance, then our forefathers ought never to have declared themselves independent—for they were greatly the minority in the British Empire."[1] Editor Reed and correspondents in the *Times* favored basing representation in both houses on the number of free white males, arguing that any other basis was "aristocracy, and must tend to subvert the liberties of the people."[2]

In December, 1835, Delegate Sevier wrote Woodruff that he had recently arrived in Washington to find that the course of Arkansas in the matter of statehood had been misunderstood.

The impression had extended widely, that Arkansas intended to form a State Government, and kick *into nonentity the Territorial authorities, without the approbation of Congress.* I have taken pains to explain this truly—have pointed out the *false issue* upon which we were likely to have been adjudged. I have informed the President, and such other of our friends as I had an opportunity to address upon the subject, that we have contemplated no such thing.

[1] *Arkansas Advocate* (Little Rock), December 11, 18, 25, 1835, January 8, 1836.
[2] *Times* (Little Rock), November 23, 30, December 7, 21, 1835. Woodruff took no stand on the issue.

Sevier went on to say that his explanation seemed "satisfactory to every body," and to urge that a republican constitution be framed and in Washington by mid-February; if this was done, "Arkansas and Michigan will be received together into the Union, without difficulty."[3]

The delegates to the constitutional convention came together January 4, 1836, in the Baptist Meeting House at Little Rock.[4] John Wilson of Clark County was elected president, Charles P. Bertrand, secretary, and Albert Pike, printer.[5] Both Wilson and Pike, notwithstanding their diverse factional allegiances (Wilson was a Sevierite, Pike a member of the opposition), had in 1835 supported the position of the south and east on representation in the convention (above).[6]

On January 5 a resolution by Sam C. Roane of Jefferson County that a state constitution should be framed and a state government established passed 49 to 1, James H. Walker of Hempstead County dissenting. The next day the convention decided to move to the Presbyterian Church, which afforded better facilities.[7]

[3] Sevier to Woodruff, December 4, 1835, *Arkansas Gazette* (Little Rock), December 29, 1835.

[4] "Meeting of the Convention," *ibid.,* January 5, 1836. Delegates to the convention were William Cummins, Absalom Fowler, and John McLain, Pulaski, White, and Saline Counties; James S. Conway, Hot Spring County; Sam C. Roane, Jefferson County; Elijah Kelly, Pike County; Grandison D. Royston and James H. Walker, Hempstead County; Josiah N. Wilson, Lafayette County; Travis G. Wright, Miller County; Andrew J. May, Union County; J. D. Calvert and Wright W. Elliott, Crittenden County; William Strong and Caleb S. Manly, St. Francis County; Henry L. Biscoe and George W. Ferebee, Phillips County; Bushrod W. Lee, Arkansas County; Thomas J. Lacy, Monroe County; John Robinson, Jackson County; Terence Farrelly, Arkansas and Jefferson Counties; John Adams, Izard and Carroll Counties; John Clark and Anthony H. Davies, Chicot County; Robert Smith, Thomas S. Drew, David W. Lowe, and Henry Slavens, Randolph and Lawrence Counties; John Ringgold and Townsend Dickinson, Independence County; Charles R. Saunders, Izard County; John F. King, Carroll County; David Walker, Mark Bean, Abraham Whinnery, William McK. Ball, James Boon, and Robert McCamy, Washington County; James Woodson Bates, John Drennen, and Richard C. S. Brown, Crawford County; Gilbert Marshall, Scott County; Thomas Murray, Jr., Pope County; Lorenzo N. Clarke, Johnson County; Andrew Scott, Johnson and Pope Counties; Walker W. Trimble, Van Buren County; Nimrod Menefee, Conway County; Joseph W. McKean, Sevier County; Richard Ellis, Miller and Sevier Counties; G. L. Martin, Greene County; and John Wilson, Clark County. John L. Lafferty successfully contested the election of Walker W. Trimble, and William D. Ferguson unsuccessfully contested that of Wright W. Elliott. On January 21 George Halbrook replaced Richard Ellis, who had resigned. There is no record of attendance by a delegate from Mississippi County. *Arkansas Constitutional Convention Journal,* 1836, pp. 3–6, 35. The journal of the convention is also printed in the January and early February issues, 1836, of the *Gazette,* the *Advocate,* and the *Times.*

[5] *Convention Journal,* 4, 7; "Albert Pike's Autobiography," *New Age Magazine,* XXXVII (December, 1929), 720.

[6] Bertrand's attitude on the question of representation is not known.

[7] *Convention Journal,* 5–6.

During the early meetings committees on various subjects—e.g., the executive, the judiciary, boundaries, and banking—were appointed to draft provisions for inclusion in the constitution.[8] Editor Pike said on January 15 that he had read the committee reports "with high gratification—for though there are some things which might be bettered, yet there are more which are beyond all praise." So far, everything had been "harmonious and peaceful."[9] David Walker of Washington County wrote his wife that "We are doing more business and in better feeling than I expected, yet the exciting question [of representation] is not yet reported."[10]

Arkansas is, one recalls, divided geographically into highlands and lowlands, the north and west being the highland area, the south and east the lowland. The north and west contained in 1835 about 58 per cent of the white population but only some 34 per cent of the slaves. The table below, derived from the territorial census of 1835, shows the black and total populations of the sections by counties.[11]

Sectional differences over the problem of the apportionment of representation in the legislature had already plagued constitutional conventions in other new Southern states. In the Mississippi constitutional convention of 1817 western Mississippi, the blacker portion of the state, had triumphed over eastern Mississippi in the apportion-

[8] See *ibid.*, 5–8. The membership of the various committees is available in Jesse Turner, "The Constitution of 1836," *Publications of the Arkansas Historical Association*, Vol. III (Fayetteville, 1911), 103, note 46.

[9] *Advocate*, January 15, 1836.

[10] Walker to wife, January 9, 1836, *Washington County Historical Society Flashback*, I (November, 1951), unpaged; W. J. Lemke, ed., "The Walker Family Letters," *Washington County Historical Society Bulletin*, No. 21 (Fayetteville, 1956), letter 76. For an account of the routine work of the convention, see Turner, "The Constitution of 1836," *Publications of the Arkansas Historical Association*, III, 101–119.

[11] These figures are based on an official abstract of a territorial census taken in 1835 (*Terr. Papers*, XXI, 1144–1145); on a detailed report of incomplete returns of the census of 1835 in the *Gazette*, August 25, 1835; and on an arbitrary adjustment of my own. The official abstract, from which the total population is taken, shows a slightly larger total population than does the report in the *Gazette*, presumably because the latter was based on incomplete returns. The *Gazette* and the abstract agree on the total number of Negroes in the Territory, but the abstract shows only the total; county figures are from the *Gazette*. Since Randolph, Searcy, White, and Saline Counties were created after the census was taken (*Arkansas Acts*, 1835, pp. 9–13, 26–31, 36–39, 84–87), the distribution of population between them and their parent counties in 1835 is not known. As a further complication, Randolph County seems to belong to the east, and Lawrence, the parent county, to the north. I have allocated one-third of the population of undivided Lawrence County to the south and east and two-thirds to the north and west. The sectional distribution of counties shown in this table has been arrived at by comparing a reproduction of a physiographic map of Arkansas in Robert Bradshaw Walz, "Migration into Arkansas, 1834–1880" (unpublished Ph.D. dissertation, University of Texas, 1958), 36, with Tanner's Map of Arkansas, 1836, in Map Collection, University of Texas Library.

	South and East			North and West	
County	Blacks	Total Population	County	Blacks	Total Population
Sevier	276	1,350	Washington	508	6,724
Miller	376	1,373	Carroll	81	1,357
Hempstead	817	2,955	Izard	155	1,873
Lafayette	1,032	1,446	Lawrence	328	2,563
Clark	203	1,285	Independence	429	2,653
Union	217	878	Van Buren	11	855
Chicot	1,364	2,471	Pope	146	1,318
Jefferson	523	1,474	Johnson	290	1,803
Arkansas	507	1,973	Scott and		
Phillips	272	1,518	Crawford	557	3,139
Crittenden	230	1,407	Conway	107	1,214
St. Francis	176	1,896	Pulaski	687	3,513
Jackson	182	891	Hot Spring	69	617
Mississippi	...	437	Pike	25	449
Randolph	164	1,281	Searcy created 1835 after census		
Monroe	57	556	White " " " "		
Greene	49	971	Saline " " " "		
Total	6,445	24,162		3,393	28,078

ment of the senate, but had failed in an attempt to establish the Federal ratio (five slaves equal three whites) for apportionment in the house.[12] In the Alabama constitutional convention two years later the "black counties" had fought unsuccessfully against the "white counties" to establish the Federal ratio as a basis of representation in both houses. They then lost an effort to give each county one member in the senate regardless of population. The final outcome of the Alabama struggle was apportionment of both houses on a basis of white population.[13] The experiences of Mississippi and Alabama served sufficient warning that Arkansas also could expect a contest over representation.

The report of the committee on the legislative branch, made on January 19 by Chairman Bates (Crawford County), did indeed break the harmonious character of the Arkansas convention. The committee called for a senate to consist of not less than nineteen nor more than thirty-three members elected by the voters of seven senatorial districts. Pending a reapportionment in 1840 on the basis of the number of free white males then returned by a census, the senate should contain nineteen members. The house was to consist of not less than fifty members nor more than one hundred, each county to

[12] Edwin Arthur Miles, *Jacksonian Democracy in Mississippi* (Chapel Hill, 1960), 33–34.

[13] Malcolm Cook McMillan, *Constitutional Development in Alabama, 1798–1901: A Study in Politics, the Negro, and Sectionalism* (Chapel Hill, 1955), 36–37.

have at least one, and no new county to be created until its population entitled it to a member. Until the first census fifty representatives were to be apportioned among the several counties.[14]

Ringgold of Independence County next submitted a minority report which, to judge from the support it received, proposed an arrangement more favorable to the north and west. Pending a census in 1837, the senate should consist of seventeen members from fourteen districts and the house of fifty-nine members apportioned among the counties. After the census the legislature should determine the size of both the senate and house and apportion the seats in both on the basis of the number of free white males, no district to have more than one senator.[15]

Soon after the majority report was taken up nearly a week later Ringgold moved that the report of the minority replace the sections concerning representation. A vote was taken and the motion carried, 26 to 24, the south and east voting against (Bates was absent, evidently because he was sick).[16]

After the failure of a motion by Farrelly of Arkansas and Jefferson Counties that the convention adjourn *"sine die"* (i.e., break up),[17] and another by Fowler of Pulaski, White, and Saline Counties to refer the report of the committee on the legislative branch, as amended, to a select committee, Murray of Pope County won a motion to reconsider his vote on Ringgold's proposition, thereby turning the previous 26 to 24 vote in favor of the proposition into a 25 to 25 tie.

Ringgold's proposition having been thus defeated, Drew of Randolph and Lawrence Counties proposed another amendment to the majority report on representation. The legislature was to cause a census to be taken every four years, beginning in 1838, and apportion representation in the senate among districts according to the number of free white males. There should be not less than seventeen nor more than thirty-three senators. Until the number reached thirty-three, the senatorial ratio should be one senator for every fifteen hundred free white males. Pending the first apportionment fifteen districts should have one senator each and Washington County should

---

[14] Orville W. Taylor, *Negro Slavery in Arkansas* (Durham, 1958), 41, is completely mistaken in saying that the committee on the legislative branch "at first recommended that representation [he evidently means in both houses] be drawn from districts comprised of equal numbers of inhabitants, whether white or black . . ."

[15] *Convention Journal,* 29–32.

[16] See *ibid.,* 43.

[17] See *Gazette,* January 26, 1836.

have two. The house should have not less than fifty nor more than one hundred members. Taking five hundred free white males as the ratio until the number of representatives reached one hundred, the legislature should after the first census apportion representation among the several counties on the basis of the number of free white males, each county to have at least one representative unless, in the case of counties established in the future, its population did not entitle it to one.

Farrelly promptly moved that Drew's proposal be amended to omit the provision calling for a ratio of fifteen hundred free white males in apportioning senators. The amendment failed, 25 to 25. Fowler then won a motion to refer the report to a select committee. Drew's proposal seems not to have been brought to a vote.

The next day (January 26) Murray offered a resolution that the convention could "recognize no other basis of representation than the free white male citizens of the country." A motion by Walker of Hempstead County to table Murray's motion carried 36 to 14.

On behalf of the select committee Fowler now reported comprehensive proposals to settle the problem of apportionment. The senate should consist of not less than seventeen nor more than thirty-three members. The legislature should cause a census to be taken in 1838, and every four years thereafter, in order to alter the senatorial districts so that each contained an equal number of free white males. The number of senators might not exceed twenty-five as long as the state had fewer than five hundred thousand inhabitants. Until the number reached twenty-five, the ratio of representation should be one senator to fifteen hundred free white males. Pending the first census, there should be sixteen districts, each except Washington County, to have one senator; Washington should have two. The house should begin with fifty-four members, never have more than one hundred, and be reapportioned after every census on the basis of the free white male population; each county was to receive at least one representative, and no new county to be established without population sufficient to entitle it to one representative. The number of representatives might not exceed seventy-five as long as the state had fewer than five hundred thousand inhabitants. Until the number reached seventy-five, the ratio should be one representative for every five hundred free white males.

By a vote of 28 to 22, the north and west opposing, the convention adopted Fowler's report.[18] Thus the difficulty over the matter of

[18] *Convention Journal*, 38–44.

representation ended in compromise. According to Woodruff, there were

to be 17 senators—8 on each side of the *imaginary line* which some dema-
gogues have attempted to draw through the Territory (or State that shortly
is to be), and one to the centre district, which is composed of the counties of
Pulaski, White and Saline.[19]

Woodruff's statement was nearly accurate. Of the sixteen senatorial
districts, seven were in the south and east, six in the north and west,
and three cut across the sectional line. Assuming that districts crossing
the sectional line would elect senators favorable to the sections in
which a majority of the inhabitants resided, the north and west (including in it the district comprising Pulaski, White, and Saline Counties which Woodruff did not count in either section) would have a
total of nine senators, and the south and east, eight. The nine senators
from the north and west would represent about 24,685 whites, the
eight from the south and east, about 17,717 whites. Approximately
54 per cent of the white population in 1835 being male,[20] a senator
in the south or east would represent on the average about 1,196
white males, a senator from the north or west, about 1,481. These
arrangements were to prevail only until 1838.[21]

Presumably another part of the compromise, which Woodruff
did not mention, was the manner of handling representation in the
house. The south and east were allowed twenty-four representatives,
leaving thirty to the north and west. A member of the house from
the south or east would represent on the average about 399 white
males, one from the north or west, about 444. Again, as in the case
of the senate, the disproportion would presumably last in this form
only until 1838, though the small free white population of certain
counties, mostly in the south and east, might continue to give them
an overrepresentation in terms of white males.

On January 30, 1836, the convention adopted the constitution by
a vote of 46 to 4, Ball, Boon, McCamy, and Roane dissenting, and
shortly afterward adjourned.[22] Editor Pike congratulated

the country upon the happy termination of the deliberations of the Convention. The difficulties apprehended were fortunately not realized—and the
constitution, as finally signed gave general satisfaction to the members of that

---

[19] *Gazette*, January 26, 1836. See also *Advocate*, January 29, 1836.
[20] The percentage of males in the white population is derived from the detailed
census in the *Gazette*, August 25, 1835.
[21] See *Arkansas Acts*, 1838, pp. 1–2.
[22] *Convention Journal*, 50–52.

body. Sach [Such], we trust too, will be its effect among the people. We, for one, give it our almost unqualified approbation.[23]

The constitution, as finally completed, vested the executive power in a governor elected for a term of four years. In mild conformity with the principle of rotation in office, he was forbidden to serve for more than eight years in any twelve. The president of the senate and speaker of the house were next in line of succession to the governorship. A secretary of state was to be selected by the legislature for a term of four years, an auditor, a treasurer, and circuit attorneys for terms of two.

The judicial power was vested in a supreme court, circuit courts, county courts, and justices of the peace. The legislature might, if necessary, establish corporation and chancery courts. The supreme court was to be composed of three judges, one a chief justice, elected by the legislature for terms of eight years,[24] and having appellate jurisdiction only. Circuit judges were to be elected by the legislature for four-year terms, and to have original jurisdiction in criminal and civil cases. Justices of the peace were to be elected for two-year terms by the voters in the townships and preside over the county courts, which had jurisdiction in certain local matters.

Members of the house and of the senate were to have terms of two and four years, respectively. Meetings of the assembly were to be held biennially. The legislature might incorporate a state bank and such branch banks as were required for "public convenience," and might also incorporate a bank "calculated to aid and promote the great agricultural interests of the country." No bill of divorce was to be passed. An executive veto might be overridden by a majority of the whole membership in both houses. The lower house should have sole power to impeach, and all impeachments were to be tried by the senate. Laws should be passed from time to time "calculated to encourage intellectual, scientific and agricultural improvement." On the important subject of slavery, the assembly was forbidden to emancipate slaves without the consent of the owners or to prevent emigrants from bringing slaves into the state, though it could prevent slaves from being brought into the state as "merchandise" and "oblige" slaveholders to treat them "with humanity." Slaves on trial were not to be deprived of "an impartial jury," and when convicted of a capital

---

[23] *Advocate,* February 5, 1836.

[24] The report of the committee on the judiciary set the term of supreme court judges at six years, but the convention raised it to twelve, and then reduced it to eight. *Convention Journal,* 12, 33–35. Pike thought they should serve during good behavior, or at least ten years. *Advocate,* January 15, 22, 29, 1836.

offence they should "suffer the same degree of punishment as would be inflicted on a free white person."

Other provisions dealt with the organization of a state militia; required the state to encourage internal improvements; prohibited poll taxes "for other than county purposes"; and forbade the authorization of lotteries by the state. All property "subject to taxation" should be taxed "according to its value." Until otherwise provided by law, Little Rock was to remain the seat of government.[25]

The Arkansas constitution continued the democratic trend which had been evident in several other state constitutions framed in the previous two or three decades.[26] No property qualifications were required either to hold office or to vote. Officeholding was, however, restricted to persons acknowledging existence of a God, and voting was to be *viva voce* and limited to free white males. The governor was to be elected by the people, and might therefore be independent of the legislature, though lesser state officials and judges of the higher courts were to be chosen by that body. Local officers—sheriffs, coroners, surveyors, treasurers, constables, and justices of the peace—were to be popularly elected.

A comparison of the Arkansas constitution of 1836 with the five Southern state constitutions framed since 1819 (Alabama, 1819; Missouri, 1820; Virginia, 1830; Mississippi, 1832; Tennessee, 1834)[27] would seem to indicate that Arkansas neither made any notable innovations nor drew slavishly upon any particular model. Earlier constitutions, except that of Virginia, provided for popular election of the governor. Only Virginia required property qualifications for voting. A majority of these constitutions provided for judges of the higher courts to be elected by the legislature, usually to serve during good behavior. All except Virginia provided for local officers to be elected locally. The provisions in the Arkansas constitution pertaining to slavery were essentially the same as those in the

[25] *Arkansas Constitution* (1836) in Francis N. Thorpe, ed., *The Federal and State Constitutions . . . ,* 59 Cong., 2d sess., Doc. 357 (7 vols., Washington, 1909), I, 268–286; William McK. Ball and Sam C. Roane, compilers, *Revised Statutes of the State of Arkansas, Adopted at the October Session of the General Assembly . . . 1837 . . .* (Boston, 1838), 3–41; *Gazette Extra,* February 4, 1836; *Gazette,* February 9, 1836; *Advocate,* February 5, 1836; *Times,* February 8, 1836; *Constitutional Journal* (Helena), March 8, 1836.

[26] See Charles S. Sydnor, *The Development of Southern Sectionalism, 1819–1848* (Baton Rouge, 1948), 275–288; Fletcher M. Green, *Constitutional Development in the South Atlantic States, 1776–1860: A Study in the Evolution of Democracy* (Chapel Hill, 1930), 201–253.

[27] These constitutions are in Thorpe, ed., *Federal and State Constitutions,* I, 96–116, IV, 2049–2063, 2150–2167, VI, 3426–3444, VII, 3819–3829.

Alabama, Mississippi, and Missouri constitutions, and the sections relating to the amending process and to the changeover from territorial to state government were almost identical in wording with the parallel sections in the Missouri instrument.

To accompany the constitution the convention framed (for congressional approval) an ordinance which proposed, among other things, that the state be given (1) section sixteen in every township of public land for use of schools, (2) two sections per county for the erection of an academy in each county, (3) all salt springs and the townships on which they were located, (4) the Hot Springs and four sections of land surrounding them, and (5) eight hundred sections for internal improvements.[28]

Charles F. M. Noland left Little Rock with the constitution and ordinance on February 5.[29] He was, however, delayed en route,[30] and copies of the constitution in the *Gazette* and *Gazette Extra* arrived in Washington before Noland did. On March 2 Sevier wrote Woodruff that the copy in the *Gazette* "will answer for an investigation of the subject," but that the Committee on Territories could not report a bill for Arkansas until the official copy arrived. A bill to admit Michigan had already been reported out by the committee.[31] When Noland finally appeared on March 8 Sevier was unhappy to learn that he had brought only a single copy of the constitution addressed to the Secretary of State. Even before his arrival, however, the committee had agreed to report a bill without an official copy of the constitution. Sevier expected no difficulty in obtaining acceptance of the constitution, but the ordinance was a different matter; "the pruning knife, with a heavy hand, will have to be used—or it will not go through."[32]

On March 10, 1836, President Jackson transmitted to Congress "a report from the Secretary of State communicating the proceedings" of the Arkansas constitutional convention.[33] In the Senate James Buchanan of Pennsylvania promptly moved reference to a select committee. John M. Clayton of Delaware moved that the reference be to

[28] Clarence E. Carter, ed., *Territorial Papers of the United States,* Vol. XXI, *Arkansas Territory, 1829–1836* (Washington, 1954), 1189–1191.

[29] *Times,* February 8, 1836; *Gazette,* March 29, 1836.

[30] See *Advocate,* April 22, 1836.

[31] Sevier to Editor, March 1, 2, 1836, *Gazette,* March 29, 1836. See also Sevier to Editor, January 8, 11, 1836, *ibid.,* February 9, 1836.

[32] Two letters of Sevier to Editor, March 8, 1836, *ibid.,* April 5, 1836.

[33] See Secretary of State to President, March 9, 1836, and President to Congress, March 10, 1836, *Terr. Papers,* XXI, 1186–1191.

the select committee on Michigan's application for statehood. But Buchanan's motion prevailed by a non-sectional vote of 22 to 17.[34]

Sevier wrote Woodruff on March 14 that a bill for the admission of Arkansas would be reported to the House from the Committee on Territories as soon as the chairman could "get the floor." "Don't be astonished," he said, "if we should have another *Missouri discussion upon the subject of slavery.*"[35] On March 21 a bill was reported and referred to the Committee of the Whole, but the House seems to have taken no further action at that time.[36]

In the Senate next day Buchanan of the select committee to consider Arkansas' application for admission reported a bill for that purpose. The bill was read once and ordered to a second reading, but further consideration was postponed.[37]

Ten days later in the Senate Thomas Hart Benton of Missouri, who was sponsoring the Michigan bill, answered objections to Michigan's having framed a constitution without an enabling act by saying that the case for both Michigan and Arkansas was "clear and strong," the right of Arkansas to statehood resting upon the Louisiana Purchase treaty "and her numbers being indisputably sufficient, and larger than the population of several of the new States was at the time of their admission."[38] Buchanan pointed to the fact that Tennessee had in 1796 framed a constitution and been admitted into the Union without prior congressional authorization. Congress had "the unquestionable power of waiving any irregularities in the mode of framing the constitution, had any such existed."[39]

After a number of close divisions, non-sectional in character, the Michigan bill passed the Senate on April 2.[40] Sevier observed that the vote "throughout" the proceedings was almost "a complete party vote."[41]

Immediately upon passage of the Michigan bill the Senate, on

[34] *Register of Debates in Congress*, 24 Cong., 1 sess., XII (March 10, 1836), 782; *Congressional Globe*, 24 Cong., 1 sess., III (March 10, 1836), 240.

[35] Sevier to Editor, March 14, 17, 1836, *Gazette*, April 12, 1836.

[36] *House Journal*, 24 Cong., 1 sess., 547.

[37] *Register of Debates*, 24 Cong., 1 sess., XII (March 22), 934; *Globe*, 24 Cong., 1 sess., III (March 22), 275.

[38] *Register of Debates*, 24 Cong., 1 sess., XII (April 1), 1033–1036; *Globe*, 24 Cong., 1 sess., III (April 1), 311–312.

[39] *Register of Debates*, 24 Cong., 1 sess., XII (March 30, April 1), 1011–1015, 1037–1046; *Globe*, 24 Cong., 1 sess., III (April 1), 311–312.

[40] *Register of Debates*, 24 Cong., 1 sess., XII (April 1, 2), 1032–1048, 1050–1052; *Globe*, 24 Cong., 1 sess., III (April 1, 2), 311–312, 313.

[41] Sevier to Editor, April 1, 1836, *Gazette*, April 26, 1836.

motion of Buchanan, took up the Arkansas bill. A motion by Arnold Naudain of Delaware that the Senate adjourn failed, 27 to 11. Next, the bill was amended so "as to provide more effectually against any difficulties as to the boundary with the western Cherokees." After "some brief remarks" by John C. Calhoun of South Carolina, Henry Clay of Kentucky, Thomas Ewing of Ohio, Benton and others, William R. King of Alabama moved that the Senate adjourn. There was, he argued, no reason to hurry consideration of the bill

as the other House could not act on both bills at once, and as there were no such objections to this bill as had been made to the one for Michigan. He had such a perfect confidence in the disposition of the Senate to pass this bill, that he was willing to delay it another day, to give to those members who wished an opportunity of examining into its details, being fully persuaded that they would find nothing in it to object to.

King's motion was defeated by a non-sectional vote of 18 to 16.

Buchanan hoped the Arkansas bill would be acted on promptly and be sent to the House simultaneously with the Michigan bill. The argument that some members had not had time to examine the bill was invalid because a copy had been distributed to every senator a week ago. Notwithstanding Buchanan's wishes, the Senate, after ordering the bill to be engrossed for a third reading, adjourned for the day.[42]

When the bill was taken up again two days later, Benton observed that

on the presentation of these two great questions [Arkansas and Michigan bills], those gentlemen who had charge of them were so slightly affected by the exertions that had been made to disturb and ulcerate the public mind on the subject of slavery as to put them in the hands of Senators who might be supposed to entertain opinions on that subject different from those held by the States whose interests they were charged with. Thus the people of Arkansas had put their application into the hands of a gentleman representing a non-slaveholding State [Buchanan]; and the people of Michigan had put their application into the hands of a Senator [Benton] . . . coming from a State where the institutions of slavery existed; affording a most beautiful illustration of the total impotence of all attempts to agitate and ulcerate the public mind on the worn-out subject of slavery.

Speaking next, Benjamin Swift of Vermont declared that he would not vote for the Arkansas bill because the framers of the state constitution "had made the institution of slavery perpetual." Buchanan replied with some exaggeration that "this constitution was more

---

[42] *Register of Debates*, 24 Cong., 1 sess., XII (April 2), 1052–1053; *Globe*, 24 Cong., 1 sess., III (April 2), 313–314.

liberal [in regard to slavery] than the constitution of any of the slaveholding States that had been admitted into the Union." But no matter, the Missouri Compromise had permanently settled the question of slavery "in the new southwestern States." Though Thomas Morris of Ohio disliked the slavery provision in the constitution, he would vote for the Arkansas bill because he believed it to be his "duty" under the Federal constitution to do so. Others opposed the measure because the constitution had been framed without an enabling act. A vote taken on final passage carried 31 to 6, Swift, Clay, Nehemiah R. Knight of Rhode Island, Alexander Porter of Louisiana, Samuel Prentiss of Vermont, and Asher Robbins of Rhode Island opposing.[43]

Editor Woodruff, a supporter of the Van Buren–Johnson ticket for President and Vice-President,[44] surmised from the proceedings in the Senate that Arkansas was

solely indebted to the friends of the [Jackson] Administration and of Messrs. Van Buren and Johnson, for the passage of the bill for our admission through that body—and that Judge White [presidential candidate from Tennessee] voted against us, and with Clay, Calhoun, & Co., on every *party vote* that was taken. His voting for Arkansas, on the final passage of the bill for her admission, entitles him to no thanks from her citizens, as he had previously left no effort untried to prevent the passage of the bill for the admission of Michigan, on the passage of which depended the success of our application for admission.

In the same issue as his editorial, Woodruff reprinted an article from the Washington *Globe* asserting that the attitude of "the opposition" to the Michigan and Arkansas bills arose "from a knowledge" that the admission of Michigan and Arkansas now would weaken their "strength in the next Presidential election, and their dwindling phalanx in the Senate." Every "stratagem" had been employed by "the misnamed whigs" to deprive Michigan and Arkansas "of their unquestionable rights."[45]

In the House on June 6, 1836, Sevier obtained passage of a resolu-

[43] *Register of Debates,* 24 Cong., 1 sess., XII (April 4), 1053–1058; *Globe,* 24 Cong., 1 sess., III (April 4), 315–316. Henry Clay later presented "several petitions" signed by Philadelphians remonstrating against admission of Arkansas because of the clause "in her constitution prohibiting any future legislation for the abolition of slavery," and James Buchanan presented one from a meeting of the Society of Friends in Philadelphia. Both Clay and Buchanan disagreed with the petitions, all of which were laid on the table. *Register of Debates,* 24 Cong., 1 sess., XII (April 12, April 25), 1134–1135, 1277–1278; *Globe,* 24 Cong., 1 sess., III (April 12, April 25), 346, 395.

[44] *Gazette,* January 12, April 26, May 10, 1836.

[45] *Ibid.,* April 26, 1836. See also Helena *Constitutional Journal,* April 21, 1836; St. Louis *Missouri Argus,* April 22, 1836.

tion that the Arkansas and Michigan bills be considered two days thence and every day thereafter except Fridays and Saturdays until the matter of their admission was settled.[46] When on June 8 the Michigan bill came up for consideration ahead of the Arkansas bill, Henry A. Wise of Virginia sought to reverse the order. Forthwith Francis Thomas of Maryland asked why "Southern men" should

now make an effort to give precedence to the bill for the admission of Arkansas into the Union? If they manifest distrust, must we not expect that fears will be entertained by Northern members, that unreasonable opposition will be made to the admission of Michigan? Let us proceed harmoniously, until we find that our harmony must be interrupted.

After some debate Wise "modified" his proposal by moving to refer both bills to the Committee of the Whole with instructions that they be incorporated into one bill. John M. Patton and James W. Bouldin, both Virginians, opposed Wise's motion. Though Patton thought the Michigan bill should be allowed to hold its present position, he believed

it would be well to require of the House (or rather of the non-slaveholding portion of the Union) to give some unequivocal guarantee to the South that no difficulty would be raised as to the reception of Arkansas in regard to negro slavery.

Dixon H. Lewis of Alabama favored Wise's motion. Because Arkansas' constitution permitted slavery, Lewis looked "upon the Arkansas question as . . . the weaker of the two, and for that reason I would give it precedence." "We of the South want a hostage, to protect us on a delicate question; and the effect of giving precedence to the Michigan bill is to deprive us of that hostage."[47]

Finally, after considerable discussion, the House committed both bills to the Committee of the Whole. The Michigan bill, considered first, encountered the same objections that had been raised in the Senate. On June 9 it was laid aside and the Arkansas bill taken up.[48] When this was done Stephen C. Phillips of Massachusetts, complaining that it was after midnight and that he was "exhausted in body and mind" and did not "feel that it was his duty to remain and consent to the precipitate action by which it was evidently intended to force through the committee two bills of the importance of those under consideration," moved that the committee rise. The ensuing

[46] *Register of Debates,* 24 Cong., 1 sess., XII (June 6), 4186; *Globe,* 24 Cong., 1 sess., III (June 6), 533.

[47] *Register of Debates,* 24 Cong., 1 sess., XII (June 8), 4207-4209; *Globe,* 24 Cong., 1 sess., III (June 8), 537-538.

[48] *Register of Debates,* 24 Cong., 1 sess., XII (June 8, 9), 4209-4259; *Globe,* 24 Cong., 1 sess., III (June 8, 9), 538-539, 542.

vote of 92 to 17 against Phillips's motion revealed that the committee did not have a quorum. Sevier promptly requested Phillips to withdraw his motion, but Phillips refused. The committee then rose and John Reed of Massachusetts moved that the House adjourn. The vote of 98 to 24 against adjournment showed that the House now had a quorum, and it went back into Committee of the Whole on the admission of Arkansas. David Sprangler of Ohio promptly moved that the committee rise and the ensuing vote, 95 to 15 against the proposal, fell short of a quorum. Again the committee rose. But this time the chair ordered a call of the House, lasting from about 1:30 A.M. to 4:30 A.M.[49] According to John Quincy Adams 81 absentees were "returned without excuse" and 20 to 30 members brought in "under custody" of the Sergeant at Arms.[50]

Back in Committee of the Whole, Adams moved to amend the Arkansas bill to say that nothing in it should be construed as an assent by Congress to the provision in Arkansas' constitution "in relation to slavery and the emancipation of slaves." Caleb Cushing of Massachusetts supported Adams's motion, saying that he had been charged with sundry memorials from citizens of Massachusetts and New Hampshire remonstrating against the provision because it would make slavery "perpetual," and that he himself could not "ratify or sanction a constitution of government which undertakes . . . to foreclose in advance the progress of civilization and of liberty forever."

Gideon Hard of New York also spoke in favor of Adams's amendment. He did not believe Congress could under the Federal constitution interfere with slavery in the original states, but there was "no compact existing between the General Government and any of the new States or the Territory of Arkansas, whereby it has conceded to them the right to barter in human flesh . . ." Congress had not by the Missouri Compromise "surrendered any power, or yielded any jurisdiction"; if it had, it had done so by "a mere legislative act, that could not bind" future Congresses. Because the bill before the committee would confer either liberty or perpetual slavery on millions of persons yet unborn he thought it to be momentous in character. Thus in view of its importance, he could see no "good reason" why it should be "recklessly pushed through amidst darkness, fatigue, and confusion . . ."

[49] *Register of Debates*, 24 Cong., 1 sess. XII (June 9), 4259–4260; *Globe*, 24 Cong., 1 sess., III (June 9), 542.
[50] John Quincy Adams, *Memoirs* (edited by Charles Francis Adams, 12 vols., Philadelphia, 1874–1877), IX, 292–294.

When it came to a vote after further debate, Adams's amendment was defeated, 98 to 32. So also was a motion by Adams that the committee rise.[51]

Later in the proceedings William Slade of Vermont proposed that Arkansas should not be admitted until an elected convention should remove the constitutional prohibition of freeing the slaves without the consent of the owners, and provided that no Negroes or mulattoes born or brought into the state after admission be "subjected to slavery." Slade's motion was discussed but rejected without a record vote.

Evidently hoping to postpone final action, Wise now entered upon a filibuster, yielding several times to motions that the committee rise. Finally, at 11 A.M. (one hour after the session of June 10 was to have commenced), the committee rose and reported the Michigan and Arkansas bills. The House then adjourned.[52]

Four days later the two bills passed the House with relative ease. Though Adams moved an amendment to the Arkansas bill identical with the one he had proposed in Committee of the Whole, it was never brought to a vote. The division on final passage of the measure was 143 to 50.[53]

Senator Thomas Hart Benton later explained that the "struggle" in the House was

not to pass the two bills, but to bring them to a vote. This was the secret of the arduous session of twenty-five hours in the House. Besides the public objections which clogged their admission—boundaries in one, slavery in the other, alien voting, and (what was deemed by some), revolutionary conduct in both in holding conventions without authority of Congress; besides these public reasons, there was another cause operating silently, and which went more to the postponement than to the rejection of the States. This cause was political and partisan, and grew out of the impending presidential election, to be held before Congress should meet again. . . . The new States, it was known, would vote, if now admitted, for Mr. Van Buren; and this furnished a reason to the friends of the other candidates (even those friendly to eventual admission, and on which some of them were believed to act), to wish to stave off the admission to the ensuing session.[54]

[51] *Register of Debates*, 24 Cong., 1 sess., XII (June 9), 4260–4277; *Globe*, 24 Cong., 1 sess., III (June 9), 542. Adams said the vote on his proposed amendment was 90 to 32. *Memoirs*, IX, 294.

[52] *Register of Debates*, 24 Cong., 1 sess., XII (June 9), 4278–4281; *Globe*, 24 Cong., 1 sess., III (June 9), 543.

[53] *Register of Debates*, 24 Cong., 1 sess., XII (June 13), 4291–4295; *Globe*, 24 Cong., 1 sess., III (June 13), 550–551.

[54] Thomas Hart Benton, *Thirty Years' View; or, A History of the Working of the American Government for Thirty Years, from 1820 to 1850* (2 vols., New York, 1854), I, 637–638.

One suspects that if Arkansas' admission had been postponed until after the election, as many people evidently wished, she would have encountered greater opposition from Northerners on the score of slavery.

The act of admission, approved June 15, 1836, provided boundaries identical with those in the act creating Arkansas Territory (above, Chapter I) except that the western boundary was to be that described in the Cherokee treaty of 1828.[55] Arkansas would elect one representative to the next Congress. The new state would compose one Federal judicial district to be presided over by a judge appointed by the President who would also appoint a marshal and an attorney. The people of Arkansas were never to interfere with the disposal of the public lands nor levy a tax on any United States lands in the state. All non-local Federal laws were extended over the new jurisdiction.[56]

Congress also passed a supplementary act, approved June 23, 1836, to the act of June 15. The supplementary act "rejected" the ordinance of the constitutional convention and offered in its stead five "propositions" for the "free acceptance or rejection" of the state legislature. These proposals would grant to the state (1) section sixteen of each township of land for use of public schools, (2) all publicly owned salt springs not exceeding twelve in number, together with six sections of land adjoining each spring, (3) five per cent of the net proceeds from the sale of public lands in Arkansas for internal improvements, (4) and five sections of land for completing the state house. Two townships of land previously granted to Arkansas for a seminary of learning would be "vested in and confirmed" to the state for appropriation by the legislature to the use of a seminary of learning.[57] One notices that several provisions of the ordinance were incorporated in the supplementary act and that others were included with certain modifications.[58] The supplementary act was accepted in October, 1836, by the first state legislature.[59]

The act of June 15 did not mean that Arkansas passed immediately out of territorial status, for statehood could not be achieved until

---

[55] Congress probably sought to allay excitement among the Cherokee and the Choctaw Indians produced by the ambiguity of the Arkansas constitution on the western boundary and a provision in the ordinance looking toward retrocession to Arkansas of all lands ceded to the Cherokee and the Choctaw Indians after 1824. See *Gazette,* March 15, April 19, 1836; William Armstrong to Elbert Herring, and Herring to Armstrong, March 22, April 27, 1836, *Terr. Papers,* XXI, 1190–1191, 1200–1201, 1215.

[56] 5 *U.S. Stat. at L.* (1850), 50–52.

[57] *Ibid.,* 58–59.

[58] See *Terr. Papers,* XXI, 1189–1191, notes 18–31.

[59] Thorpe, ed., *Federal and State Constitutions,* I, 267–268.

a state government had been organized. In the first state elections held in August James S. Conway defeated Absalom Fowler and Alexander S. Walker for the governorship, and Archibald Yell beat William Cummins for Congress. Van Buren was the choice of the voters for President. Benjamin Johnson was appointed by the President to be Federal judge, Elias Rector, marshal, and Thomas J. Lacy, district attorney.[60]

The state assembly convened September 12 and the next day heard the valedictory of the outgoing territorial governor, William S. Fulton, and the inaugural address of the incoming state governor, James S. Conway. Thus on September 13 Arkansas entered upon her new status.[61]

[60] D. A. Stokes, Jr., "The First State Elections in Arkansas, 1836," *Arkansas Historical Quarterly*, XX (Summer, 1961), 126–150; Marie Cash, "Arkansas Achieves Statehood," *ibid.*, II (December, 1943), 304–308; *Terr. Papers*, XXI, 1207, note 82, 1233.

[61] "Gov. Fulton's Valedictory" and "Inauguration of the Governor," *Gazette*, September 13, 1836; *Terr. Papers*, XXI, 1254. Less than a week later the state legislature elected Fulton and Sevier to be United States senators.

CHAPTER THIRTEEN

Conclusion

PROMINENT AMONG THE INFLUENCES shaping the character of Arkansas territorial politics was the behavior of the governors. James Miller seems to have pursued a neutral course and to have left the Territory with the best wishes of everyone. George Izard, on the other hand, befriended Henry W. Conway and Chester Ashley, and quarrelled with his private secretary, the Cherokee Indian agent, the legislature, and Robert Crittenden, thereby contributing to the development of factionalism. John Pope, the first politician appointed governor—Miller and Izard were military men—took a still more active part in factional politics. His successor, William S. Fulton, was also politically minded. Of the four, only Fulton strongly desired the office, and only he stayed consistently at his post.

The many and often protracted absences of the governors made the secretaryship a post of considerable power and importance. Crittenden served in the capacity of acting governor nearly half his tenure as secretary. In the absence of Governor Miller, he helped organize the territorial government, later advanced it to the second grade, and in time gathered around himself a formidable array of political adherents. Fulton likewise acted as governor during much of his tenure as secretary, though his service seems less conspicuous than Crittenden's.

One notices that a large majority of the territorial politicians were former Kentuckians and Tennesseans. This fact as it pertains to Tennesseans accords with Robert B. Walz's finding that Tennessee, 1834–1850, furnished more white migrants to Arkansas than any other state. But in regard to Kentuckians it is completely out of line with Walz's figures showing that Kentucky ranked tenth as a source of white population.[1] The great number of Tennesseans in Arkansas

[1] Robert Bradshaw Walz, "Migration into Arkansas, 1834–1880" (unpublished Ph.D. dissertation, University of Texas, 1958), 115–116.

presumably contributed to the conspicuous success of Henry W. Conway and Ambrose H. Sevier in winning elections to Congress. Both men were natives of Tennessee who had lived in Missouri before coming to Arkansas. It may be that Sevier benefited also from the fame of his late great uncle, John Sevier of Tennessee,[2] though one notices that Ambrose himself never attempted to capitalize upon his relative's name. Sevier's relationship to Superior Court Judge Benjamin Johnson, formerly of Kentucky, whose brother was the prominent Richard M. Johnson, perhaps made him more acceptable to erstwhile Kentuckians.

The territorial period witnessed the formation and rise of a powerful family combination in Arkansas politics. As early as 1823, when Henry W. Conway first won election to Congress, the Conway family began wielding an important influence in public affairs. Henry's brother, James S., later became surveyor general of Arkansas Territory and the first governor of the state. Another brother, Elias N., enjoyed a similar career. Upon Henry's death in 1827, his cousin, Ambrose H. Sevier, who was also the son-in-law of Superior Court Judge Benjamin Johnson, became delegate. Sevier was a United States senator from 1836 to 1848, and Johnson held a Federal judgeship from 1836 to 1849. Benjamin's son, Robert W. Johnson, served during the early statehood period in both houses of Congress.[3] The Conways were also related to the Rectors. William Rector, as surveyor general of Missouri, Illinois, and Arkansas Territory, was probably responsible for the appointment that brought his nephew, Henry W. Conway, to Arkansas in 1820.[4] Wharton and Elias Rector, cousins of Henry W. Conway, were supporters of Conway and Sevier in territorial politics and themselves held several minor offices.[5] Another cousin, Henry M. Rector, later became governor, though, according to Josiah H. Shinn, he was not a member of the "Conway-Johnson dynasty."[6]

[2] Josiah H. Shinn, *Pioneers and Makers of Arkansas* (Little Rock, 1908), 206–207; William Alphonso Walker, Jr., "Tennessee, 1796–1821" (unpublished Ph.D. dissertation, University of Texas, 1959), 14–164.

[3] Shinn, *Makers of Arkansas*, 202, 204–205, 397

[4] See *ibid.*, 393, 397; Lonnie J. White, "Arkansas Territorial Politics, 1824–1827," *Arkansas Historical Quarterly*, XX (Spring, 1961), 23–25.

[5] See Clarence E. Carter, ed., *Territorial Papers of the United States*, Vol. XIX, *Arkansas Territory, 1819–1825* (Washington, 1953), 872, 874, Vol. XX, *Arkansas Territory, 1825–1829* (Washington, 1954), 721–722, Vol. XXI, *Arkansas Territory, 1829–1836* (Washington, 1954), 291, 320–321, 1207; G. W. Featherstonhaugh, *Excursion Through the Slave States* . . . (2 vols., London, 1844), II, 240.

[6] Shinn, *Makers of Arkansas*, 401–402.

One of the most significant developments during the territorial period was the rise of factionalism. Robert Crittenden, in his capacity as acting governor during the absences of Governor Miller, built up through use of the patronage the first significant political following in the Territory. In consequence of a difficulty between him and Henry W. Conway in 1827, a new faction, led by Conway, emerged and supplanted the Crittenden clique as the dominant faction in territorial politics. Of no little importance to the success of the Conway faction was the staunch support of William E. Woodruff's *Arkansas Gazette,* for over ten years the only newspaper in the Territory.

Both factions, until Andrew Jackson became President, adhered to Adams in national politics. Thenceforth the Conway faction, more appropriately called the Sevier faction after Conway's death in 1827, supported Jackson in national politics, while the Crittendenites for the most part favored Henry Clay. Why the *Advocate,* established in 1830, should have professed to be a Jackson paper and at the same time supported Crittenden men in territorial politics is not clear; one suspects that the Crittendenites, recognizing that Jackson was more popular than Clay in Arkansas, hoped to draw support from among Jackson's friends.

The Sevier faction was greatly strengthened in 1829 by the accession of John Pope and William S. Fulton, both prominent Jackson men, to the governorship and secretaryship, respectively. Though Pope and Fulton took active parts in politics they were prevented using the patronage to build up followings, for an act of Congress obtained by Sevier in 1829 had made elective the civil and military officials previously appointed by the governor.

Owing presumably to the frontier environment, territorial politics was violent, name calling and differences often leading to fights and duels. Whether killing an opponent in a duel in Arkansas Territory hurt the successful duellist as a public figure is not easily ascertained. Andrew Scott, who killed a fellow superior court judge, failed to obtain reappointment as judge and election to Congress, but was subsequently elected to the legislature and the constitutional convention. C. F. M. Noland, who fatally wounded William Fontaine Pope, became a prominent politician during early statehood.[7] Robert C. Oden, killer of the brigadier general of the militia, was later soundly de-

---

[7] See Josiah H. Shinn, "The Life and Public Services of Charles Fenton Mercer Noland," *Publications of the Arkansas Historical Association,* Vol. I (Fayetteville, 1906), 337–343.

feated in a race for the delegateship, but other factors, including Oden's own arrogant and quarrelsome personality,[8] entered into his defeat. The most difficult case was that of Crittenden and Conway. From the newspapers it appears that Crittenden was blamed by his enemies more for allegedly causing the duel than for the actual killing of Conway. The close contests between Crittenden candidates and Sevier in the special election of 1827 and the two ensuing regular elections would seem to indicate that Crittenden had not been greatly weakened. A majority of the legislature of 1831 was pro-Crittenden, and Fulton believed in 1834 that Crittenden had political friends enough to elect him to the United States Senate as soon as Arkansas should become a state. One suspects Crittenden's main political handicap was a lordly personality that the plain people did not relish.

Factions in territorial Arkansas were based largely upon men and personalities rather than upon issues and measures. Until near the very end of the territorial period sectionalism played no visible part in politics. Conversely, during the sectional struggle over representation in the convention and in the prospective state legislature, factional allegiances were not observed.

The political arena in territorial Arkansas provided training for future state politicians. It was only to be expected that young men, particularly lawyers, should come to the new frontier territory of Arkansas in the hope of making a political career for themselves. Though several of the most promising had died early or left Arkansas before 1836,[9] a considerable number, among them Sevier, Fulton, C. F. M. Noland, and William Cummins, remained to enjoy their best years after statehood.

Probably no other event in territorial affairs caused the Crittenden faction to lose and the Sevier clique to gain so much in popularity as the ten-section episode in which the Crittenden men pushed through the legislature of 1831 a bill to provide a state house by giving the public land granted for that purpose in exchange for Crittenden's residence. In the election of 1833 Crittenden's defeat at the hands of Sevier was overwhelming.

---

[8] Hiram A. Whittington to Father, December 1, 1828, in Margaret Smith Ross, ed., "Letters of Hiram Abiff Whittington, 1827–1834," *Pulaski County Historical Society Bulletin,* No. 3 (December, 1956), 11.

[9] Crittenden, Desha, Searcy, and Thomas P. Eskridge died before 1836. William Trimble, Robert C. Oden, and Thomas W. Newton returned to Kentucky. Oden died in Kentucky in 1833 and Newton subsequently came back to Arkansas to play a prominent role in state politics. Shinn, *Makers of Arkansas,* 190–194, 201, 333.

Though the Sevier faction emerged from the election of 1833 completely dominant in territorial politics, trouble between Pope and Fulton and Pope and Sevier soon threatened that dominance. It was preserved, however, by President Jackson's appointment of Fulton to be governor in Pope's stead, and by Crittenden's untimely death. After statehood the Sevier faction became the Democratic Party in Arkansas and the opposition derived mainly from the membership of the old Crittenden clique.[10]

[10] See Walter Lee Brown, "Albert Pike, Arkansas Editor," *Arkansas Historical Quarterly,* X (Winter, 1951), 406; Brown, "Albert Pike, 1809–1891" (unpublished Ph.D. dissertation, University of Texas, 1955), 123.

Bibliography

A. SOURCES

MANUSCRIPTS

Berkeley-Noland Papers. Alderman Library, University of Virginia.

John J. Crittenden Papers. Library of Congress.

John J. Crittenden Papers. Duke University Library.

Luther C. Gulley Collection. Arkansas History Commission.

Letters of Governor Izard, 1825–1828. Arkansas History Commission. Much of this correspondence is in *Publications of the Arkansas Historical Association,* Vol. I (entry below), and in *Territorial Papers,* Vol. XX (entry below).

Andrew Jackson Papers. Library of Congress; microfilm copies, University of Texas Library. Most of the few items pertaining to Arkansas Territory in this collection are also in *Territorial Papers,* Vol. XXI (entry below).

John Perkins Letters and Papers. Microfilm copies, Joint University Libraries, Nashville, Tennessee; originals in hands of Edward McGavock, Nashville.

Joel R. Poinsett Papers. Henry D. Gilpin Collection, Historical Society of Pennsylvania.

James K. Polk Papers. Library of Congress.

Robert W. Trimble Collection. Arkansas History Commission.

Jesse Turner Papers. Duke University Library.

Martin Van Buren Papers. Library of Congress; microfilm copies in University of Texas Library.

William E. Woodruff Papers. Arkansas History Commission.

NEWSPAPERS

Helena *Constitutional Journal,* 1836.

Little Rock *Arkansas Advocate,* 1830–1836.

Little Rock *Arkansas Gazette,* 1819–1836, 1873, 1919. (Published at Arkansas Post, 1819–1821.)

Little Rock *Times,* 1835–1836.

St. Louis *Missouri Gazette,* 1812.

St. Louis *Missouri Gazette & Illinois Advertiser,* 1815.

St. Louis *Missouri Gazette and Public Advertiser,* 1818–1819.

St. Louis *Missouri Argus,* 1836.

OFFICIAL PRINTED MATERIALS

Arkansas. Constitutional Convention, 1836. *Journal.*

Arkansas. Legislature. *Legislative Acts,* 1819, 1820, 1821, 1823, 1825, 1827, 1828, 1829, 1831, 1833, 1835, 1838.

Arkansas. Legislature. *Legislative Journal,* 1831.

Ball, William McK., and Sam C. Roane (compilers). *Revised Statutes of the State of Arkansas, Adopted at the October Session of the General Assembly of Said State, A.D., 1837.* Boston, 1838.

Carter, Clarence E. (ed.). *The Territorial Papers of the United States,* Vol. IX, *Orleans Territory, 1803–1812* (1940); Vol. XIII, *Louisiana-Missouri Territory, 1803–1806* (1948); Vol. XIV, *Louisiana-Missouri Territory, 1806–1814* (1949); Vol. XIX, *Arkansas Territory, 1819–1825* (1953); Vol. XX, *Arkansas Territory, 1825–1829* (1954); Vol. XXI, *Arkansas Territory, 1829–1836* (1954). Washington, 1940–1954.

Hempstead, Samuel H. (compiler). *Reports of Cases Argued and Determined in the United States Superior Court for the Territory of Arkansas, from 1820 to 1836; and in the United States District Court for the District of Arkansas, from 1836 to 1849; and in the United States Circuit Court for the District of Arkansas, from 1839 to 1856.* Boston, 1856.

Steele, J., and J. M'Campbell (eds.). *Laws of Arkansas Territory.* Little Rock, 1835.

Thorpe, Francis N. (ed.). *The Federal and State Constitutions, Colonial Charters, and Other Organic Laws of the States, Territories, and Colonies now or Heretofore Forming the United States of America.* 7 vols. Washington, 1909.

United States. Congress. *American State Papers, Miscellaneous.* Vol. II. Washington, 1934.

United States. Congress. *Annals of Congress.* 15 Cong., 1 sess., Vol. II. 15 Cong., 2 sess., Vol. III. 17 Cong., 1 sess., Vol. I.

United States. Congress. *Congressional Globe.* 23 Cong., 1 sess., Vol. I. 24 Cong., 1 sess., Vol. III.

United States. Congress. *House Journal.* 15 Cong., 1 sess. 15 Cong., 2 sess. 22 Cong., 1 sess. 22 Cong., 2 sess. 23 Cong., 1 sess. 24 Cong., 1 sess.

United States. Congress. *Register of Debates in Congress.* 19 Cong., 2 sess., Vol. III. 23 Cong., 1 sess., Vol. X. 24 Cong., 1 sess., Vol. XII.

United States. Congress. *Senate Executive Journal,* Vols. III–IV.

United States. Congress. *Senate Journal.* 23 Cong., 1 sess.

United States. Congress. *Statutes at Large,* Vols. II–V.

OTHER PUBLISHED SOURCES

Adams, John Quincy. *Memoirs.* Edited by Charles Francis Adams. 12 vols. Philadelphia, 1874–1877.

Bassett, John Spencer (ed.). *Correspondence of Andrew Jackson.* 7 vols. Washington, 1926–1935.

Benton, Thomas Hart. *Thirty Years' View; or, A History of the Working of the American Government for Thirty Years, from 1820 to 1850.* 2 vols. New York, 1854.

Featherstonhaugh, G. W. *Excursion Through the Slave States, From Washington on the Potomac to the Frontier of Mexico; with Sketches of Popular Manners and Geological Notices.* 2 vols. London, 1844.

"Official Correspondence of Governor Izard, 1825–1826," *Publications of the Arkansas Historical Association,* I (Fayetteville, 1906). This correspondence includes letters written in 1827.

James, Thomas. *Three Years Among the Indians and Mexicans.* Edited by Milo M. Quaife. Chicago, 1953.

Letter of George W. Jones to Fay Hempstead, April 9, 1888, *Pulaski County Historical Review,* I (June, 1953).

Lemke, W. J. (ed.). "The Walker Family Papers," *Washington County Historical Society Bulletin,* No. 21 (Fayetteville, 1956).

Lucke, Jesse Ryon. "Correspondence Concerning the Establishment of the First Arkansas Press," *Arkansas Historical Quarterly,* XIV (Summer, 1955).

Nuttall, Thomas. *A Journal of Travels into the Arkansa{s} Territory, During the Year 1819.* Philadelphia, 1821.

Pike, Albert. "Autobiography," *New Age Magazine,* XXXVII (December, 1929). XXXVIII (February, 1930).

———. "Letters from Arkansas," *American Monthly Magazine,* I (January, 1836).

———. "Life in Arkansas," *American Monthly Magazine,* I (March, 1836).

Pope, William F. *Early Days in Arkansas.* Little Rock, 1895.

Ross, Margaret Smith (ed.). "Three Letters of Cephas Washburn," *Arkansas Historical Quarterly,* XVI (Summer, 1957).

Ross, Margaret Smith (ed.). "Letters of Hiram Abiff Whittington, 1827–1834," *Pulaski County Historical Society Bulletin,* No. 3 (December, 1956). The originals, including a few letters written after 1834, are in the hands of Mrs. Lloyd Moreland, Austin, Texas.

Tanner's Map of Arkansas, 1836. Map Collection, University of Texas Library.

Letter of David Walker to wife, January 9, 1836, *Washington County Historical Society Flashback,* I (November, 1951).

White, Lonnie J. (ed.). "A Letter from Robert Crittenden to John J. Crittenden," *Arkansas Historical Quarterly,* XXI (Spring, 1962).

White, Lonnie J. (ed.). "The Pope-Noland Duel of 1831: A Letter from C. F. M. Noland to William Noland," *Arkansas Historical Quarterly,* XXII (Summer, 1963).

Worley, Ted R. (ed.). "A Letter of Governor Miller to His Wife," *Arkansas Historical Quarterly,* XIII (Winter, 1954).

B. SECONDARY WORKS

BOOKS

Allsopp, Fred W. *Albert Pike; A Biography.* Little Rock, 1928.

Allsopp, Fred W. *History of the Arkansas Press for a Hundred Years and More.* Little Rock, 1922.

Baylor, Orval W. *John Pope, Kentuckian; His Life and Times, 1770–1845.* Cynthiana, Kentucky, 1943.

Bemis, Samuel Flagg. *John Quincy Adams and the Union.* New York, 1956.

Crittenden, H. H. (compiler). *The Crittenden Memoirs.* New York, 1936.

Green, Fletcher M. *Constitutional Development in the South Atlantic States, 1776–1860: A Study in the Evolution of Democracy.* Chapel Hill, 1930.

Hallum, John. *Biographical and Pictorial History of Arkansas.* Vol. I. Albany, 1887.

Hamer, Philip M. (ed.). *Tennessee, A History, 1673–1932.* 4 vols. New York, 1933.

Heitman, Francis B. *Historical Register and Dictionary of the United States Army, from its Organization, September 29, 1789, to March 2, 1903.* 2 vols. Washington, 1903.

Hempstead, Fay. *A Pictorial History of Arkansas.* St. Louis, 1890.

Hempstead, Fay. *Historical Review of Arkansas.* 3 vols. Chicago, 1911.

Herndon, Dallas T. *Why Little Rock Was Born.* Little Rock, 1933.

———. *Annals of Arkansas, 1947.* 4 vols. Little Rock, n.d.

———. *Centennial History of Arkansas.* 3 vols. Little Rock, 1922.

Houck, Louis. *A History of Missouri.* 3 vols. Chicago, 1908.

Lossing, Benson J. *The Pictorial Field-Book of the War of 1812.* New York, 1868.

McMillan, Malcolm Cook. *Constitutional Development in Alabama, 1798–1901: A Study in Politics, the Negro, and Sectionalism.* Chapel Hill, 1955.

Miles, Edwin Arthur. *Jacksonian Democracy in Mississippi,* Chapel Hill, 1960.

Moore, Glover. *The Missouri Controversy, 1819–1821.* Lexington, 1953.

Quaife, Milo M. (ed.). *The John Askin Papers.* 2 vols. Detroit, 1931.

Reynolds, John Hugh. *Makers of Arkansas History.* Dallas, 1905.

Shinn, Josiah H. *Pioneers and Makers of Arkansas.* Little Rock, 1908.

Shoemaker, Floyd Calvin. *Missouri's Struggle for Statehood, 1804–1821.* Jefferson City, 1916.

Sydnor, Charles S. *The Development of Southern Sectionalism, 1819–1848.* Baton Rouge, 1948.

Taylor, Orville W. *Negro Slavery in Arkansas.* Durham, 1958.

Thomas, David Y. *Arkansas and Its People; A History, 1541–1930.* 4 vols. New York, 1930.

United States. Congress. *Biographical Directory of the American Congress, 1774–1927.* Washington, 1928.

ARTICLES

Brown, Walter Lee. "Albert Pike's First Experiences in Arkansas," *Arkansas Historical Quarterly,* X (Spring, 1951).

Brown, Walter Lee. "Albert Pike, Arkansas Editor," *Arkansas Historical Quarterly,* X (Winter, 1951).

Cash, Marie. "Arkansas in Territorial Days," *Arkansas Historical Quarterly,* I (September, 1942).

Cash, Marie. "Arkansas Achieves Statehood," *Arkansas Historical Quarterly,* II (December, 1943).

Cheves, Langdon. "Izard of South Carolina," *South Carolina Historical and Genealogical Magazine,* II (July, 1901).

Eno, Clara B. "Territorial Governors of Arkansas," *Arkansas Historical Quarterly,* IV (Winter, 1945).

Eno, Clara B. "Old and New Capitols of Arkansas," *Arkansas Historical Quarterly,* IV (Autumn, 1945).

Foreman, Carolyn Thomas. "William Bradford," *Arkansas Historical Quarterly,* XIII (Winter, 1954).

Gravley, Ernestine. "William Edward Woodruff, Pioneer Arkansas Journalist," *Arkansas Historical Quarterly,* XIV (Summer, 1955).

Johnson, Boyd W. "Benjamin Desha," *Arkansas Historical Quarterly,* XIX (Winter, 1960).

Kennan, Clara B. "Arkansas' Old State House," *Arkansas Historical Quarterly,* IX (Spring, 1950).

Montagno, George L. "Matthew Lyon's Last Frontier," *Arkansas Historical Quarterly,* XVI (Spring, 1957).

Newberry, Farrar. "Some Notes on Robert Crittenden," *Arkansas Historical Quarterly,* XVI (Autumn, 1957).

Robinson, William A. "Matthew Lyon," in Allen Johnson and Dumas Malone (eds.), *Dictionary of American Biography* (20 vols., New York, 1928–1936), XI, Larned—MacCracken.

Rose, U. M. "Chester Ashley," *Publications of the Arkansas Historical Association,* III (Fayetteville, 1911).

Rose, U. M. "John Pope—An Unfinished Sketch," *Publications of the Arkansas Historical Association,* IV (Conway, 1917).

Ross, Margaret Smith. "The Cunninghams: Little Rock's First Family," *Pulaski County Historical Review,* I (June, 1953).

———. "The Territorial Militia," *Pulaski County Historical Review,* III (September, 1955).

———. "Cadron: An Early Town That Failed," *Arkansas Historical Quarterly,* XVI (Spring, 1957).

Scroggs, Jack B. "Arkansas Statehood: A Study in State and National Political Schism," *Arkansas Historical Quarterly,* XX (Autumn, 1961).

Sherwood, Diana. "When Governor Miller Bought Crystal Hill," *Pulaski County Historical Review,* I (September, 1953).

Sherwood, Diana. "The Code-Duello in Arkansas," *Arkansas Historical Quarterly,* VI (Summer, 1947).

Shinn, Josiah H. "The Life and Public Services of Charles Fenton Mercer Noland," *Publications of the Arkansas Historical Association,* I (Fayetteville, 1906).

Stokes, D. A., Jr. "The First State Elections in Arkansas, 1836," *Arkansas Historical Quarterly,* XX (Summer, 1961).

Thomas, David Y. "George Izard," in Allen Johnson and Dumas Malone (eds.). *Dictionary of American Biography* (20 vols., New York, 1928–1936), IX, Hibben—Jarvis.

Vaughn, Myra McAlmont. "A History of the Old State House," *Publications of the Arkansas Historical Association,* III (Fayetteville, 1911).

Walz, Robert B. "Arkansas Slaveholdings and Slaveholders in 1850," *Arkansas Historical Quarterly,* XII (Spring, 1953).

White, Lonnie J. "The Arkansas Territorial Election of 1823," *Arkansas Historical Quarterly,* XVIII (Winter, 1959).

————. "James Miller: Arkansas' First Territorial Governor," *Arkansas Historical Quarterly,* XIX (Spring, 1960).

————. "Disturbances on the Arkansas-Texas Border, 1827–1831," *Arkansas Historical Quarterly,* XIX (Summer, 1960).

————. "The Election of 1827 and the Conway-Crittenden Duel," *Arkansas Historical Quarterly,* XIX (Winter, 1960).

————. "Arkansas Territorial Politics, 1824–1827," *Arkansas Historical Quarterly,* XX (Spring, 1961).

————. "Arkansas Territorial Indian Affairs," *Arkansas Historical Quarterly,* XXI (Autumn, 1962).

————. "Dividing Missouri: The Creation of Arkansas Territory," *Bulletin of the Missouri Historical Society,* XVII (April, 1961).

————. "Kentuckians in Arkansas Territorial Politics," *Register of the Kentucky Historical Society,* LX (October, 1962).

Williams, Edwin Marshall. "The Conway-Crittenden Duel," *Arkansas Historical Review,* I (February, 1934).

Worley, Ted R. "An Early Arkansas Sportsman: C. F. M. Noland," *Arkansas Historical Quarterly,* XI (Spring, 1952).

UNPUBLISHED MANUSCRIPTS

Brown, Walter Lee. "Albert Pike, 1809–1891." Unpublished Ph.D. dissertation, University of Texas, 1955.

Daniel, Vivian. "Territorial Development of Arkansas." Unpublished M.A. thesis, University of Texas, 1929.

Ferguson, John Lewis. "William E. Woodruff and the Territory of Arkansas, 1819–1836." Unpublished Ph.D. dissertation, Tulane University, 1960.

Walker, William Alphonso, Jr. "Tennessee, 1796–1821." Unpublished Ph.D. dissertation, University of Texas, 1959.

Walz, Robert Bradshaw. "Migration into Arkansas, 1834–1880." Unpublished Ph.D. dissertation, University of Texas, 1958.

White, Henry Ford. "The Economic and Social Development of Arkansas Prior to 1836." Unpublished Ph.D. dissertation, University of Texas, 1931.

Index

Absentee judges: problem of, 26–27
Adams, John: 184 n.
Adams, John Q.: 50 f., 89 n., 90 f., 100, 106, 197 f., 203
Admission bills (Arkansas): 164, 166–167, 192–199
Alabama Territory: 5, 186
Alexander, John: 95 n., 157 n.
Allen, William O.: 23, 28–30, 67, 203
Allen-Oden duel: 28 f., 67, 203
Anderson, Richard C., Jr.: 14
Andrews, Robert: 34
Arbuckle, Matthew: 39
Arkansas Advocate: 90 f., 102, 104–105, 108 ff., 114 ff., 119, 123 f., 127, 130 n., 134–135, 137–139, 141 f., 144, 146, 149, 156, 161 f., 165, 168, 173, 183, 203
Arkansas Gazette: 21, 34, 36 f., 40, 43, 48–49, 52, 55, 63, 72 f., 78, 86–87, 94, 98–100, 102, 106, 109–111, 114–116, 122–124, 127, 134, 139, 143 n., 144, 146 f., 150, 156, 161, 164 f., 167, 169, 203
Arkansas Herald: proposed, 99 n.
Arkansas Post: 3 f., 7, 16, 20 f., 23, 25, 28, 30 n., 36 n., 62 n., 105, 117
Arkansas Territory: created, 3–17; government organized, 18 ff., 201; government advanced to second grade, 21–22, 201
Ashley, Chester: 31, 32 n., 71, 72 n., 74–76, 79, 90 n., 94, 100–101, 103, 105–108, 114, 121, 124, 128–131, 133, 136–138, 142 n., 148 nn., 149 f., 152, 154, 159 f., 176, 201
Austin, Stephen F.: 22, 30

Ball, William McK.: 120–121, 127 n., 128–130, 137 n., 138, 184 n., 189
Banks: 57, 138, 171, 176, 182, 185, 190
Barber, David: 57–58
Barbour, James: 55, 57–59, 60–61
Barbour, Philip P.: 14
Barfield, George C.: 77, 95 n.
Barkman, Jacob: 23, 55
Barry, William T.: 91
Barton, David: 92

Basset, Burwell: 11
Bates, Edward: 22 n.
Bates, Frederick: 22
Bates, James Woodson: 20, 22–23, 28 n., 29 n., 33–35, 37–38, 43 ff., 47, 49, 52 ff., 61 ff., 86 n., 89 n., 113, 135, 139, 152, 184 n., 186 f.
Bates-Conway controversy: 37–38, 43–45
Batesville: 96
Bean, Jonathan L.: 53 f.
Bean, Mark: 77, 95 n., 157 n., 174 n., 176 n., 177 n., 184 n.
Bean, Robert: 35, 46, 55
Benton, Thomas Hart: 50, 193 f., 198
Bertrand, Charles P.: 99–102, 104 f., 108–109, 110 n., 117, 119–123, 127, 129–131, 132, 136 n., 137 f., 141, 142 n., 143 n., 149 f., 152, 154–155, 161, 173 n., 182, 184
Bertrand-Woodruff quarrel: 99–102
Bibb, Charles S.: 139 nn.
Bibb, George M.: 139 n., 167 nn.
Billingsley, James: 34, 95 n.
Biscoe, Henry L.: 46, 55, 135 n., 184 n.
Blount, Rueben J.: 125 n., 128 n., 129 n.
Boon, James: 184 n., 189
Boswell, Hartwell: 28, 57, 120
Boswell, James: 125 n., 129 n., 157 n.
Bouldin, James W.: 196
Boundaries: of Territory, 5–7, 16; of state, 185, 199
Bowman, John: 75
Bradford, James M.: 91 n.
Bradford, William: 33 f., 37 ff., 55 f., 66 n.
Brearly, David: 50
Brice, William: 75–76
Bridges, Edmund H.: 125 n., 129 n., 131 n.
Briggs, Robert: 21
Brown, Richard C. S.: 95 n., 125 n., 128 n., 133, 136, 176 n., 177 n., 184 n.
Bryan, James: 30
Buchanan, James: 192–194, 195 n.
Bullitt, George: 7 n.
Burrill, James, Jr.: 15
Burton, Hutchins G.: 90–91
Burton, Robert: 88

Bussy, Ellitt: 121
Butler, A.: 91 n.
Butler, Benjamin F.: 176, 181
Buzzard, Jacob: 157 n., 176 n.
Byrd, Richard C.: 97, 128, 148 n., 157 n.
Byrnside, James: 95 n., 157 n.

Cadron: 25, 30 f.
Calaway, John: 55
Caldwell, Charles: 95 n., 98 n., 102–103 n., 124, 125 n., 127, 129 n., 130 f., 136 n., 158, 176 n.
Calhoun, John C.: 139, 194 f.
Call, Richard K.: 52
Calvert, John: 125 n., 128 n.
Calvert, J. D.: 184 n.
Calvert, John W.: 54
Capital location issue: 30–32, 105
Carroll, William: 90
Carter, Elijah: 46
Cassidy, Henry: 4, 20, 22, 26
Chamberlain, Jason: 26
Chicot: 96
Clark, David: 23, 46
Clark, Edwin T.: 77, 95 n., 103
Clark, James: 77, 95 n., 157 n.
Clark, John: 125 n., 128 n., 157 n., 176 n., 177 n., 184 n.
Clark, William: 53 f.
Clarke, Lorenzo: 184 n.
Clay, Henry: 9, 11, 56, 59 f., 63, 89–91, 104, 108–109, 117, 123–124, 139 f., 151 f., 194 f., 203
Clayton, Alexander M.: 139 n., 168
Clayton, John M.: 192
Cobb, Thomas W.: 14
Cocke, John H.: 88, 111–112, 149
Collins, Moses: 125 n., 129 n.
Collinsworth, James P.: 147
Constitution of 1836: provisions of, 188–192; congressional objection to slavery provision in, 194 ff.
Convention of 1836 (constitutional): 172–192, 204
Conway, Elias N.: 80 n., 182, 202
Conway, Henry W.: 28, 32 n., 37 ff., 47, 49, 50 n., 51 ff., 56, 63, 65 ff., 73 ff., 83–87, 90, 101, 106 n., 118 f., 142, 152, 201 ff.
Conway, James S.: 53, 88 n., 125 n., 142 n., 184 n., 200, 202
Conway-Crittenden quarrel and duel: 67 ff., 78 ff., 85, 87, 101, 106 n., 118, 142, 152, 204
Conway faction: mentioned, 87, 106, 203
Conway family: 47, 53 f., 141 f., 202
Cook, Daniel P.: 51
Counties: creation of, 4, 25, 30, 47, 57, 82, 89, 97, 161, 181

Court system: 7, 16, 30, 36, 46 f., 57, 82–85, 88 f., 93, 96 f., 120, 126, 134, 161, 185, 190, 199
Craig, Silas: 147 f.
Crawford, William H.: 152
Crittenden, John J.: 14, 19, 135 n., 170, 171 n.
Crittenden, Robert: 19 ff., 24 f., 29, 31, 32 n., 35–38, 39 n., 46 f., 50 n., 51 f., 55–56, 59–65, 68–73, 74 n., 76 n., 77 ff., 84–87, 89–90, 92, 98 f., 101, 103–106, 112 f., 114, 116–118, 120 f., 123, 124 n., 125, 127–131, 134–137, 139, 141–142, 144 ff., 148 n., 149–158, 163, 169 n., 170–171, 173 n., 201, 203–205
Crittenden, Thomas: 79 n.
Crittenden-Bates difficulty: 61–65, 84, 152
Crittenden-Eskridge altercation: 155–158
Crittenden faction: 87, 90, 93, 104, 111, 114 ff., 120, 124–125, 127, 130, 135 f., 139–140, 145–146, 149–150, 152 n., 155, 163, 170–171, 184, 201, 203–205
Crittenden-Izard quarrel: 55–56, 59–61, 65, 103, 201
Crittenden-Woodruff hostility: 62 n., 70–73, 86–87, 101, 125, 127, 141
Cross, Edward: 107, 127 f., 135, 143
Crutchfield, Peter T.: 124, 125 n., 128 n., 133
Crystal Hill: 31 n.
Culbreth, Thomas: 12 n.
Culp, Thomas: 46
Cummins, John: 4
Cummins, William: 92 f., 142–147, 156, 158, 176 n., 177 n., 179 f., 184 n., 200, 204
Cunningham, Matthew: 87, 105, 127 n., 138–139
Cushing, Caleb: 197

Davidson, John: 4
Davidsonville: 4, 96, 99 n.
Davies, Anthony H.: 184 n.
DeBaun, James: 32 n.
Democratic Party: 205
Desha, Benjamin: 79, 83, 113, 115 ff., 141, 153–154, 204 n.
Desha, Joseph: 116
De Soto, Hernando: expedition of, 3
De Tonti, Henri: 3
Dickinson, Townsend: 46, 184 n.
Dillard, John: 77, 88
Districts of Arkansas, Louisiana, and New Madrid: 3 f.
Douglass, Jesse: 95 n., 125 n., 129 n.
Drennen, John: 184 n.
Drew, Thomas S.: 184 n., 187 f.

Duane, William J.: 147
Duelling law (1820): passed, 29–30; bill to amend vetoed, 47; mentioned, 49–50; amended, 57; indictment for violation of quashed, 87
Dunlap, John: 88
DuVal, Edward W.: 58–59

Edwards, Ninian: 14, 15 n.
Election: of 1819, 21–25; special, of 1820, 29; of 1821, 33–36; of 1823, 37–47; of 1825, 52–55; of 1827, 66–81, 83, 86–87, 106; special, of 1827, 83–87, 94, 204; special, of 1828, 88; of 1829, 92–95, 204; of 1831, 111, 114–125, 152 n., 204; of 1833, 141–157, 160, 163, 168, 204 f.; of 1835, 174; of 1836 (state), 200
Eller, David G.: 128 f., 148 n.
Elliott, Elias A.: 32 n.
Elliott, Henry: 32 n.
Elliott, Wright W.: 95 n., 157 n., 176 n., 184 n.
Ellis, N. Dandrige: 176 n., 177 n., 178
Ellis, Radford: 23, 30–31
Ellis, Richard: 184 n.
English, John: 23, 30–31
Eskridge, Thomas P.: 32 n., 37 f., 50, 135, 143, 155, 157–158, 204 n.
Evans, Onesimus: 176 n., 177 n.
Ewing, Joshua: 46
Ewing, Thomas: 166 f., 194

Factionalism: mentioned, 42 f., 59, 65, 90, 97, 110, 141, 143, 155, 201, 203
Farrelly, Terence: 46, 77, 95 n., 125 n., 128 n., 129 n., 131, 157 n., 184 n., 188
Fayetteville: 181–182
Ferebee, George W.: 103, 127, 184 n.
Ferguson, William D.: 95 n., 184 n.
Field, John P.: 158
Field, William: 102 f., 135 f., 137 n., 138, 157, 171, 174 n.
Fillingim, Samuel: 125 n., 128 n.
Fiscal matters: of Arkansas Territory, 29, 36, 46 f., 55–56, 81 f., 96 f., 109, 115, 126, 134, 165
Fish, Thomas: 23, 30–31, 35
Forts: mentioned, 39–41, 56, 67, 94, 96
Fowler, Absalom: 124, 127, 143, 176 n., 177 n., 178, 179 n., 180, 184 n., 187 f., 200
Fowler, John H.: 77, 88
Franchise law of 1829: 93, 95, 97, 203
Fulton, John T.: 95, 126
Fulton, William S.: 92, 98–100, 102–104, 109, 113 f., 128 n., 135 f., 139, 140 n., 143, 145 n., 159–161, 163,

167–168, 171, 175–177, 181, 200 f., 203–205

Gaines, Edmund P.: 39
Gaines, William H.: 147
Gambling: 96 f., 122–123, 139, 143, 145, 191
Garrett, John T.: 100–101
Gibson, John: 125 n., 128 n.
Graham, J. E.: 166 n.
Grundy, Felix: 166

Hackett, William P.: 125 n., 129 n.
Halbrook, George: 184 n.
Hampton, Daniel W.: 147
Hanks, Fleetwood: 95 n., 125 n., 128 n.
Hanscome, Aaron: 55, 77 n.
Hard, Gideon: 197
Hardin, Joab: 23, 30–31
Hardin, Joseph: 4, 30 f., 32 n., 44, 77, 95 n.
Harrington, Bartley: 55
Harris, Egbert: 143, 145 n.
Harrison, William Henry: 14
Hartfield, Benjamin H. G.: 125 n., 129, 131
Hawthorn vs. *Hightower*: 62–64
Hayward, Elijah: 146 f.
Helena: 48, 94, 96, 161
Helena *Herald*: 166, 175
Henderson, Joseph: 88, 128, 148, 154
Hickman, William: 88
Hill, John: 157 n., 176 n.
Hines, John: 35, 55
Hogan, Edmund: 4, 29, 35, 54 n., 56 n., 77, 86, 88
Holland, Nehemiah: 125 n., 128 n.
Horner, William B. R.: 23, 30–31, 35, 46
Hoskins, Josiah: 55
Hot Springs: 96, 192
Howard, Benjamin: 4
Howell, Laban: 176 n., 180
Howell, O. V.: 143, 145 n.
Hudspeth, George: 77, 95 n., 125 n., 128 n., 129, 157 n.
Hughes, Isaac: 125 n., 129 n.
Humphreys, William: 46, 77, 88
Hunt, Andrew J.: 173, 175, 182 n.

Indian matters: of Arkansas Territory, 7, 23, 26, 29, 34, 36, 39–40, 46–47, 52 f., 55–58, 68–70, 72, 74–76, 82–84, 88 f., 93 f., 97, 111, 132, 134, 194, 199
Ingram, William: 125 n., 129 n.
Internal improvements: of Arkansas Territory, 25 f., 39 f., 47, 57, 67, 82–84, 93 f., 96 f., 116, 134, 141 f., 151, 173, 191 f., 199

Izard, George: 51–52, 55 ff., 63, 65, 74, 81–83, 88 f., 103, 106, 141, 201
Izard, Mark W.: 176 n.
Izard, Ralph: 51

Jackson, Andrew: 51, 90–92, 97 f., 99 f., 104 f., 107–109, 111, 116 f., 138–140, 145, 151 f., 158, 160–162, 168, 171 f., 175 f., 192, 195, 203, 205
James, Jesse: 35
Janes, William: 34
Jefferson, Thomas: 91, 171 n.
Jeffery, Johoiada: 54
Johnson, Benjamin: 27, 83, 102, 135, 138, 142–146, 158, 200, 202
Johnson, John: 77, 95 n.
Johnson, Richard M.: 19, 26 f., 166, 168, 170, 195, 202
Johnson, Robert W.: 202
Johnston, T. W.: 72
Jones, George W.: 79
Jouett, Charles: 19 f., 26 f.
Judkins, James W.: 157 n., 176 n.

Keatts, James B.: 112
Kelly, Charles: 61
Kelly, Elijah: 176 n., 184 n.
Kentuckians: in terr. politics, 28, 201–202
King, John F.: 184 n.
King, William R.: 194
Knight, Nehemiah R.: 195
Kuykendahl, James M.: 54
Kuykendall, Amos: 77, 95 n., 157 n., 176 n.

Lacy, Thomas J.: 168, 184 n., 200
Lafferty, John L.: 176 n., 184 n.
Land matters: of Arkansas Territory, 17, 25, 30 ff., 34, 37, 39 f., 45–47, 53 f., 57, 67, 70–73, 81–84, 89, 93 ff., 102, 105, 107 f., 116, 118, 126, 128, 130, 134, 137 f., 141 f., 146–148, 153, 158–159, 162–163, 164, 192, 199
Langford, Eli: 34 n.
La Salle, Robert Cavelier de: 3
Latting, Andrew: 46
Latting, Henry: 147
Laycock, Abner: 8
Lee, Bushrod W.: 149, 176 n., 184 n.
Leeper, Matthew: 155
Legislature: of 1819, 20; of 1820, 23–26, 29–31; of 1821, 34–37; of 1823, 46–47; of 1825, 54–57; of 1827, 77, 81–83; of 1828, 88–89; of 1829, 95–98; of 1831, 125 ff.; of 1833, 157–163; of 1835, 176–182; of 1836 (state), 200
Letcher, Robert P.: 20, 26–27
Lewis, Dixon H.: 196
Lewis, Meriwether: 4

Lewis, William: 30
Lewis, William B.: 171
Lincecum, Green B.: 125 n., 129 n.
Lindsay, James: 166 n.
Litchfield, David: 77
Little Rock: 30–32, 36, 40, 67, 70 ff., 92, 96 f., 99, 104 ff., 134, 137, 146, 148 nn., 154, 168, 178, 184, 191
Little Rock conference: of 1823, 37–38
Little Rock *Political Intelligencer:* 168 f., 173
Little Rock *Times:* 173, 174 n., 182 f.
Livermore, Arthur: 13
Livingston, James: 125 n., 128 n.
Louisiana: 3–4, 9–10, 174 f., 193
Lowe, David W.: 184 n.
Lowndes, William: 11
Lucas, John B. C.: 50
Lyon, Matthew: 33–36

McArthur, John: 21, 62 n.
McCampbell, James: 169
McCamy, Robert: 125 n., 128 f., 131, 184 n., 189
McDonald, Edward: 23
McElmurry, John: 23
McFarland, Lydia: 74–75
McKean, Joseph W.: 176 n., 177 n., 184 n.
McKenzie, James H.: 125 n., 129 n., 131 n.
McKinney, David E.: 102 f.
McLain, John: 184 n.
McLane, Louis: 9, 16, 147, 158
McLane, Neil: 20, 24, 28 n., 34
McLean, John: 46
McNair, Alexander: 50
McRee, William: 54 n.

Magness, Morgan: 125 n., 128 n., 157 n., 176 n.
Magness, Perry G.: 4
Manly, Caleb S.: 95 n., 120–121, 125 n., 128 nn., 133, 135, 184 n.
Marshall, Gilbert: 95 n., 184 n.
Martin, Allen: 124, 157 n.
Martin, G. L.: 184 n.
Mathers, Thomas: 46, 95 n., 176 n., 177 n.
May, Andrew J.: 184 n.
Medical bill (of 1831): 132–133
Menefee, Nimrod: 79, 125 n., 128 nn., 132, 137, 184 n.
Mercer, Charles F.: 13
Michigan Territory: 164–167, 172, 182, 184, 192–196, 198
Milam, Benjamin: 113
Miles, Benjamin L.: 95 n., 146

Militia: 23, 56, 82, 93, 96 f., 134, 136, 161, 191
Miller, James: 18–19, 23–25, 28 n., 29, 31, 50, 52, 59, 62 n., 201
Mississippi Territory: 5, 8, 185 f.
Missouri Compromise: 16, 174, 195, 197
Missouri Territory: 4 ff., 17, 20, 22, 24 f., 193
Monroe, James: 18, 25 ff., 49, 50 n., 51
Montgomery, William: 55, 77, 79–81, 95 n.
Mooney, Daniel: 34, 46
Moore, Charles: 76
Moore, Thomas: 62
Moore, William F.: 157 n., 176 n., 177 n.
Morris, Thomas: 195
Morrow, Jeremiah: 14
Morton, Elijah: 29
Murphy, Benjamin: 30, 31 n., 34
Murphy, Richard: 4
Murray, Thomas, Jr.: 184 n., 187 f.

Naudain, Arnold: 166, 194
Newton, Thomas W.: 63, 78–79, 81, 204 n.
Nicks, John: 46, 55, 83
Noland, C. F. M.: 79, 80 n., 113–114, 152 n., 153 n., 192, 203 f.
Noland, William: 113 n.

Oden, Robert C.: 28, 31, 32 n., 49, 59, 66 ff., 79, 86, 203–204
Ogle, Alexander: 14
O'Hara, William: 30
Ordinance of 1836: 192, 199
Organic Act (Arkansas): 5–17, 20, 22, 24 f., 60, 95 n., 159, 175
Orr, David: 125 n., 129 n.

Patton, John M.: 196
Patton, William B.: 125 n., 129 n.
Peel, John W.: 78 n.
Peeler, Richard: 29
Pelham, William: 162
Pennington, Isaac: 77, 125 n., 129 n.
Philbrook, Nathaniel: 31, 32 n.
Phillips, Stephen C.: 196–197
Phillips, Sylvanus: 23, 79–81, 95 n.
Pike, Albert: 19, 79 n., 116, 161, 163, 173, 175, 179, 181 n., 183 ff., 189–190
Poinsett, Joel R.: 51
Polk, James K.: 161
Polk, Thomas: 46
Pope, James: 125 n., 128 n.
Pope, John: 91–92, 95 ff., 102–114, 126, 127 n., 130–138, 140, 142 n., 143, 146–151, 153, 158–163, 167–172, 201, 203, 205

Pope, William Fontaine: 112–114, 203
Pope, Worden: 90 n.
Pope-Cocke duel: 112
Pope-Fulton breach: 159–161, 163, 167–168, 171
Pope-legislature of 1831 clash: 130 ff.
Pope-Noland duel: 112–114, 203
Pope-Sevier breach: 107–108, 112, 114, 168, 170, 172
Population: of Arkansas, 6, 21 n., 81, 111, 174, 178, 185 f., 189
Porter, Alexander: 166, 195
Prentiss, Samuel: 195
Presidential election: of 1824, 51, 152; of 1828, 91, 100, 109; of 1832, 139 f.; of 1836, 166, 175–176, 195, 198, 200
Pseudonymous newspaper writers: 19, 40 ff., 52 ff., 61 ff., 68 ff., 75 ff., 85, 87, 99 ff., 106 ff., 117 ff., 127, 131, 144, 147, 148 n., 153 n., 156, 165, 168, 173 f., 181

Quarles, Tunstall: 19
Quarles, William: 55, 62, 64

Randolph, Lewis: 171
Rector, Elias: 80 f., 112, 128, 200, 202
Rector, Henry M.: 202
Rector, Wharton: 79 f., 95 n., 174 n., 202
Rector, William: 54, 202
Rector family: 54, 202
Reed, John: 62
Reed, John (of Mass.): 197
Reed, John H.: 182 f.
Reyburn, William P.: 79, 99 n., 153
Rhea, John: 13–14
Rice, C. E.: 173 n.
Riley-Bradford affair: 41–43
Ringgold, John: 77, 79, 176 n., 177 n., 184 n., 187
Roane, Samuel C.: 28, 34, 37 n., 38, 46, 72, 107–108, 128, 143, 184, 189
Robbins, Asher: 195
Roberts, Brown C.: 176 n., 180
Robertson, George: 5–6, 11 f., 18, 20, 26–27
Robinson, John: 184 n.
Rorer, David: 94
Royston, Grandison D.: 184 n.
Russell, William: 30, 32, 148 n.
Rutherford, Samuel M.: 125 n., 128 n., 157 n., 162

Sampson, Zabdiel: 12 n.
Saunders, Charles R.: 184 n.
Schweppenheizer, Mynheer: 157
Scott, Andrew: 19 f., 24, 28 n., 31, 48–50, 65, 83 ff., 90, 125 n., 127, 128 nn., 131 n., 133–134, 137, 143, 184 n., 203

Scott, George W.: 21, 28, 113–114
Scott, John: 5 f., 20, 28 n.
Scott, Thomas W.: 125 n., 128 n., 133
Scott-Hogan fight: 86
Scott-Selden duel: 48–49, 65, 203
Scrobey, Matthew: 46
Scull, James: 21, 79 n., 97, 162 n.
Searcy, Richard: 62, 64, 66 n., 83 ff., 92 ff., 204 n.
Sectionalism (terr. and national): 8–16, 178–181, 183, 185–190, 192–199, 204
Selden, Joseph: 27, 48–50, 65
Seminary of learning: 25, 67, 81, 96, 158, 161, 199
Sevier, Ambrose H.: 46 f., 55–57, 72 n., 77–79, 83, 85–88, 89 n., 90, 91 n., 92 ff., 98, 107 f., 111–112, 114 f., 117 ff., 125, 130 f., 134, 138 f., 141 ff., 148 n., 149, 151–158, 160, 161 n., 162 n., 163–168, 170, 172–174, 183 f., 192 f., 195, 200 n., 202–204
Sevier, John: 202
Sevier-Conway-Johnson family: 47, 141–142, 174, 202
Sevier-Cummins altercation: 142–146, 158
Sevier faction: 87, 90, 100, 103 f., 106, 108, 112, 114 f., 117, 120, 123 ff., 130, 134, 137, 139 f., 145 f., 150, 156 f., 163, 168, 170, 184, 203–205
Sevier-Newton duel: 78 f.
Sharp, Solomon P.: 18
Shaw, William: 157 n., 176 n.
Shryock, Gideon: 149 n.
Simms, William D.: 28
Sinclair, Robert: 125 n., 128 n., 129 n., 157 n.
Slade, William: 198
Slaughter, Robert F.: 22
Slavens, Henry: 184 n.
Slavery: 3, 8–16, 57, 82, 90, 97, 110, 164 f., 172–174, 178 f., 181, 185–186, 190–199
Smith, Bernard: 146
Smith, C. S.: 166 n.
Smith, Jefferson: 182
Smith, Robert: 125 n., 128 n., 184 n.
Sprague, Peleg: 167
Sprangler, David: 197
Statehood: 81, 85, 94, 109–111, 115 f., 120, 126, 141, 158, 164–167, 172–182, 183–200, 204 f.
State house: 31, 36, 96 f., 126 ff., 138–140, 146–151, 158–160, 163, 167 f., 204
Steele, John: 166 n., 168–169
Stevenson, William: 23, 30 f.
Stevenson, William W.: 153

Stillwell, Harold: 125 n., 128 n., 157
Stillwell, Joseph: 29, 31
Strong, William: 184 n.
Strother, George F.: 14
Swift, Benjamin: 194–195

Tait, Charles: 14
Talbot, Frederick: 125 n., 128 n., 133, 157 n.
Tallmadge, James: 8, 14
Taylor, John K.: 156
Taylor, John W.: 8 ff.
Ten section bill: of leg. of 1831, 127–131, 133 ff., 163, 204
Ten section grant: 126 ff., 138, 146 ff., 158–160, 162–163
Tennessee: 28, 182 n., 193, 201–202
Thomas, Francis: 196
Thomas, Jesse B.: 15 n.
Thompson, John: 27
Thorn and Cook: 150
Thousand-acre grant: 142, 146 ff., 159 f., 163
Thurmond, Thomas J.: 157 n., 162
Tidwell, Roland: 125 n., 129 n., 157 n., 176 n.
Tindall, Thomas H.: 23, 30 f., 35
Tipton, John: 166 f.
Trimble, John: 28, 49
Trimble, Robert: 18
Trimble, Walker W.: 184 n.
Trimble, William: 20, 28 n., 32 n., 35, 37 f., 49, 107, 120, 125 n., 127, 128 n., 133, 142 n., 204 n.
Trotter, George J.: 135 f.
Tucker, Peyton: 34, 157 n.

Van Buren, Martin: 168, 170 f., 195, 198, 200
Voting laws: 36, 41, 142, 161, 191

Walker, Alexander S.: 4, 22, 54, 83, 95 n., 200
Walker, David: 106 n., 176 n., 177 n., 179–181, 184 n., 185
Walker, Felix: 9
Walker, J. Hardeman: 7 n.
Walker, James H.: 176 n., 177 n., 179, 184
Wallis, Perly: 22
Ward, William: 76
Washington (Hempstead Co.): 83
Webster, Daniel: 167
Weigart, George: 149 f.
Weir, John: 95 n., 77
Wells, John: 125 n., 129 n.
Wheeler, Amos: 31
Whinnery, Abraham: 125 n., 128 nn., 133, 176 n., 179 f., 184 n.

White, Hugh L.: 176, 195
White, John T.: 147, 148 n.
Whitman, Ezekiel: 12
Whittington, Hiram A.: 67 n., 71 n., 77 n., 151 n., 176 n.
Wickliffe, Charles A.: 91
Williams, John: 14
Williams, Lewis: 10
Williams, Thomas H.: 14
Williamson, John: 157 n., 176 n., 177 n.
Wilson, John: 35, 46, 55, 77, 95 n., 125 n., 128 n., 133, 157 n., 176 n., 184
Wilson, Josiah N.: 184 n.
Wilson, Stephen R.: 35
Wirt, William: 25
Wise, Henry A.: 196, 198
Witter, Daniel T.: 55, 77, 88, 122 n., 125 n., 128 n., 129 n.
Wolf, Charles: 125 n., 128 n., 129

Wolf, Jacob: 77, 95 n., 125 n., 157 n., 176 n.
Woodruff, William E.: 21 f., 25, 27, 37, 48 f., 62 f., 70 ff., 81 n., 85–87, 90, 91 n., 92 n., 93 f., 97, 98 n., 99–102, 110–114, 116–119, 121–125, 127, 129 f., 131 n., 132, 134 ff., 142 n., 143 n., 148 n., 149 ff., 161, 165, 166 n., 167–170, 172–175, 177–179, 182 n., 183, 189, 192 f., 195, 203
Woodruff-Fulton squabble: 167–168
Woodruff-Menefee fight: 132
Woodruff-Pope squabble: 168 ff., 172
Wright, Clayborn: 34, 55
Wright, Travis G.: 184 n.

Yell, Archibald: 200
Yeomans, William T.: 110 n.